April/56

# Voltaire and the State

# Voltaire and the State

BY CONSTANCE ROWE

IN LITTERIS LIBERTAS

1754·1893

COLUMBIA UNIVERSITY PRESS

NEW YORK 1955

PUBLISHED IN GREAT BRITAIN, CANADA, INDIA, AND PAKISTAN
BY GEOFFREY CUMBERLEGE: OXFORD UNIVERSITY PRESS,
LONDON, TORONTO, BOMBAY, AND KARACHI

*Library of Congress Catalog Card Number:* 55-9097

MANUFACTURED IN THE UNITED STATES OF AMERICA

TO THE MEMORY

OF MY FATHER

# Preface

For well over one hundred and fifty years, Voltaire has commanded the attention of scholars. His ideas on religion and philosophy have been discussed by innumerable critics. His political and social views have likewise provoked bitter controversy. Though the author of *Candide* has been considered from every conceivable angle, a coordinated report on his theory of the nation and of international relations has heretofore been lacking. The subject has been merely touched on by his long line of biographers, and what evidence they have produced is contradictory and fragmentary.

The purpose of the present study is to examine the personal patriotism of one of the world's greatest champions of free thought and free inquiry and secondly, to determine where in the scale of human loyalties he, as a philosopher, would assign love of country. This can be done by no mere listing of such statements as he consciously voiced in his writings. A philosophy of patriotism and the role of the nation in world civilization is necessarily based on certain key concepts. These are the object of national allegiance, the terms of the implicit social contract which underlies all government, and lastly, a definite stand toward the advancement of the homeland by military conquest and economic power. On all such matters the attitude of Voltaire must be tested and explained.

The idea which emerges is that Voltaire led France toward a new conception of the nation. His was not the French and

continental view of patriotism as a blind worship of a king, a
native land, and inherited traditions which the patriot is in duty
bound to revere and cherish. He pointed the way toward the
modern American concept of allegiance to the State as embodied
in a constitution preserving man's fundamental liberties. Laws
based on "natural law," a just distribution of economic burdens,
and the safe-guarding of inalienable human rights, these to Voltaire were the essential cornerstone of man's duty toward his
fellow man. Such, he believed, were the original and ideal aims
of all organized society. Their fulfillment by the State was then
not a matter of national politics, but an ethical obligation toward
mankind, and at all points of the compass, universal and invariable.

We Americans have a somewhat overpatriotic tendency to
speak of the universal rights embodied in our Constitution as if
they were invented by our Founding Fathers. Yet many of these
"primitive and inalienable rights" were defined and fought for
by Voltaire before Thomas Jefferson was born. To Voltaire
human personality was inviolable, the individual the unit of
social organization. More than any one thinker, with the possible
exception of Montesquieu, he inspired our Constitution, just as
he inspired the French Declaration of the Rights of Man. Benjamin Franklin was his warm admirer, and Franklin's grandson,
Voltaire, the so-called Skeptic, blessed with the memorable words,
"God and Liberty."

Franklin and Jefferson were "constructive thinkers." Voltaire
has been called a "destructive thinker." The line between "constructive" and "destructive" thinking can be extremely fine.
Voltaire lived in the old world, under a system, where, by the
"divine right of kings," Church and State were one. The Temporal Power he could not criticize without also attacking the
Spiritual Power. Yet he was a practical man and his real interest
was in the State and in the obligation of the State toward
mankind.

Forgetful of these bygone conditions, our age finds it fashionable, upon occasion, to disparage Voltaire. Yet, if in the "world-garden," Jefferson was able to plant and build, Voltaire could only clear the land for a greater freedom.

Both reason and sentiment had their share in the Frenchman's philosophy of the nation. Whenever he was obliged to choose between loyalty to the France already created by historical forces, and his own universal, rational ideals for an equitable State, Voltaire chose the latter. Still, his was also a patriotism of sentiment. He felt keen delight in such characteristic aspects of his own nationality as the French language, French culture, French history, and French society. He had great faith in the civilizing mission of his own country as regards Europe and the world.

His personal concept of the bond between an individual and his country, as finally summed up in his *Philosophic Dictionary,* includes both the homeland and the State, both *la patrie* and *l'Etat.* To the nationalist theory of the French Revolution, Voltaire made a substantial contribution. For throughout his writings he insisted that the individual should depend for his welfare neither on God, nor the sovereign, nor his regional home, but on his nation—*la patrie* in the classical liberal sense invoked by the patriots of '93. Inspired by his personal love for France, by his longing to live as a philosopher unmolested in his native land, he fought to establish within French boundaries a trustworthy state.

The chapter "The Bond with La Patrie" traces the course of this life-long struggle. Examined in the earlier part are the nature and strength of the bond that held him to the France he inherited: his personal response to such characteristic aspects of the French way of life as Catholicism, classicism, and last but not least, the art of society. So captivated was the young Voltaire by this real *patrie* that he often tended to minimize the injustices and corruption of the autocratic French state, of the Bourbon monarchy. Next he himself met up with a flagrant injustice. A bodily attack against him had been planned and carried out by the Chevalier de Rohan, his social superior. The outrage therefore remained unpunished and unpunishable.

Voltaire then realized that the mutual interchange of rights and duties between the State and the citizen, which the initial social contract implies, had for himself ceased to function. In any vital or true sense, he had no country. For he had no hearth-land upon which he could depend for the defense of his fundamental liberties. Rejected, as it seemed, by his homeland and his government, he spent his term of banishment in England. There he obtained a glimpse of constitutional government.

The latter half of the same chapter shows how the epicurean Frenchman, in love with his native land, gradually evolved into a philosopher dedicated to world-wide principles of social justice. Many of these he had seen in workable practice in England. Yet their fulfillment he himself wished to enjoy not on the shores of a foreign country. He recrossed the channel, determined that reason and human rights should find official acceptance in his homeland, in the France he so bitterly loved.

France as a political entity he first sought to reshape through the sovereign, by personally winning over to his ideas Louis XV, the head of the established order. Yet when such an attempt failed, he fought for justice, tolerance, and humanity outside French boundaries, or, as soon as he dared, at Ferney, poised for escape, on an obscure wooded corner of his national soil.

His final return to his native capital without official permission and as an affront to Louis XVI gives proof that before the oncoming tide of ideas even a monarch is powerless. France and Paris had placed the seal of approval on those philosophic requirements Voltaire had set for the government of all nations. At last the philosopher had triumphed in his native land.

His rational concept of the nation is scrutinized in the following two chapters of this book. The one traces the growth of his idea of *la patrie* from his earliest light verses to his final *Philosophic Dictionary* statement of the basic contract between the State and the citizen. Analyzed next are those rights and liberties which according to Voltaire make up the actual terms of the social contract.

His views on the ethics of international relations reveal him as a cosmopolitan, humanitarian patriot, or, to express this historic term more simply, a "world patriot."

The passive title "world citizen" has been used to denote a person who can feel at home in any country. A "world patriot," though, may be described as one who actively fights for and upholds the rights of all the globe's inhabitants, regardless of race, nation, class, or creed. In this same sense, Washington, Jefferson, and Franklin were also world patriots. For while upholding human rights within their own loved nation, they were contributing to the freedom of their larger country, the world.

# Acknowledgments

THE WRITER is grateful to the many scholars, living and dead, American and native French, who have offered her advice and guidance with this research. She has appreciative memories of the late Professors Paul Hazard, Louis Cons, Horatio Smith, and especially the late Professor Arthur Livingston, who first suggested that a study of Voltaire and the State be made.

For suggestions on economics she is indebted to Dr. Charles W. Cole, now president of Amherst College, who taught history in the Graduate School of Columbia University at the time this essay was written. Acknowledgment is also made to Professor Mirkhine-Gutzévitch of the Ecole Libre des Hautes Etudes for comments on the nationalist theory of the French Revolution.

The writer, most of all, wishes to express her profound debt of gratitude to Professor Norman L. Torrey. For his sympathetic advice and inspiring guidance have proved an unceasing aid in this research.

CONSTANCE ROWE

*April, 1955*

# Contents

# Voltaire and the State

# Introduction

Few french authors or indeed, few authors in any country have provoked more passionate controversy than Voltaire. In life, his writings won him both warrants of arrest and the highest tributes from royalty. After his death, men quarreled over the resting-place of his bones. The so-called patriots of the French Revolution carried his remains in a triumphal procession to the Paris church now known as the Panthéon. Yet ardent supporters of the restored Bourbon kings fulfilled in another way their patriotic duty. The remains of Voltaire and those of Rousseau were dug up, carted outside the city, and thrown in a dump.

The bones of Voltaire no longer exist as "bones of contention." Nor in the mid-twentieth century can they be consigned by an illiberal government to a posthumous exile. Instead, a Minister of the Vichy Régime ingeniously saw fit to banish Voltaire's statue. The empty pedestal remains, and, for such a thinker, this chance memento seems humorously out of keeping. A pedestal Voltaire never needed. He was above it, and also, at times, beneath it.

In France, however, living or dead, Voltaire remains inescapable. On this point his compatriots seem to agree. "Voltaire is so French," states a modern literary critic, "both in his virtues and faults, so impossible to imagine outside France, that we could no more disown him than we could disown ourselves."[1]

The dazzling crystallization of the so-called French genius

and national character that the philosopher embodied was recognized by even his most hostile critics. Says Ferdinand Brunetière:

There are perhaps greater names in the history of French literature, three or four, at most; there are certainly names more honorable and more justly honored; there is none more French, none more a faithful image or mirror of ourselves; there is none more European and, I may as well admit, none more universal than the name of Voltaire.[2]

Nevertheless, the creator of *Candide,* in whom national tendencies were generally believed to have reached such a brilliant synthesis, has at the same time been accused of lack of patriotism. The late-nineteenth-century scholar and critic, Emile Faguet, went so far as to say:

Voltaire has no patriotism and no idea of homeland. . . . The article "Patrie" in the *Philosophic Dictionary* is given over to an obscuring of the idea of homeland, to a questioning whether there is anyone who can be sure that he has a country, and concludes that a patriot can only be a poor specimen of a man.[3]

While this judgment is more or less confirmed by Brunetière[4] and Cornou,[5] Edmé Champion in a brief but penetrating study insists on Voltaire's patriotism in a special chapter.[6] Aulard, an outstanding authority on the French Revolution, places the Sage of Ferney at the head of France's liberal and humanitarian patriots.[7]

Such estimates reveal less the patriotism or lack of patriotism of Voltaire than the conception of national allegiance held by the individual critic. "A patriot," according to Merriam-Webster, "is one who loves his country and zealously supports its authority and interests." The question remains. In exactly what does "love of country" consist; secondly, in what policies of government, in what standards for human relations do the true interests of the nation lie?

The *New English Dictionary* compiled by Sir James A. H. Murray casts hardly any more light on this complex subject. A "patriot" is here defined as, "one who disinterestedly or self-sacrificingly exerts himself to promote the well-being of his country; one whose ruling passion is the love of country; one who maintains and defends his country's freedom or rights."

These terms are likewise open to broad and conflicting interpretation. For, needless to say, ideas on how to promote the nation's well-being are continually at variance and any allusion to a country's rights must at best be vague.

All definitions may agree that patriotism is "love of one's country." Yet equally intelligent and public-spirited men differ widely as to what is meant by one's country, who one's compatriots are, and what sort of conduct logically results from the patriotic attitude. As one modern authority makes clear:

Most civil wars—those of secessionists or home-rulers against unionists or nationalists, of colonials against the mother-country, of Catholics against Protestants, of republicans against monarchists—have been wars between patriots.[8]

Indeed, in the France of the *ancien régime,* the majority of men would have agreed that patriotism meant to love and serve *le roi et la patrie,* king and country. However after 1740 it became increasingly apparent that these two words represented antagonistic entities. For the "authority" of the State as embodied in the king failed to support the "interests" of that vast heterogeneous mass of people who constituted the country or nation.

The lifework of Voltaire was centered in his ceaseless effort to compel the ancient Bourbon monarchy to espouse the welfare of his fellow Frenchmen. More than any pre-revolutionary thinker, except perhaps Rousseau, he helped prepare public opinion for that transfer of patriotic allegiance from the person of a sovereign and his House to a people willingly united in the possession of their primitive liberties. These basic human prerogatives the eighteenth century called "natural rights."

His love and zeal for his country he proved by striving to establish within French boundaries a trustworthy political organization. To do this he identified himself with no hidebound faction. Nor was he primarily interested in techniques of government. He merely defined for all thinking people those universal claims of reason which he believed should be enforced by the State.

In his eyes the State was reasonable and therefore sound when it guaranteed to the individual such "natural rights" as liberty of person and property, freedom of speech, press, and assembly, liberty of conscience, and trial by jury. National policies he considered just when they promoted equality of opportunity, assigned the economic burdens of the nation to those best able to carry them, and regardless of rank or religion, rewarded ability. For the goal of government should be the common good or "the greatest good of the greatest number."

He would call any political system unreasonable and unsound whose dealings, whether with individuals within the nation or with the foreign powers outside, have no other sanction than the "right of the strongest."

Since nationalist philosophies so seldom agree, all opinions on the patriotism of any man must remain inconclusive. Our purpose is therefore to set down as objectively as possible Voltaire's idea of *la patrie,* his reading of the implicit social contract between the State and the citizen, and lastly, his views on the ethics of international relations.

While a few lovers of their country have claimed Voltaire as their prophet, in nineteenth-century France the majority of so-called patriots turned from him with aversion. Such reactions depend on the position to which national devotion is assigned in the hierarchy of man's loyalties.

If to a reader of the *Philosophic Dictionary,* patriotism means a deep attachment to the native soil, the unquestioning acceptance of the nation's political institutions, and an externally imposed duty to exalt a national abstraction rather than the human beings who give this idea life and meaning, then, as judged by such a person, Voltaire was unpatriotic indeed.

If, however, love of country is measured by delight in the

accomplishments of the native land in the past, in the hope of even greater national glory to be won in the future; if the support of the country's interests means the fight for laws that safeguard the rights of the individual, and conditions conducive to his material and intellectual advancement, thus enabling the homeland to contribute richly to world civilization, then, judged by such a standard, the author of *Candide* was the greatest of patriots.

This divergence of viewpoint is clearly reflected in the estimates of Voltaire by those writers and historians, who, from 1789 until the late nineteenth century, have molded French opinion. A brief survey of their leading judgments gives ample evidence that the eighteenth-century thinker was considered patriotic or unpatriotic, a credit to his country or a force of corruption, merely according to whether the critic himself had a liberal or conservative view of the nation.

In the opinion of Condorcet, whose *Life of Voltaire* first appeared in 1789, the leader of European Enlightenment was a great humanitarian patriot, humanitarian in his devotion to man's rights, patriotic in his delight in national achievements.[9] Thus he was judged by a critic who chose as his object of patriotic allegiance those basic human liberties which found full documented expression in the Declaration of the Rights of Man. Such, Condorcet believed, are the invariable terms of the social contract, and unless they are enforced, no nation can be the true homeland of its citizens. The zeal and fervor of the patriot should consist in striving for the orderly fulfillment of these rights and liberties on national soil.

The same cosmopolitan humanitarian principles both Condorcet and Voltaire would apply to international relations. They believed that the homeland would be patriotically served not by adding new territory to her borders, but by a policy of peaceful cooperation with other members of the European family of nations.

When the forces of royalist reaction set in, the patriotism of the Sage of Ferney received a very different appraisal. Such a change in attitude is evident in the writings of Vicomte Bonald, whose works won wide popularity during the Bourbon Restoration.

To this sincere lover of France and founder of traditional nationalism, Voltaire was seen as a bad angel. Accuses Bonald:

He brought misfortune upon Europe by leading France astray, France, the head of this great body. He brought misfortune upon France by implanting with his philosophy the scorn of serious matters and the esteem for frivolous ones.[10]

The writer of these lines was convinced that national allegiance was equivalent to a fervent support of the Faith of the homeland, a veneration for the ancient monarchy, and an emotional loyalty to those feudal institutions which had created France and given this great country her national identity. Both Bonald and his like-minded contemporary Joseph de Maistre looked upon a divinely revealed Catholicism as the cornerstone of European civilization, the custodian of public morals, and the indispensable support of any temporal authority. That the leader of eighteenth-century Enlightenment had used his peerless intellectual gifts to shatter this view of the world and make the nation serve not a monarch by "Divine Right," but a human purpose (and such a contemptible purpose as individual happiness) provoked denunciations from the defenders of absolutism. De Maistre goes so far as to brand Voltaire and eighteenth-century philosophers in general as agents of national disintegration and social chaos. Of the Patriarch of Ferney's final triumphant return to Paris this writer exclaims angrily:

Paris crowned him. Sodom would have banished him. When I perceive what he was capable of doing and what he did do, his inimitable talents inspire in me a sort of holy rage that must remain nameless. Suspended between admiration and horror, sometimes, I would like to raise to him a statue . . . but by the hand of the executioner.[11]

There were nevertheless different shadings in these judgments
of Voltaire by the prophets of reaction. Chateaubriand recognized in the eighteenth-century thinker a confirmed apologist of
monarchy, of the established order. Therefore he accused the
author of *Candide* of being inconsistent. For in an age when
Church and State were indissolubly united, to attack the Spiritual
Power was equivalent to an attack upon the Temporal Power.[12]
Chateaubriand, though, fails to note that the reverse is equally
true. Nor does he admit that were the union of these two governing bodies solemnly respected, any criticsm of either would
become an impossibility.

To Bonald, De Maistre and Chateaubriand, Voltaire was
decidedly unpatriotic. For none of the critics believed in the
right of an individual to choose his homeland, or that the State
exists to promote the welfare of the citizen. They inclined to the
view that a man was assigned to a given country by fate, hopelessly committed to it by language, and obliged automatically to
remain faithful to its traditional institutions. Such unthinking
loyalty to a native land was noble and natural.

In the *Genius of Christianity,* Chateaubriand devoted a sentimental chapter to the idea of *patrie,* homeland. This primitive
and therefore laudable emotion, he said, was discernible even
in the members of the animal world where it was expressed in
the devotion of birds to their nests and their habit of remaining
in flocks. The relationship between the individual and his native
land must be kept equally unsullied by reason or reflection. For
should such an element intrude, patriotism might lose much of
its primeval vitality.[13]

Later in the writings of such mid-nineteenth-century liberals
as Lamartine, Quinet, and Michelet, Voltaire was restored to
the glory conferred upon him by the closing years of the
eighteenth century. Those Bourbon kings famed for having
"learned nothing and forgotten nothing" had been tried out
again and failed. The nominally liberal rule of Louis Philippe
had likewise ended in failure. On the eve of the Revolution of

1848, for a public disenchanted with monarchy, writers and historians began to reinterpret the message of eighteenth-century philosophers.

Both Lamartine and Michelet came to the bold conclusion that Voltaire and the thinkers of the Age of Reason were not agents of national disintegration, but heralds of social progress and more equitable conditions for Frenchmen. Michelet believed that the Revolution and the excesses of the Terror were brought about by the financial bankruptcy of the realm left by Louis XV. The poet Lamartine and the historian Michelet felt persuaded that if the author of the *Philosophic Dictionary* had denied and assailed Christian dogma, he and his followers had advanced and defended Christian works. If they seemed to be enemies of the Word, they were still apostles of the devout disinterested deeds Faith should have inspired.

In his *History of the Girondists,* Lamartine looked upon the reforms of the French Revolution as the complement of Christianity, and the belated application of essential Christian precepts to earthly society. Of these precepts, one of the most fundamental and neglected was the dignity and importance of every human being. The bond between all men that Christians call the Brotherhood of Man eighteenth-century philosophers referred to as the world-wide fraternity of reason. Such thinkers were therefore in harmony with the spirit of true Faith. For in the name of *fraternité,* of universal humanity, they demanded for each fellow man the fulfillment of his inalienable rights.[14]

Lamartine beheld Voltaire as a salutary personification of reason. In the light of his mockery, all the man-made errors, cruelties, and abuses stood revealed as far too ridiculous to exist. Thanks to him, the human race learned to laugh at itself.[15]

The protection of the poor and the weak was the historic duty of organized Christianity. Yet at this task the Church of the *ancien régime* had failed. Her moral influence she had neglected to use in behalf of earthly justice and charity. This truly Christian work had therefore to be taken over by others, by philosophers inspired by the spirit of universal truth. The view of eighteenth-century philosophy as a corrective and purifying influence on the Church herself was expressed by the historian Quinet. Dramatically he declared: "Voltaire is the Exterminating Angel sent by God to chastize his sinful Church."[16]

Michelet, the "Republican Bossuet,"[17] whose *History of France* is a sort of mystic pontifical discourse on the march of his countrymen to the left, also praises the work of "Enlightenment." The mid-nineteenth-century historian believed that the old Bourbon monarchy, and the Church which supported it, had betrayed the trust of the French people, a patient devoted people who for so long had given these institutions their deepest loyalty and allegiance.[18] Voltaire he honored for his espousal of the well-being of the common man, for his fury at social injustice, and for his tireless ability to act on his convictions. In his *History of the Revolution,* the first volume of which appeared in 1847, the same year as Lamartine's *History of the Girondists,* he paid him the glowing tribute:

From all the evil that fanaticism and tyranny have ever done in the world, it would seem that Voltaire was the sufferer. Martyr, universal victim; he it was, who was slaughtered on St. Bartholomew's Eve; he, it was, who was burnt at Seville; he, again whom the parlement of Toulouse broke on the rack with Calas. Voltaire, almost eighty revives. . . . While still breathing, he is raised from the tomb by a voice, the voice that was at the core of his existence, the voice of humanity. . . . Old athlete, yours is the crown! Here you are again, the victor of victors. Throughout a century with every method of combat, every arm and every doctrine you pursued without ever swerving, one interest, one cause, the saintly cause of humanity. . . . And you have been called a skeptic! And you have been called variable![19]

To these idealistic liberals, patriotism meant more than the duty to exalt or be submissively faithful to a France already created by historical determinism. They viewed the State as designed for the individual rather than the individual for the State. The bond between the citizen and the homeland should consist in the mutual fulfillment of rights and duties.

At the close of the century, which had given rise to the sentimental traditionalism of Bonald and Chateaubriand and the equally sentimental liberalism of Lamartine and Michelet, traditional nationalism came of age with the thoughtful conservatism of Taine. In 1872, after the disastrous Franco-Prussian War and the anarchy brought about by the Paris Commune, the positivist thinker made extensive researches into French history.

The frequent governmental upheavals of the nineteenth century he explained as a part of his country's slow convalescence after the French Revolution. From this drastic operation the patient had never fully recovered. In his *Origins of Contemporary France,* Taine described eighteenth-century philosophy as a dangerous drug, the components of which were scientific inquiry, Cartesianism, and the habit of abstraction so characteristic of the French classical mind and spirit.[20] Isolated, these elements were harmless and salutary. Yet in the particular compound of them brewed by Voltaire, Rousseau, and the philosophers, they had become a deadly poison.

This poison was well-nigh fatal because it had maddened France into breaking with her past. Drunk and reeling, the nation had therefore started forth on new paths not chartered for flesh-and-blood Frenchmen. These roads had been designed instead, and most alluringly, for a phantom-abstraction known as universal man, who carried with him a bundle of even more mythical rights.[21] Progress along the shadowy highway had led to national anarchy and lasting confusion.

As a positivist more concerned with what *is* or *has been* than with those things which *ought to be* or *might be,* Taine saw modern France as a product of the ancient French monarchy, the Catholic Church, and a strong regional aristocracy. These basic elements in the structure of society had imposed a national

pattern of thoughts, customs, and behavior from which Frenchmen could never successfully break loose. This fact, so Taine
believed, the citizen should accept.

The Frenchman should realize that he owes a debt of honor
not only to his country of the present, but to his country of
preceding generations and centuries. He should piously recon-
struct the ancient institutions, and intelligently preserve and
restore the customs and traditions of his native land. For these
are inalienable parts of France and their influence an inescapable
element in his own thoughts and consciousness as a Frenchman.
The flaws in the inherited national framework are known flaws
and as such the more remediable. Thus *faute de mieux,* on this
same noble social edifice bequeathed by times past, all thoughtful
architects of the future should build.

Though Taine, with his scientific pessimism, recoiled particularly from the idealistic optimism of Rousseau, he saw in
Voltaire an aseptic force of reason, cleansing the time-honored
social structure of parasitic moss and fungus. Nevertheless on
this venerable façade the Voltairean acid proved too corrosive.
The author of the *Origins of Contemporary France* could only
exclaim appalled at the horrors, hypocrisies, crimes, and evils
which the Sage of Enlightenment had exposed throughout all
his writings: "In what a deep dark closet politics and religion
hide their dirty linen!"[22]

Of such injustices and abuses of the *ancien régime,* the
nineteenth-century thinker was almost as well aware as his
eighteenth-century predecessor. Yet while faith in reason and
science taught Voltaire to hope for better things, this same faith
taught Taine to submit to historical forces with despairing
resignation. Of the famed gaiety of Voltaire in the face of such
disheartening facts of society, the positivist historian believed
that he had penetrated the secret:

Concerning all that [evils and abuses] one must laugh so as not to
cry, and still back of this laughter there are tears. He finally laughs,
he hides a profound sadness, a sorrowful pity. . . . Note well, how-

ever. Gaiety is still a pulse-spring, the last in France to hold a man upright, the best tonic to keep the soul intact with all its force and resistance in a century when men and women too felt obliged to die like persons of good company with a smile and an epigram.[23]

In spite of this praise, Taine nevertheless held Voltaire, Rousseau, and their followers severely responsible for precipitating such a national convulsion as revolution. For these thinkers had viewed the individual as the essential unit of social organization. Their scheme of things had implied that the individual is free to choose his actions.

To Taine man was a mere product of such historical deterministic forces as "race," "environment," and "epoch."[24] Just as plants are rooted to the earth in which they were originally sown, so is a human being materially and psychologically bound to the soil of the native land. Away from his original social and regional grouping, he can know neither happiness nor true fulfillment.

The scientific determinism of Taine furnished the point of departure for a new nationalist philosophy which disregarded the individual as a moral and intellectual entity. *The Origins of Contemporary France* became the Bible of reactionaries. It provided the social and political groundwork of that integral nationalism propounded by Barrès and by Maurras, the royalist-minded founder of *L'Action Française*.[25] That traditionalism, innocent and elevated in Bonald and Chateaubriand, thoughtful, though defeatist in Taine, fused into a new fanaticism at the time of the Dreyfus Affair. To Barrès, Maurras, and Frenchmen dominated by the sentiments these writers exploited, the State stood as a supreme and glorious entity. This entity had an existence above and beyond the individuals which made up its social fabric. The object of this organization was military glory, and its institutions were designed not so much to promote justice as to create and enforce unity. Such reactionaries viewed the philosophy which in 1789 had culminated in the Declaration of the Rights of Man as dangerously destructive to authority whether religious or political.

Therefore in the opinion of Brunetière and Emile Faguet, who both stood firmly against the revision of the Dreyfus case, and who helped form the League for the French Homeland in order to meet the challenge of the pro-Dreyfus League for the Rights of Man,[26] Voltaire was indeed unpatriotic. For to these two famed critics and professors, patriotism meant zeal for national prestige, the duty to uphold public order rather than individual justice. They felt solicitous for the outward dignity of so important an institution in French life as the army. Against considerations like these, the fair and equal treatment by law, meted out to a member of a small racial minority, seemed relatively unimportant. For to patriots of this sort, the honor and glory of their country was unrelated to the rights of French citizens.

Similarly Brunetière had been indignant when in 1882 Ernest Renan had told his hearers at the Sorbonne that the bond between the individual and the nation was based on neither geography nor culture, but on voluntary adherence, on the spontaneous devotion of a people to their common past, and on their steadfast will to share a common future.[27] Renan had stated that nations in their present form had not always existed![28] Worse still, he had more than hinted that they would undoubtedly assume new shapes in the future. The great nineteenth-century agnostic had pointed to a federation of European states as a possible solution to the dilemma of continual warfare.

To Brunetière this whole viewpoint was acutely displeasing. Heatedly he denounced those *individualistes*,[29] as he called them, who dared assume that nations exist for individuals instead of individuals for nations. The sense of homeland is "natural," "historical," and ineradicable in human nature.[30] Yet while stridently proclaiming that devotion to *la patrie* is ineradicable, he seemed to fear, at the same time, that patriotic feeling might die out. Nor did he see any contradiction in insisting upon the need for a "natural" sentiment to be artificially encouraged and stimulated. The future union of European states that Renan envisioned, even if it did end wars, still seemed, to the mind of Brunetière, a calamity. For such a union could only be founded on the ruin of the nationalist idea.[31]

So this sense of homeland must at all costs be preserved. Indeed, the noble love of country which in the past had ever inspired so much virtue, heroism, and self-sacrifice had a mystical basis.[32] The vigor of this emotion should not be impaired by the dry winds of reason. Thus, even if thinkers of such renown as Voltaire, Goethe, and Renan had estimated that patriotism, to a certain extent, is irrational, limiting, and artificially imposed on free human nature,[33] "then," challenged Brunetière, "alas for nature, and reason herself will be proved wrong!"[34]

The moral failure of the nationalism of blind sentiment and mystic exaltation has already become ominously apparent. For this nationalist philosophy refuses to take into account the equal right or the equal propensity of other peoples to exalt their own national myths and to assert their own inherent superiority and claim to dominate. In a world transformed by nuclear science, the clash of national ambitions, egotisms, and ideologies must lead eventually to mutual destruction or even global annihilation.

The role of reason is to harmonize these conflicting interests. Sentiment and intuition may well provide the fuel that energizes and propels the national vessel. Yet without reason at the controls these same admirable forces can only hurl man back to primitive chaos.

# The Bond with *La Patrie*

## THE BIRTH OF "VOLTAIRE"

THE LIFE of Voltaire represents a bitter and unending conflict between a Frenchman infatuated with his native land, and a philosopher whose first allegiance is to world-wide principles of human justice. The latter he found unrespected within home boundaries. To the mature French thinker, *la patrie* or "homeland" meant not only the territory that had nurtured him from infancy to manhood, but a land of conscious predilection, a place where he could live in safety, according to his tastes, and peacefully fulfill his intellectual destiny.

If the land of birth fails to provide such an atmosphere of liberty and assured tranquility, an individual is entitled to seek his happiness elsewhere. The choice of a "homeland" Voltaire classed as a "natural right."[1] Such a view implies that the State is of primary importance to the individual. For on the political organization he must depend for his well-being and the enjoyment of his rights. When government fails in these obligations, so the author of the *Philosophic Dictionary* makes clear, no man can feel at home, even on his own farm lands.[2] Nor could he, Voltaire, find a "homeland" within the country of his birth.

France was the land of his own predilection. A spell of mutual attraction ever existed between himself and his native land. Yet despite his keen delight in French society, French customs, and French culture, the Bourbon kingdom became

increasingly uninhabitable for a philosopher. In lands outside
France he sought freedom of expression and the tolerance and
humane dealings he demanded of the State.[3]

Though he practiced and preached the right of man to choose
his own homeland,[4] he also recognized a subtle obstacle to the
use of such a prerogative. This well-nigh insuperable obstacle he
defined with delicacy in his play *Mahomet*.

Zopire says in surprise to Palmire, who has just freed herself
from the yoke of the mother-country:

> Thus of Mohammed, you regret the bonds
> The tumult of the camps, the horrors of the desert
> This wandering nation, abandoned to confusion?

Whereupon Palmire replies:

> One's homeland is wherever the soul is held captive.[5]

The mind and heart of Voltaire were held captive not so
much in France as in Paris, his city of birth and earliest educator.
Of this metropolis he ever bore the fascinating imprint. *La patrie*
or "homeland," young Arouet would scarcely have dreamed of
seeking very far beyond the Seine and the quarter near the Pont
Neuf. For here in the salons and cafés of his native capital, the
man and the writer was as nowhere else understood and appreciated. Here he felt, in the truest sense, at home.

Absent or present, Paris always seemed to him a glamorous,
infinitely desirable siren that he must court and flatter. His loss
of Parisian favor through his quarrel with Rohan caused him
the severest shock of his early manhood. His later banishment
from the city by a Jansenist *Parlement* left upon him a mental
hurt that he went on feeling from maturity to old age. Morbidly
sensitive to Parisian criticism or approval, his thoughts and
wishes were ever turned toward the capital as the seat of refined
Epicureanism, indeed, the homeland of good company and good
taste.[6] His passionately acclaimed return to Paris a few months
before his death may be considered as a magnificent home-
coming, the apotheosis of his long career.

To understand his mature conception of patriotism, it is necessary first to examine the nature and strength of the bond which held Voltaire to his native city. For his devotion to those liberal, humanitarian principles that were later to constitute *la nation*[7] grew out of influences he absorbed in his youth and early manhood when Paris was still his home and chosen habitat.

Voltaire belonged to that enlightened, rapidly rising middle class which occupied so pivotal a place in the structure of the French nation. As he was later to observe: "This order is considerable; it governs the men at the top who think once in a while, and the underlings who think not at all."[8]

His bourgeois station rendered him more a part of the vital fabric of France than either the propertyless artisan or the idle tax-free aristocrat. For in the case of these last two classes, that steady interchange of benefits and services which membership in the nation should imply[9] had ceased to function, and they lived within the nation like guests and slaves respectively.

As a member of the third estate, the future Voltaire stood exposed to the many cruel pinches of the existing order. For in spite of a few dizzying successes in the drawing rooms of nobility, he bore the plain name of Arouet, and his circumstances compelled him to earn his own living. In Master Alain's law office he became familiar with that tangled mass of outmoded verbiage that made up his country's legal system. He met drab clerks. He touched the outer fringes of the world of big business and even gleaned hints of many a bold financial speculation.

Such experiences brought his brilliant mind into contact with material reality. Soon he learned to question those established institutions accepted by most Frenchmen as conditions of existence no less inescapable than sunrise and sunset.

He had, however, ample opportunity to know intimately the traditional three estates of French society.[10] His father had attained considerable prominence as a notary, and several grandees of the realm were numbered among his clients. Through his father, the youth became acquainted with such brilliant members of the military nobility as Richelieu and Sully. He likewise rubbed elbows with the parvenu though pretentious parliamentary nobles. In his godfather, the Abbé de Châteauneuf, he beheld a perfect example of the idle, frivolous clergy, a type almost indigenous to the soil of France.

On familiar terms with all these social groupings, young Arouet, though a bourgeois, had opportunities to watch the passions and intrigues of persons in key positions. He could note the repercussions of these private dramas on public affairs. He knew his country as a political organization and he knew it as a social salon. His love for France in this latter capacity was to remain one of the most abiding passions of his life.

In Paris, Voltaire was shaped by the most characteristic influences of his age and nation. He spent his boyhood at the aristocratic Lycée Louis-le-Grand where, at the hands of the Jesuit Fathers, he received the best education that the times afforded. In the dawning eighteenth century the Jesuits had reached the peak of royal favor. For Father le Tellier, a member of their order, had become the all-powerful confessor of Louis XIV. The Lycée Louis-le-Grand was a pillar of the monarchial system and enjoyed the beneficent protection of the Sun King himself. Thus during his school days young Arouet was exposed to the three ideals which France has clung to through all the tragic events of her history. These are, and to a large extent still remain, Catholicism, classicism, and the art of society.

The Catholicism of the Jesuit Fathers of the Lycée Louis-le-Grand was pliant and worldly. Like most men of their order they tended to isolate faith in the supernatural powers of God and the Church from too direct a connection with the stern moral code of the gospels. Insistence on rigorous standards of personal conduct might prove extremely unpalatable to the adherents they hoped to win among the great and the fashionable. So they placed their emphasis instead on the blind submission of man's intellect to the ineffable mysteries of doctrine and ritual.[11]

At the Lycée Louis-le-Grand, Voltaire may well have found evidence for his later famous statement that God was made in man's image, and not the pious reverse. As envisioned by his teachers, the heavenly hierarchy seemed to be a sort of celestial court of Louis XIV where credit and persuasion were not without their uses. As at Versailles, the prime duty of the Faithful lay in the formal recognition and correct glorification of omnipotent authority. Christianity, the Jesuit Fathers sought to uphold by their stress on the sacrosanct infallibility of such human institutions as the Church and the monarchy. As a result, the youths who accepted their teachings became, first of all, the fanatical defenders of Catholicism, and secondly, the devoted subjects of those Bourbons who in the self-congratulatory words of Louis XIV had "done so much for God."[12]

The godson of the impious Abbé de Châteauneuf was immune to such devout indoctrination. His precocious mind, long guided by that eminent though cynical churchman, refused to be subjugated by a supernaturally revealed interpretation of the universe. Nor did this orthodox vision of the world cast any spell over his imagination or emotions.

Thus the emancipation which his schoolmates often pretended, with little Arouet was a reality. For unlike most of these boys he had never known any sentimental associations with the Faith of his native country. In love with life, he recoiled from any religion or philosophy which regards earthly happiness as inconsequential. Keen distaste he felt for that monastic ideal of holiness which counsels man to withdraw from all that earth has to offer of beauty, work, and pleasure. If such a course finds favor with heavenly authority, then, he reasoned, the ways of Heaven are inapplicable to the affairs of earth, and earth in turn has even less to contribute to the workings of Heaven.

Voltaire found the Jesuits congenial because they had a tendency to maintain this same sharp cleavage between natural and supernatural phenomena. To insure faith against the questionings of reason, they seemed to place religious beliefs, principles, and practices in an acknowledged sphere of the miraculous denied all connection with actual life.[13] To young Arouet this sphere of revelation remained closed. He chose instead the way of reason. Yet so conducive to incredulity was this complete separation of reason and revelation that the mature philosopher could use their lack of bearing upon each other most skillfully.

With sly irony, the author of the *Essay on the Manners and Minds of Nations* admits his incompetence as a mere mortal to comment on the divinely mysterious events recorded in the scriptures. Indeed, man with his feeble reason has often wondered why, with God as their leader, the Israelites were nevertheless obliged to flee the Egyptians, and why the cavalry of the latter was so numerous when all their horses had apparently succumbed to the plague.

To these countless objections there is only one answer. God willed it, the Church believes it, and we too should believe it. . . . It seems clear that the history of God should in no way resemble the history of Man.[14]

So beyond human comprehension were these workings of celestial authority that actions which in Moses and Joshua were divinely sanctioned would be considered reprehensible from the standpoint of lay morality. By appealing to universal natural law, Voltaire wished to call attention to the falsity, cruelty, and capriciousness which, so he judged, characterized much supposedly divine intervention in human affairs.[15] As a philosopher he had declared war on that sanguinary spirit of superstition which the Church of his day seemed to abet and encourage. His weapon was reason. Yet in recognizing reason and revelation as two distinct sources of knowledge and in keeping these two spheres separate, he owed to his Jesuit training a method of attack at once diabolical in finesse and safe for the attacker.

Still, reason to Voltaire was not, as some critics have believed, a "panacea for all human ills," a magical power to judge correctly, or a lay substitute for the gift the devout call "revelation."

"Reason," said Voltaire in the article "Enthusiasm" of the *Philosophic Dictionary,* "consists in seeing things unfailingly as they are." In his estimation "reason" is not truth in itself, but the conscious will to search for the truth and to do so with fearless integrity. Such integrity of judgment can be achieved only when the mind is permitted free inquiry and when the individual is sufficiently master of himself to remain mentally unshackled by passions, authoritarian doctrines, self-interest, partisan feeling, or vanity. Reason, as Voltaire saw it, is the fruit of intellectual honesty, and such thinking, far from being "soulless," often requires the highest qualities of mind and soul.

During his years as a pupil of the Jesuits he formed those strong cultural ties which helped to bind him irrevocably to his native country. While in his early teens, he acquired a lasting passion for the artistic heritage of his nation.[16] No more able custodians of classical culture could be found than the learned Jesuit Fathers. In early eighteenth-century France, a worship of pagan Antiquity coexisted in placid harmony with a rigorous and formal Catholicism. If the Jesuits, as priests, were inclined to shun the philosophic aspect of classical culture, they stressed above all the aesthetic grandeur of Latin literature. They dwelt in ancient Rome and Greece as in a spiritual cultural homeland and extolled this vanished civilization as the greatest monument to a purely human development.

Their talented pupil was therefore taught to revere French classicism as the creative appropriation by France of rules and standards that were the heritage of a Golden Age, never to be surpassed in later centuries. Uninterrupted by studies of science or modern European history, he spent his boyhood writing smooth translations of Virgil. French odes, eclogues, and epigrams he was taught to compose according to favorite Latin models.

From his art-loving masters he acquired his life-long conviction that the canons of literary excellence had been established once and for all by the incomparable Ancients. The Patriarch of

Ferney like the schoolboy of Louis-le-Grand would respond with
fervor to any perpetuation by his compatriots of the aesthetic
ideals of antiquity. In 1778, the very last year of his life, he
defended the French classical tradition against Mrs. Montague,
an English woman of letters. Racine she had compared unfavor-
ably with Shakespeare. In her opinion the harmony and grace
of the French dramatist were artistic qualities far inferior to the
poetic exuberance of the Shakespearean imagination. To such
statements the Sage of Ferney replied:

I was the first to extract from the genius of Shakespeare a little of
that gold which lies still embedded in the mud of his century. I
have never been swayed by national prejudice.[17]

By "extracting gold from the genius of Shakespeare," Voltaire
was referring to his own adaptations from the English poet and
his work in popularizing the beauties of the Bard on the European continent. National prejudice, it is true, he never consciously allowed to dictate his artistic judgments.

His literary taste, though, remained a prisoner of his early
training. The fearless intellect of Voltaire, which in religion and
matters of government dared everything, accepted in art a set
of infallibles. The same classical precepts, taught him in his
youth by Father Tournemine, he cherished, even at eighty-four,
as ultimate revelations on the achievement of literary perfection.

A third national characteristic that he developed and acquired
under Jesuit tutelage was his skill at the art of good manners.
Taste and a sense of correct form in both life and literature
were always an essential part of his genius. While still a schoolboy, he received a thorough training in all the typically French
social graces. He learned to discuss without pedantry any subject, no matter how weighty. He could flatter playfully and
realistically, and as an extra-curricular activity, he could stab
with that daintily cruel literary weapon know as the "epigram."

His Jesuit teachers were masters of etiquette both urbane
and celestial. From early youth, the future dinner-guest of kings

became familiar not only with correct usage, but with the intricate conventions of the French court. Like those young aristocrats, his fellow-students, he became an accomplished model of poise and *savoir faire.*

His actual station was in the middle class. Yet his training and formative influences fitted him only for a life in the highest circles. The conflict inherent in this equivocal position proved an irresistible stimulus to his ambition and a torment that fretted and harassed his youth.[18]

Young Arouet left school already molded by two national ideals which were to determine the course of his later existence. These two French passions were classicism and urbanity. Contact with classical art set the elegant, harmonious pattern for the poet and playwright. His graceful urbanity won him sufficient friends in high places to make his future campaigns as a reformer possible. As a youth any realization of the literary goals he set for himself merely rendered his social ambitions more attainable.[19] In turn, the ease of tone and persuasive lightness of touch he learned from aristocratic salons found expression in his prose, and explains the wide circulation of his writings on the most profoundly philosophic subjects.

His formal classical education had provided him with his passport for *la patrie des honnêtes gens,* and though this land of culture and taste might well spread out regardless of national boundaries, the domain had, so he believed, a capital. To young Arouet and to the mature Voltaire, the name of it was Paris.

As he entered upon the world, young Arouet found his intimate personal inspiration in that spirit of hedonism so prevalent in the Paris of his early manhood. Religion he saw represented by a dying king who, hoping to save his royal soul, turned over the affairs of France to a set of hypocritical priests and rapacious religious councilors. For such superstition and abuse of power the future Voltaire felt outright contempt. In preference to such so-called Christians, he aligned himself with the intellectually honest worshipers of the god Bacchus and the philosopher Epicurus. Readily he embraced the deistic paganism of Abbé Chaulieu, the leader of that company of learned libertines who called themselves the "Epicureans of the Temple."[20]

While the favorite of this group, the young poet discovered a philosophic justification for his own personal will to enjoy fully of this world with scant thought for the Hereafter. Amidst the banqueters of the "Temple" the hedonism of ancient Rome and Greece lived again in all its crude simplicity. To Chaulieu and his band the supreme object of man's existence was the attainment of pleasure and the ingenious avoidance of all kinds of pain. This paganism was best fulfilled through the fat benefices attached to the Catholic office of *abbé*.[21] Indeed, that champion of earthly values, Voltaire, was started on the path of his lifework by the idle parasitic clergy his own vitriolic pen did so much to destroy and discredit. His subtle method of attack he owed in part to his Jesuit training.

The originator of the mighty battle-cry of *Ecrasez l'Infâme* was a product of the Latin Catholic world. For the form of his genius and his habits of mind, he was indebted alike to libertinism and to Catholicism. *Libertin* ideas gave him his private impetus as a social philosopher, and *libertinisme* such as practiced by Ninon, St. Evremond, and the sharp-witted old banqueters of the Temple exists only in a Catholic culture. In Latin France *libertinisme* stood in relation to Catholicism as the "other side of the medal." Since Catholicism by its very nature is incapable of modification, the individualistic, hedonistic spirit that found expression in libertinism took revenge upon the Church by spearing her with sarcasms and in usurping the materially profitable offices of her inner organization. In a society where Church and State were one, the rejection of revealed religion entailed the questioning of the authority back of all laws and institutions. Libertine in the matter of religious belief came inevitable to mean libertine as regards morals and customs as well.[22]

Thus young Arouet at twenty voiced the same Epicurean

maxims as the eighty-four-year-old revelers who welcomed him so heartily to the banquets of the Temple. Like them he celebrated the earthly pleasures of love and delicate feasting, while he personally gloried in the less robust delights of poetry and witty conversation. Sorrow he would drown in a voluptuous refreshment of the senses, and death he would face with stoical acceptance.[23]

Nevertheless the libertine precepts which summed up the life experience of Abbé Chaulieu merely served Voltaire as a point of departure. At eighty the master was a jovial Silenus who notwithstanding his years of revelry still maintained a firm hold on reason. The disciple at the same ripe old age had evolved into a social reformer, a philanthropist, and a humanitarian philosopher.

The originality of Voltaire, as a person and as a thinker, is that he divested hedonism of its selfishly individualistic implications. Man must enjoy. He himself had an inborn claim to what the American Declaration of Independence was later to name "the pursuit of happiness." But others, he as firmly believed, have also the right to enjoy, and in order that this right of all may be fulfilled, reason should achieve an effective balance between egotism and altruism.

His once flippant exposure of moral hypocrisies and incongruities gradually ripened into a relentless often destructive analysis of the leading institutions of his nation. The law, the Church, and the monarchy he judged not by any ideals they theoretically represented, but by their actual contribution to the greatest good of the greatest number. His mature opposition to the ecclesiastical code was founded not on antipathy to principles that sought to cheat his individual instincts of their natural satisfaction. He fought monasticism as an obstacle to the successful social expression of the forces of self-interest and self-perpetuation. He felt persuaded that the renunciation of terrestrial pleasures and responsibilities inherent in such teachings would result in a negation of the purpose of all civilizations, and, as viewed by Voltaire, this purpose could be paradoxically described as a great communal effort toward individual happiness.[24]

The years from 1716 to 1726 marked the first phase of his life-long struggle between his epicurean delight in his Parisian homeland and his growing dissatisfaction with the autocratic French state. His imprisonment by the regent for poems he was only rumored to have written struck the blow that shocked him into writing an epic poem. In this expression of literary patriotism he made a fervent plea for liberal and humane principles of government.

During his eleven-month incarceration in the Bastille he not only found his direction as a writer. He discovered unsuspected within himself a courage, a fortitude, and a will for justice that neither prison, exile, age, nor maladies could ever weaken.[25] To this Titan he felt stirring within him he gave the name "Voltaire."

The Titan had come alive, but remained for a while quiescent. For his stay in the Bastille had enhanced the prestige of the society-poet, and at this stage in his life, the poet nursed a predominant ambition. He wished members of nobility to accept him as an equal.[26]

The self-named Voltaire challenged as yet no essential principle of the existing order. In such plays as *Œdipus, Artémire,* and *Mariamne* he stressed, it is true, the common mortality of kings and the perils of superstition. Daring ideas like these, however, were certain to find favor with a free-thinking aristocracy jealously critical of the power of king and priest. Such topics were introduced in other plays of the era.[27]

Offered a pension by the monarch who, a short while ago, had imprisoned him, the author of *Œdipus* responded with a remark which, true or false, well reflects his attitude of mockery and personal contentment with conditions as he found them: "I should appreciate it if Your Majesty would take charge of my board. Yet I beg Your Highness to provide no longer for my lodgings."[28]

Still, Philip of Orleans continued to take charge of his lodgings and upon the mere appearance of the anonymous satire the *Philippics,* the young Voltaire was denied admittance to the capital. With scant complaint against a regime which permitted such arbitrary injustice, he blithely accepted the hospitality of Mme la Maréchale de Villars.

His complacency in the face of official persecution increased in exact proportion to his popularity with the nobility. In 1716 when first charged with literary *lèse majesté,* he had felt restless and resentful, even in spite of the delightful refuge provided him by the Duc de Sully.[29] Yet in 1719, a fashionable young playwright, completely at home in the world of society, his banishment from Paris for a few months aroused in him little more than lighthearted indifference. The spring he had passed in long visits to the country château of Sully and the Duc de Richelieu. Summer could just as well be spent at Villars where he could talk astronomy to the fascinating Maréchale: "I pass my life from castle to castle,"[30] he wrote gaily to Mme de Mimeure.

His appearance at Fontainebleau in 1725 to witness the marriage of Louis XV and Marie Leczinska marked the apotheosis of Arouet, the social climber. His foothold in the French court he had obtained the preceding year when this inner circle was staying at Chantilly. Now offered the house at Fontainebleau of Mme de Prie, the queen's best friend, he had the opportunity to take part in all the festivities of the royal wedding. He flattered the young queen and received from this future royal adversary a pension of 150 livres. He was thirty-one years old and the author of a celebrated epic poem. His conquest of both the "court" and the "town" was complete.

His visit to court, nevertheless, represents an uncomfortable moment in the growing tension between Arouet, the dazzled flatterer of French society, and Voltaire, the fearless critic of the monarchy. His correspondence proves that despite his successes he remained beneath the surface a bored and restless courtier.[31] From the pursuit of mere enjoyment, his writing had begun more and more to lure him away.

This inner transformation was hastened by an event of far reaching consequence, a wholly unforeseen quarrel with a grandee of the realm. Upon his return from court, his plebeian origin was sneered at by a Rohan and he, a commoner born Arouet, had dared talk back.

Thrashed by the lackeys of a worthless aristocrat, the first poet in France came into brutal firsthand contact with those bitter injustices inherent in the social structure. On the shoulders, too humble for a Rohan to strike in person, the full weight of the caste system had fallen instead. A few months before Voltaire had numbered among his friends even the newly married royal couple. But now he was an outcast. A tide of class feeling had risen against him and he found himself ostracized from circles where he had been a favorite from earliest youth.

The Rohan episode served as the first break in his attachment to the soil of his native homeland. Injustice by the autocratic rule of the French state he had already suffered. Yet, by those nobles for whose enormous profit the machinery of government functioned, he had, to all appearances, been welcomed as a friend and equal. His hedonistic delight in the charm, wit, and elegance of his French homeland had rendered him somewhat callous to the shortcomings of France as a political entity. Now expelled from the "salons" he was obliged to call upon the State to protect his rights as a French citizen.[32]

By the laws of the kingdom, death was the accustomed penalty for an unprovoked act of violence. Yet his adversary not only remained free, but took prompt measures to rid himself of an absurd bourgeois poet who was fool enough to believe that any statute in the legal code could be effective against a Rohan. Snatched from his useless attempts at vengeance, Voltaire found himself clapped in the Bastille as a common laughingstock who had made of himself a public nuisance.

In prison he learned that the class prejudices bred by the monarchical system were stronger than friendship, justice, royal favor or disfavor, or any conceivable law of the land. The Duc de

Sully had gladly shielded him from the displeasure of the regent. Yet he would take not one step against the abuse of his friend by the Chevalier de Rohan. When the enforcement of law worked to the disadvantage of the privileged classes, all processes of justice remained paralyzed. With neither friends nor any impartial authority to uphold his natural right of liberty of person, Voltaire felt literally and spiritually abandoned. The State had failed him. The society of his homeland had remorselessly rejected him. Therefore, on April 29, 1726, when banished to within fifty leagues of Paris, he made up his mind to leave France and sail for England.[33]

Nevertheless when the author of the *Henriade* embarked for England, he had no intention of settling there permanently. He meant only to draw a curtain of absence, in hopes of effacing from the mind of Paris his recent humiliation. He had also a literary purpose for the trip to England. Imprisonment by the regent had first moved him to celebrate with escapist ardor his country's greatest monarch. Now ill-treated by both the homeland and the State he again turned to Henri IV for comfort.

The clandestine edition of the *Henriade* which he had published at Rouen failed entirely to satisfy him, for his text was often mutilated by errors and omissions. On the supposedly freer soil of a Protestant nation he had long dreamed of bringing out a de luxe edition of his national epic poem. The moment had now come when superbly printed and illustrated, as well as corrected and embellished, his Henri IV should invade and reconquer France from a foreign vantage point. For the scene of this endeavor he chose the impious land across the channel.

His firsthand discovery of England made on the mind of Voltaire an unforgettable impression. After his disillusionment with his native country he now discovered a national organization on which the common man could rely for support and protection. As he pointedly reminded his own nation in his famous discussion of English government in the *Philosophic Letters*:

On these shores you hear nothing about high, medium or low justice, nor of hunting privileges on the lands of a citizen who may not fire so much as a shot in his own field.[34]

Deploring the days before the rights of ordinary mankind were recognized in England, he declared with a warm new-found sympathy for the bourgeois and artisan classes:

The people, the most numerous, the most self-respecting and therefore the most respectable part of the population, the group made up of those who study law and sciences, business-men and artisans, in a word everyone not a tyrant, was regarded by them [the nobles] as animals beneath the status of man.[35]

On this side of the channel he beheld a government which ruled by an impartial body of laws and not by the caprice of the king, his mistress, or his confessor. Whenever the sovereign forsook his role as custodian of the constitution or failed to uphold the precious document, revolution followed—yet a revolution for the conservation of liberty and not a sedition resulting from intrigue.

This historical observation Voltaire made clear to his compatriots in the *Philosophic Letters*:

The French think that the government of this island is more stormy than the surrounding ocean. True; yet only when the King himself begins the tempest; only when he tries to make himself the master of a ship of which he is nothing but the First Mate.[36]

The check and balance of the parliamentary system appealed to him no less than the Newtonian laws of attraction. Under the eye of royal authority the nobles and the people strove to harmonize their conflicting interests for the sake of the common good.

The House of Commons represented the majority of British citizens. A principal function of this organ was therefore the regulation of taxes.

England provided Voltaire with a definite standard by which to judge the customs and institutions of his native country. The

*Philosophic Letters* are less a description of the English political system than a criticism of France in the light of comparison with a freer nation. He noted that in liberal England, clergy and nobility alike shared the financial burdens of the kingdom. So the poor were saved from misery.

In his discussion of the sore subject of taxes he abandoned all show of detachment and struck boldly at some of the most prevalent French abuses:

. . . each gives not according to his rank (which is absurd) but according to his income; there is no *taille* or *capitation arbitraire* but a workable land tax. . . . The amount of the tax is always the same, even if the revenues from land might have increased; thus no one is oppressed and no one complains. The feet of the peasant are not bruised by wooden shoes; he eats white bread; he is well dressed; he need not fear that if he adds to the number of his live-stock or covers his roof with tiles, his taxes for the next year will be raised.[37]

England thrilled Voltaire. For in this land which had attained greatness not by war but by commerce, the average citizen could live with a fair amount of dignity and security. Ability was rewarded regardless of rank. Freedom of worship was permitted so long as the exponents of the many religious sects did not disturb the peace or curtail the liberty of their fellow Englishmen. The peculiar practices of the various faiths enjoyed the full protection of the law, and Quakers kept their hats on even before the officers of the crown.

The whole English system of government, which is designed as a mighty bulwark against the infringement of "natural rights," caught hold of his mind and imagination with the force of a sudden revelation. Ever afterward he saw in the British constitutional monarchy the closest approximation of how the nation as a political entity should protect the individual.[38]

In England he explored the state of man in a foreign country whose customs and institutions were anathematized across the channel. His unique aim was no longer to be the pet of "high society." He set about to investigate almost all classes and conditions of Englishmen. In Falkener, whose home he shared at Wandsworth, he saw the best type of English merchant—liberal, cultivated, and proud that the trade he practiced contributed to the economic upbuilding of the nation. Undoubtedly Voltaire had this friend in mind when in his discussion of commerce in the *Philosophic Letters* he compared the usefulness of a powdered French lord, who plays the role of the menial in a king's ante-chamber, and the merchant, who as the author aptly put it, "from his business office gives order to Sumatra and Cairo and contributes to the happiness of the world."[39]

Through Falkener he met other intelligent members of the middle class of England. P. Delme, the brother-in-law of his host, was an important dignitary in the city of London and offered the French exile considerable information about the workings of the municipal government.

The author of the *Henriade,* however, made his inevitable appearance in the fashionable drawing-rooms of London. In men like Bolingbroke, Hervey, Chesterfield, and Peterborough he beheld a cosmopolitan, charmingly polite aristocracy who cultivated the arts and eagerly fraternized with men of letters. In the circle of these brilliant lords he became friendly with some of the best English writers of their era. He met his fellow classicist, Pope, and Swift, his only rival in the realm of satire. He knew the Whig poets Young and Thomson. Gay showed him the immortal *Beggar's Opera* before it reached the play-boards. Anxious for an inside view of politics he even courted the friendship of such an archetype of professional politician as Doddington.

Determined to observe the English people and the mores which gave them their honesty and vitality, he went, as he himself said, from the court to the stock exchange, from a synagogue to a Quaker meeting. He conversed with lordly politicians and with boatmen on the Thames. From his firsthand researches he concluded that mutual respect and cooperation between social classes were the outcome of a government which allowed its citizens a fair degree of civic freedom. More social justice than existed in France was indeed possible without an overthrow of law, decency, or even monarchy.

In "royalist-republican" England he found among the upper classes none of the sturdy uncouthness or indifference to culture that he had noted in the comparatively free land of Holland. In Britain he discovered a society fully as brilliant and fascinating as the Parisian world of fashion. In the splendor of Bolingbroke's mansion in Pall Mall he watched (though less often than he would have us believe) the interaction of literature, politics, and "high society." For in England the nobles did not dance the minuet in a vacuum. They actively participated in the affairs of their country. Whether they used their political power for good or for ill such aristocrats as Bolingbroke, Oxford, or Peterborough were at least men of action and not detached guests who merely resided within the nation. Since the younger sons of great nobles felt it not beneath them to engage in commerce, echoes of the international world of trade and big business reached many a smart gathering.[40]

Though in France the nobles delighted in the company of men of letters they often treated them as contemptuously as clowns or gypsies. Here such was the respect for ability that literature as a profession was highly honored and literary men were entrusted with important public offices. Poets could exchange ideas with lords on a footing of upright independence and not demean themselves by base flattery.

So intoxicated was Voltaire with British liberty and so badly did his homeland fare in comparison with liberal England that in the Fall of 1726 he wrote scornfully to Thiriot in English: "I fear, I hope nothing from your country." Stating a wish to see his friend in London he asserted vehemently:

You will see a nation fond of their liberty, learned, witty, despising life and death, a nation of philosophers; not but that there are some fools in England, every country has its madmen . . . but by God, English wisdom and honesty is above yours.[41]

"English wisdom," notwithstanding, the reading public of Britain seemed somewhat apathetic toward his cherished epic poem. Accordingly the author applied for permission to return to France. In the Spring of 1727 he finally obtained a permit from the French authorities to reenter Paris and remain there for a three-month time limit. His actual banishment was now officially over. It was tacitly understood that if he behaved to the satisfaction of the authorities during the probationary three-month time limit, his permit would become indefinitely extended. However, well pleased with the political system on the English side of the channel and busy in congenial surroundings, Voltaire remained well over a year in voluntary exile.[42]

For his whole life had now become centered in ideas, their expression, and their dissemination. If he had contemplated a return to France, his intention was primarily to try to gain those subscriptions to the *Henriade* still withheld from him by England, the "nation of philosophers." But his British prospects brightened. So he decided to remain in order to market his epic poem, and also to complete his exploration of his adopted country.

If Voltaire had once used literature as an aid in social climbing, in England he climbed chiefly for his literary and financial advancement. His first object was to express to the world a faith in liberty and tolerance which had been passionately reaffirmed in the light of recent evidence. His second goal was to acquire a financial capital which could protect him in his coming struggle against the enemies of enlightenment.

While in England, the author of the *Essay on Epic Poetry* discovered both for life and literature the cosmopolitan ideal. As with unexampled energy and ingenuity he personally advertised his epic poem in the drawing-rooms of London, he discovered that between men of taste and intellectual eagerness there exists a bond which transcends the political boundaries of nations. Between those who share wit, elegance, politeness, and learning, the isolating barriers of nationality prove relatively ineffective. For in this international fellowship of good company the differences in customs, education, and outlook caused by nation merely challenge witty analysis and provoke fruitful comparison.[43]

In England Voltaire beheld a nation which as a political entity ranked far above his native country. In addition to this, he found that in cultivation and urbanity, English society could rival the most brilliant circles of Paris. However, if England compared favorably with France as a government, or even as a "salon," his homeland stood supreme in the realm of culture. This lifelong conviction he was fond of asserting, especially on those occasions when the English had won from his countrymen a military victory.[44]

Voltaire nevertheless admired many English writers among his contemporaries. He appreciated the polished elegance of Pope and the savagely ironic humor of Swift. In Congreve he recognized a master of the comedy of manners. Yet as soon as he turned from the narrow literary sphere marked by such distinguishing features of his century as classicism and political pamphleteering he stepped into an alien world. In Shakespeare and Milton the English literary genius had reached its most characteristic expression. Yet to the former pupil of Father Tournemine these giants of literature remained in a sense merely brilliant and fascinating enigmas. Voltaire could have denied Shakespeare's claim to greatness and still be in agreement with such eminent Englishmen as Pope, Shaftesbury, Chesterfield, and Bolingbroke. Nevertheless the author of the *Essay on Epic Poetry* was one of the first persons to call to the attention of Europe the genius of Shakespeare.

In his excited response to this greatest of English poets, the author of *Œdipus* was torn between his native art instinct and a taste formed by his early training in the French classical tradition. Emotionally and aesthetically, he was swept off his feet by those scenes of swift action and inspired poetry which abound in Shakespearean drama. Yet rationally he condemned the methods by which this English dramatist created such beauty.

Shakespeare he looked upon much as a Church Father might look upon a saintly heretic. This author had defied all the consecrated rules of verse and drama bequeathed to writers of taste by the incomparable Ancients. He had violated the dramatic unities. He had introduced low characters and strewn the stage with corpses.[45] Nevertheless despite these unpardonable crudities in style and subject, Shakespeare had arrived at effects of rough magnificence. This sublimity he had achieved unaided by rules, and by his untutored genius alone.

While Voltaire admired Shakespeare, not only his French classical training, but a temperamental antipathy separated him from Milton. Still, his criticism of *Paradise Lost* shows that he at least glimpsed some of the beauty of this poet. He called attention to the harmony between the style and the subject of the celestial epic. The poem had a "majesty combined with ill humor" which the French critic considered a characteristic of the English literary genius.[46]

Also he was charmed, though puzzled, at the predominantly Anglo-Saxon conception of love as portrayed by Milton in the passion so innocent yet unabashed of Adam and Eve in the Garden. As a product of a Catholic culture whose recognition of man's right to terrestrial happiness had come chiefly through *libertin* channels, Voltaire wrote of love as an "amiable weakness," the more glamorous because theoretically forbidden. He now noted that in the Puritan poet, Milton, love became a virtue at once strengthening and legitimate. Struck by this harmonious acceptance of man's earthly needs by a writer so dominated by theological concepts, the author of the *Essay on Epic Poetry* remarked:

. . . in all other poems love is regarded as a weakness. Milton alone raises love to the level of a virtue. With a chaste hand the poet raises the veil which usually covers the pleasures of this passion. He transports the reader to a garden of delights. He seems to make him taste there the pure though voluptuous happiness with which Adam and Eve are filled. The poet thus rises no higher than human nature, but higher than human nature corrupted by Original Sin; and since such love is without example or equal, so is the poetry without example or equal.[47]

Voltaire designed the *Essay on Epic Poetry* as part of his extensive publicity campaign to market the *Henriade*. He believed that a discussion of the comparative merits of national epics would stimulate the interest of the English reading public in his forthcoming poem. However, as was so often the case, this purely personal, practical aim became his point of departure toward a new philosophic discovery. From his own reaction to Shakespeare he learned that there are beauties which impose themselves on the aesthetic sense in defiance of the particular taste formed by a national culture. He therefore concluded that beauty like "natural law" was unalterable and universal.[48]

In his *Essay on Epic Poetry,* Voltaire attempted to combat national prejudice with intellectual analysis. For he desired to broaden the sympathy of all countries so that the nations of the globe might appreciate each other's masterpieces. The cosmopolitan appreciation he envisioned would enable connoisseurs throughout the world to estimate just what qualities in literature did belong to "good sense" or universal beauty.[49]

Of the artistic advantages of such a cultural *rapprochement* between nations he gave the following concrete example:

Would each Nation attend a little more than they do to the Taste and Manners of their respective Neighbors, perhaps a general good Taste might diffuse itself through all Europe from such an intercourse of Learning and from that useful Exchange of Observations. The English stage, for example, might be cleared of mangled carcasses and the style of their tragic authors, come down from this Metaphorical Bombast to a nearer Imitation of Nature. The French would learn from the English to animate their Tragedies with more action and would contract, now and then, their long speeches into shorter and warmer sentiments.[50]

His attitude toward English literature reveals that Voltaire was essentially a literary patriot. If in his effort to appreciate a foreign culture he divested himself (as far as he could) of national prejudice, he did so as no dreamy aesthete. His native country, he hoped, would reap the benefits of his cultural impartiality.

When he first introduced Shakespeare to his compatriots, he sought less to enjoy him than to make use of him. He would enrich the literature of his homeland by adding to the formal perfection of French drama the vitality, sustained action, fire, and color of the English dramatist.[51] Later in 1752, when Shakespearean influence became dominant, Voltaire showed himself in his true role as guardian of the French classical tradition.

His attitude, however, was wholly consistent. Though he ridiculed *Hamlet* as the work of a "drunken savage," a play which would be rejected by the lowest populace of France or Italy, he thus reasserted Shakespeare's claim to genius:

But among these gross irregularities which still disfigure the English drama, making it even to-day so absurd and so barbarous, one finds, strangely enough in *Hamlet* flashes of sublimity and of the most amazing genius.[52]

In France, the dramatic devices of the Bard had been sufficiently utilized. The time had come to banish the savage uncouth playwright from the shores of *la patrie*.

Similarly, through all his indefatigable explorations of English politics, literature and society, Voltaire never lost sight of the advancement of his native country. His true aim was to improve the lot of mankind on this mediocre planet. Yet this he could do best by starting with that segment of the planet in which fate had originally placed him.

By the spring of 1728 he rapidly lost interest in his adopted country. He had by now successfully launched the *Henriade;* in the *Philosophic Letters* he would bring to the land of his birth the enlightenment of England. The island of his exile had already served for him its purpose. He now had a definite standard for the constructive criticism of his native France.

He had arrived in England a gay *libertin* poet of intellectual fearlessness. Upon his return early in 1729 to France he had crystallized into a philosopher. He longed for French friends and familiar haunts in Paris.[53] Yet no more was he intent upon reconquering his once enviable position in Parisian society. Stronger than his territorial attachment to his homeland, stronger than his love for the glittering social life of the French capital, was his determination to emancipate his countrymen from the forces of darkness and superstition.

He sailed for France resolved that reason and those rights of man based on reason should find a home in France.


## THE SAGE OF FERNEY

AFTER his return from England, Voltaire gave his first allegiance less to the real France than to universal principles of justice, tolerance, and humane dealings. These he wished to see established within the boundaries of his native land. Thus he refused to accept that loved France, already created by historical determinism. With all the force of his genius, he strove to win over men's minds to a belief in liberal policies, and the will to enlighten and improve the State.

The first of such efforts was the *Philosophic Letters*. The appearance in print of this work, together with the *Commentary on the Thoughts of Pascal*, provoked in 1734 that warrant of arrest which drove him into hiding at Cirey. There his long association with Mme du Châtelet developed. The oppressive power of French literary censorship he would go on defying so long as the breath of life were in him. In case of need, he would escape across the border to nearby Lorraine. In this small principality no officers of the Crown would have the authority to arrest him, for Lorraine was independent of French rule.

During the years from 1734 to 1740, the author of the *Philosophic Letters* was safe in Paris only so long as friendly influences predominated in the royal ministry. In 1736 friends in the

capital warned him that even from far-off Cirey he must flee.
A saucy trifle of his called *The Worldling* had enraged the French
clergy. In a few gay rhymes he had dared to question the cleanliness of Eden and the comfort of man's first parents, Adam and
Eve.[54] Yet the ecclesiastical persecution visited upon the author
was in this instance merely a pretense. His real offense was still
the *Philosophic Letters*. In fear of seizure by the police, he drove
off in disguise to Brussels. In Belgium and Holland he remained
in hiding from the authorities of his homeland for two full
months.

Meanwhile a foreign prince looked on and built his schemes
around the famous writer, a prince who hoped some day to lure
him from his native land.

That lifelong conflict between the Frenchman loving his
native land and the philosopher, whose first allegiance was to
world-wide principles, centers in its first phase around Frederick
of Prussia.[55] In August, 1736, when this prince first chose him
as a philosophic master, Voltaire saw and seized what seemed to
him an incredible opportunity. Here was his long-awaited chance
to influence a monarch to benefit humanity.

Disappointed that his own sovereign upheld those forces of
darkness and superstition which had condemned the *Philosophic
Letters,* the thinker hoped to make of his royal disciple an
enlightener, a king who, unlike other kings, would be a liber-
ator and not an oppressor of men.[56] Human progress was his
aim. So any advancement toward this goal in far-off Prussia
seemed to him fully as important as in France. For, as he himself once said, when even a corner of the earth is won for
enlightenment that light soon spreads.[57] Nothing then can stop it.

Furthermore, Voltaire the Frenchman felt drawn toward a
Prussian prince who, culturally, chose France as his adopted
country. He flattered His Highness on his bad verses in the
French language and, in obedience to his request, corrected them.

So, in 1740, when after four years of correspondence Prince
Frederick sent him a copy of his *Anti-Machiavelli,* his French

mentor saw the triumph of all his teachings, the fruit of all the discourses he had penned his royal follower on the wretched futility of war and the kingly duty of keeping the peace. The Italian politician Machiavelli had written that the relations between sovereign states can only be founded on force and intrigue. Prince Frederick, though, was of another opinion. In his lofty-minded treatise he refuted Machiavelli's whole system of politics and pleaded for international relations based on good faith and morality.

Voltaire called the *Anti-Machiavelli* the only book worthy to be written by a king for "fifteen hundred years," and proclaimed that it should become the "catechism of kings and their ministers."[58]

A few months later, upon mounting the throne, the royal author voiced the same peace-loving sentiments. The two correspondents met, and Voltaire, the so-called skeptic, came away convinced that the prince he had trained for the kingship would prove to be a civilizer of infinite possibilities. But an unforeseen event now disturbed the balance of power in Europe.

On October 20, 1740, the Emperor Charles VI died, leaving the throne of Austria and his Hapsburg domains to his young and inexperienced daughter, Maria Theresa. In this royal demise lay the grounds for many a dynastic quarrel. Would Frederick, now king, abide by the peaceful principles of his *Anti-Machiavelli?* Or would he yield to the temptation of a war of aggression?

When Frederick promptly astonished Europe by a lightning capture of Austrian-held Silesia, Voltaire suffered one of his life's severest disappointments. Gone forever were his hopes of establishing in Europe a new Arcadia where peace, plenty, and the arts would prosper. For a moment the French philosopher seemed to wonder if this Solomon of the North was worth his time and effort.[59] Frederick, after all, was only a king like other kings. Should he, Voltaire, not scrap his illusions and make the best of reality?

He swallowed the bitter pill and even congratulated his powerful friend on his victories.[60] Yet the depth of his disillusionment in his once promising royal disciple is clear in a letter to Cideville of March 13, 1741:

That fabled cat changed magically into a woman was said to chase after mice the instant she saw them. Thus a prince drops his philosopher's cloak to take up the sword, as soon as he sees a province that suits his convenience.[61]

Since Frederick had proved to be not an enlightener but a menacing hero, Voltaire decided to exploit him for personal and patriotic purposes. As a practical man and a philosopher, he aimed to improve the lot of his fellow beings on this not-so-good planet. Yet he would begin by reshaping France as a political entity. To do this he would work through his king, the human embodiment of the State.

Spurred on by his near success in molding Prussian Frederick, he now hoped to make of his own king an enlightened ruler. Besides, the philosopher was tired of a life in semi-hiding. Once secure in a post at Versailles, he would try to gain the intimate confidence of French Louis. By diplomatic service he could make himself eligible for such an honor. His royal Prussian admirer held in his hands the balance of power in Europe. King Frederick must therefore be won over to the support of French interests. If this could be done, he, Voltaire, would find a way.

Not until the June of 1743 was his patriotic offer accepted. When he started off on his fourth visit to his friend, the king of Prussia, he actually left Paris, charged by the minister of foreign affairs with a secret diplomatic mission. His expenses were paid for by the king of France. First, he was subtly to influence the Prussian ruler to renew his alliance with France. Secondly, he was to warn this monarch about allowing King George of England and Hanover to intervene in the continental struggle. A Britain fighting on the Austrian side would endanger the interests of both France and Prussia.

Indeed, in 1743 France was left fighting a war without

strategic object.[62] The nation had joined Prussia in the general attack on the territories of the Hapsburg empress. Yet not the conquest of Austria for a Prussian-controlled duke of Bavaria but the coexistence of approximately equal states advanced the true interests of the French. The year before, Prussia had consolidated the conquest of Silesia and concluded at Breslau a separate peace with Austria. French peace offers, though, were refused. So France was committed to the war, unaided by her Prussian ally.

At a time when the French kingdom needed to defend herself and her colonies against England, membership in the coalition of Spain, Sardinia, and Bavaria against Austria proved a disastrous drain on the energies of the nation. In the words of the historian Walter Dorn: "There were few errors in the history of France more calamitous than this decision to join in the assault against Maria Theresa."[63]

For France, the only way out of the military impasse was to induce Prussia to reenter the war as her active ally, or at least to back up a former partner with effective material aid. Could Prussia be made thus to conform to French wishes? To bring about such a result, Voltaire dared count on his own personal influence with a Prussian monarch who, for seven long years, had proclaimed himself his admirer.

In the interests of diplomatic secrecy, the French authorities pretended that the famous Frenchman was leaving France as a result of his quarrel with the Academy. To give credence to this belief, the *Death of Caesar* was banned at the Comédie Française. The secret emissary went straight to The Hague where he gave out word that he was there on literary business. Once in the Dutch capital, however, he charmed with attentions and flattery the pleasure-loving young Prussian ambassador. From this strategically placed person he tried to obtain facts on the international situation in regard to Prussia.[64]

In Berlin, amidst all the festivities of his royal visit, the Frenchman never lost sight of his secret mission. In vain he sounded out Frederick as to his moves on the European continent. Cleverly, but to no avail, he formulated that famous questionnaire designed to trick the king into revealing his true intentions toward Europe and toward France in particular. He worked for his national objective even at the peril of royal displeasure. Upon hearing that the king planned a trip to Bayreuth to visit his sister, he suspected that this excursion had a political significance. So despite the reluctant permission granted him by the monarch, he had the patriotism or the impertinence to trail along.

As the royal manner toward him stiffened, the Frenchman was made to feel his ambiguous position as diplomatic spy in Prussia. Still undaunted, he asked his royal host for that special letter to Louis XV which he believed would so add to his credit in his own land. Frederick however refused. Ironically he expressed his regret that the philosopher had with him no papers as ambassador.

Voltaire, nevertheless, had guessed right. The visit to Bayreuth masked a move which had direct bearing upon the international situation. Frederick had heard rumors of that forthcoming alliance between England, Sardinia, and Austria which was contracted at Worms on September 13, 1743. At once he recognized the threat to his recently acquired Silesia. For the consolidation of the conquest more territory was needed. So he meant to strike again, but at his own time, and with appropriate backing. Therefore his sojourn to Bayreuth served merely as an excuse to visit many German princes and diplomatically mobilize them against the House of Hapsburg. Before resuming hostilities he wished to make sure of their support and unqualified loyalty.

From his intimacy with Podewils, Frederick's attaché at The Hague, Voltaire knew of the probability of this venture. Energetically he seconded the king in his attempt to stir into action the princes of the Empire. As a Frenchman, though, he wanted aid for France. In a private conversation he urged the young Margrave to obtain from his royal brother-in-law an army of some ten thousand. Should the prince accomplish this, then, so said Voltaire, France would grant him a subsidy, and one large enough to maintain another ten thousand men in Franconia throughout the winter.

On the whole, though, the secret emissary discovered scant information on matters of state not available to Valori,[65] the official French ambassador to Prussia. The writer-diplomat learned, first of all, that since the treaty of Breslau, Frederick no longer considered himself a French ally; secondly that both England and Holland were bidding for the aid of Prussia; thirdly, that inside Germany the Prussian king was master. The secret informant felt reasonably certain that in spite of a few vague promises, Frederick would not offer the French much material assistance. For he was using them to fight for him a war he would reenter at his good pleasure.

Determined to succeed in the charge entrusted to him, even upon his return to France, Voltaire persisted in his efforts. With the official permission of the French ministry he entered into a secret correspondence with Podewils, the frivolous Prussian ambassador at The Hague whom he had already courted and flattered. Through this friendly intermediary he schemed to work on the mind of Frederick for a re-signing of the Franco-Prussian alliance. He therefore sent to The Hague information and propaganda which, reaching his royal friend at the discretion of the ambassador, would favorably dispose him toward France and dispel his well-known ideas on the "softness of the French."[66]

Few matters of state, though, were more of a foregone conclusion than the renewal of the alliance between France and Prussia. If the Prussian monarch were to conserve Silesia, he needed in Europe an ally. Between a hostile England, an uncertain Russia, and the southern European powers in the enemy orbit, the French nation seemed his only possible strong support. Meanwhile, France hopelessly committed to a coalition war with no bearing on her national interests, had a similar need of Prussia. Yet the alliance between the two countries signed six months after his return from Berlin seemed to crown with success the loyal efforts of the philosopher-diplomat. He now possessed a modest, though legitimate claim to favor with the court of Louis XV.[67]

His attitude toward his French king reveals that in Voltaire the concept of the nation, as the hearth of individual liberties, was often subconsciously warring with traditional dynastic patriotism. The lifework of the author of the *Discourse on Man* was to arouse all thinking people to indignation at the misuse of power and the exploitation of the poor and weak inherent in the political system. Yet, while attempting to carry on this work, he sought favor and employment from the head of the established order. Louis XV he judged coldly as the "stupidest of kings," and he had neither liking nor esteem for this ruling Bourbon. Nevertheless, more than the brilliant congenial Frederick, more than the most flattering patronage from any crowned head in Europe, he desired to stand well with the sovereign of his own nation.

As the first man of letters in France, Voltaire could find neither rest nor peace until he obtained from the descendant of Henri IV and Louis XIV full recognition for his services to literature. Deluded by his own weakness for the glamor and pageantry of court life, he persuaded himself that he could win over personally those individuals who officially or unofficially governed the affairs of the kingdom. Secure in the confidence of his king, he would soon be granted admission to the secret meetings of the royal council. Thus, he, a philosopher, might at last have his chance to influence the policies of the State.[68]

His alternate wooing and flouting of Versailles are explained by the basic impossibility of his attempt to retain royal favor while working against those time-honored injustices referred to as the "royal interests." The treasury of the realm was filled by a system of taxation which exempted from financial responsibility both the nobles and clergy and which paid for court extravagance out of the earnings of the French people. These abuses Voltaire tried all his life to destroy.

Well aware of the initial paradox in his mere presence at court he wrote to Thiriot in 1745: "I crash here the gates of the Temple of Fortune, and am as out of place at Versailles as an atheist in church."[69]

Just as with royal protection he hoped to combat the evils of monarchy, he sought patronage from the Pope while attacking the abuses of Catholicism. First he sent Benedict XIV some artful and outrageous compliments on the genius of his pontifical writings. Next, upon due encouragement, he gathered up sufficient courage to ask permission to dedicate to His Holiness himself the forbidden play, *Mahomet*. On September 19, 1745, he received the Apostolic Benediction and waved in the face of the French capital the Pope's acceptance of the dedication of a play which Lord Chesterfield as well as all Paris had justly recognized as a covert attack on the fanaticism of revealed religion. So he could say again as he had said long before this final triumph: "I am on fine terms with His Holiness. At present, let the devout beg my protection for both this world and the next."[70]

Voltaire's conquest of the powers of Church and State ended merely in the defeat of his main objectives. By 1747 he had reached the height of royal favor. He was Historiographer of France at an annual income of two thousand francs and Gentleman of the Chamber to His Majesty Louis XV. He was the friend of Pompadour, the woman who ruled the king, and the "dutiful" son of Pope Benedict XIV. Yet in his struggle to pursue his aims as a philosopher, he had not outwitted the highest powers in the kingdom. Instead with honors and dignities they, so it seemed, had subjugated him.

This fact he had glimpsed as soon as he had been appointed Royal Historiographer. Bored and irritated, he wrote to d'Argental: "Here I am employed in all honor to write anecdotes. But I shall write nothing and not earn my wages."[71]

His literary commitments as royal historian and court entertainer left him no time for his serious writings.[72] The scholarly researches he had undertaken at Cirey, the *Essay on the Manners and Minds of Nations,* and the *Century of Louis XIV,* he was forced to abandon. A literary slave to the dictates of his king, the Royal Historiographer complained that he spent the whole day hunting up anecdotes and the whole night making up rhymes.[73] The greatest writer and thinker of his age had become, as he himself said, a "court jester at fifty."[74] Yet despite his saccharine flattery of Louis XV, despite his outward catering to the taste of Versailles, he never once compromised with the basic principles of his philosophy.

The Voltairean message is present in all his court trifles. The *Poem on Fontenoy* and the *Temple of Glory* breathe the same hatred of war, the same impartial fairness toward other nations, and the same appreciation of the arts of civilization that the author expressed throughout his writings. These ideas were merely wrapped up in discreet layers of verbal and allegorical tinsel.

A crafty Voltaire had sought the favor of royal authority as a rampart of defense against the persecution of the censors. Yet as Royal Historiographer he now awoke to find that censorship was no longer a problem. Though Voltaire was unsilenced, Voltaire had become innocuous.

When ousted from court for a literary indiscretion, he regained his personal freedom. Thanks to one temporary fall from favor he had already found time to write a number of *Philosophic Tales* that mocked at the injustices of the existing order. Free again, he shifted his emphasis from the duties of kings to the rights and interests of the French people.[75]

He was, however, not above showing off to Versailles how highly he, a disgraced courtier, was prized by His Majesty's father-in-law, the former king of Poland. So he accepted an invitation for a visit to the court of Stanislaus, now duke of the tiny principality of Lorraine. There between Mme du Châtelet

and Saint-Lambert, the philosopher found himself caught in a
personal drama—that famous love-triangle so tragic and so
farcical.

Upon the death of Emilie du Châtelet on September 9, 1749,
Frederick of Prussia judged Voltaire free of all ties which bound
him to his native country. For, so his French flatterer would
have him believe, an establishment in Potsdam and the company
of His Prussian Majesty would seem to him like Heaven on
earth. Indeed, only the fetters of duty chained him to France
and Emilie.[76]

In the clash of wills between the monarch and the marquise,
up to her last earthly moment Emilie had triumphed. Now, with
his rival safe in her grave, the king had hopes that he could
attain the object which offers of princely establishments in
Prussia, flattering entreaties, and even trickery, had so far proved
powerless to accomplish. The day, it seemed, had come when
Frederick the Great might possess Voltaire.[77]

The French philosopher, nevertheless, showed slight inclina-
tion that Fall toward any visits to foreign royalty. After the loss
of Emilie and the storms leading up to the final tragedy, he
desired peace and a permanent anchorage. He bought a Paris
house and around Christmas installed his niece, Mme Denis, as
his hostess and housekeeper. The winter he spent in a battle to
outshine in the eyes of the court his rival playwright, Crébillon.
For in the favor of Louis XV and Mme de Pompadour this
gloomy-minded dramatist had supplanted him.

Unwilling to be a "prophet without honor" in his native
France, the author of *Zaïre* and *Mérope* turned a deaf ear to
King Frederick's invitations. His thoughts were far from Prussia
when he turned the second floor of his house into a theater, and
dazzled the world of letters and fashion with superb private
performances of *Mahomet* and *Rome Saved*.

The early months of 1750 found Voltaire, to all appearances,
permanently established in Paris, tending his dramatic laurels
and, as he told King Frederick, living in domestic comfort like

"a father of a family, though without any family or children."[78]
His passion to maintain his glory as a playwright, his domestic
arrangements, indeed his personal preferences and tastes all an-
chored him firmly to France and Paris.

In the early Spring of 1750, however, *Zadig* and other *Philosophic Tales* made their sensational printed appearance. The
furious reaction they provoked in Paris only proved to Voltaire
that not in France could a writer have his say and remain
unmolested. Also, by the March of that year he had acquired a
deadly journalistic enemy, the critic Fréron, the sworn foe of
French enlightenment.

As if such enemies were not enough, in the *Voice of the Sage
and the People,* the philosopher himself had thrown to the winds
his new-found security. To shame the Church and State of his
day and age he had made such generalizations as:

A government would be no better than a kingdom of Hottentots
should a certain number of men be able to say: "Let those pay taxes
who work. We should not pay because we are idle." . . . This government would outrage God and Man should the citizens be in a position to say: "The State has given us everything. We owe it in return
nothing but prayers,"[79]

and above all so perilous an anticlerical thrust as: "The body
set apart to teach justice should begin by setting an example of
it."[80] These ideas, which to their author seemed truths, in 1793
were enforced by the blood of the Terror.

Voltaire now found Paris a dangerous place indeed. His
preference was clearly to remain in his native country,[81] and at
his own risk, he was free to do so. Yet by writing the *Voice of
the Sage and the People* he had placed in the hands of his enemies an unparalleled weapon with which to destroy him. The
former historiographer of His Majesty Louis XV looked vainly
to his master for some mark of public favor to shield him from
the wrath of priests and censors and enable him to live and write
in the congenial surroundings of the French capital. Defeated in
this hope, he was speeded off to Prussia less by the persuasion

of King Frederick than by the scathing almost revolutionary pamphlet, the *Voice of the Sage and the People.*

He arrived in Potsdam on July 10, 1750, expecting to stay only a few months and possibly spend the winter.[82] But on August 14, after weeks of festivities, the king made his famous guest an offer.

Should Voltaire decide to settle in Prussia, he would be granted the highest honor a Prussian ruler can confer upon a courtier. The Frenchman would have the post of Chamberlain, and with it, the Royal Order of Merit. A yearly pension of twenty-thousand francs would sumptuously take care of his personal expenses.

Behind him in France Voltaire saw the Bastille, warrants of arrest, the hostile glare of King Louis, the smiling mask of the Pompadour. Censors, those jailors of the mind, forever alerted against him. The *Philosophic Letters* had once been burnt by the public hangman. Hounding him today were those royal leeches and clerical hypocrites offended by the *Voice of the Sage and the People.* He was fed up and sickened by French gagging, French blinding, French suppression.

No personal injustice he had ever suffered seemed meaner than the fierce persecution visited upon him for that gay trifle, *The Worldling.* For a few gay quips on comfort and cleanliness in Eden the bigots of the realm had hunted him as if he were a beast. For eight whole weeks he had been driven into hiding in Belgium and Holland. "You will say," he wrote to his Paris confidant, d'Argental, "that fifteen years have passed since it happened. No . . . Only one day. For great wrongs are always recent wounds."[83]

So Voltaire formally accepted the invitation of King Frederick. Still, his will in the matter was not free. By an inexorable set of circumstances, he seemed compelled to choose Prussia.

"I abandon myself to my fate," he wrote to his devoted d'Argental, "and am throwing myself head first into the abyss of that fatality which rules each and all of us."[84]

In Prussia, Voltaire hoped to find in a rarefied atmosphere of his native land, the intellectual freedom France denied him. Like himself King Frederick had rejected the God of the Scriptures, though not in order "to serve Man better."

The religion of Frederick was the State. For the supposed interests of this abstract entity, he violated all laws for international relations, subordinated his personal wishes, and readily sacrificed the good of his people. Yet his devotion to the Prussian state carried with it no sentiment for the country, Prussia. The spiritual homeland of Frederick was France. Life, however, had assigned him to the role of king of Prussia. This great role he continued to play superbly, even though his sentimental and cultural allegiance he gave entirely to France.[85]

To Voltaire Prussia seemed bearable only because life there remained dominated by the culture of his homeland. At the Prussian court the French language was spoken exclusively. His Majesty's circle of intimates were, with extremely few exceptions, brilliant renowned Frenchmen. The philosopher-historian met princes and princesses of the blood, nurtured in his own language, whose favorite amusement was to act in private performances of the greatest French dramas. The rough German tongue, so everyone of the court agreed, was fit only for soldiers, cooks, and horses. The king himself was a poet, and his verses he wrote in French.

Delighted at such evidence of the cultural ascendancy of his nation the author of the *Century of Louis XIV* declared in a letter to his niece: "Our language and literature have made more conquests than Charlemagne."[86]

Nevertheless, scarcely four months were over, when Voltaire felt the full weight of that territorial homesickness which was to throb so painfully in his letters to d'Argental and Mme Denis. To his niece he confided as early as December 1750:

I am writing to you beside a stove, with a heavy head and a sad heart, gazing out on the river Spree, because the Spree flows into the Elbe, the Elbe into the sea; the sea receives the waters of the Seine, and our Paris house is quite near this river, Seine, so I say: "My dear child, why am I in this palace, in this study-room, facing out on the Spree and not sitting beside our own hearth?"[87]

Exasperated at a life under royal surveyance, bedevilled with intrigues, sick at heart and surrounded by enemies, he declared in this same letter:

Oh what remorse I feel, my dear child! How poisoned is my happiness! How short life is! How sad it is to seek happiness away from you and what remorse I would feel should I find it![88]

His first choice had been neither to start forth on the journey to Potsdam in July 1750, nor to remain permanently at the court of King Frederick. His long confidential letter to the Duc de Richelieu, written during the last two weeks of August, 1750, gives proof that for a smile from France he would have sacrificed Frederick, Potsdam, and his fat Prussian pension.[89] Yet he would not return to his own country to face ridicule or suppression.

In Prussia, Voltaire gathered ammunition for the great battle against religious intolerance he would later wage at Ferney. During the years from 1750 to 1753 he wrote his *Defense of Lord Bolingbroke;* also that anti-orthodox deistic article known as the *Sermon of the Fifty.* A large part of the *Essay on the Manners and Minds of Nations* was then composed and to the *Century of Louis XIV* were added the final touches. A retouching of *Micromégas* dates from this era as well as that superb summing up of his own philosophy which the author entitled *Poem on Natural Law.* Published at Dresden was the Walther edition of his entire collection of writings.

Into the nature of man and man's institutions the aging thinker was learning to probe still deeper. In the company of a "Sage on the Throne" and Frenchmen free from all the prejudices of their nation, inspiration was provided him for those incisive articles which served as a beginning for his *Philosophic Dictionary.* Of all the weapons in his intellectual arsenal this last was perhaps the mightiest.

Nevertheless, such advantages as he enjoyed in Berlin and Potsdam were not to be his forever. The same irrepressible wit and hatred of injustice which made his life in France so stormy, inevitably prepared the way for his exit from Prussia.

When the French mathematician, Maupertuis, falsely and cruelly accused his former friend, Koenig, of forging certain Leibnitz letters (of which the original texts were unobtainable) Voltaire entered the quarrel. With his formidable pen, he opened fire on the unjust accuser. That Maupertuis was his own compatriot, a favorite of King Frederick, and the royally appointed president of the Berlin Academy, in no way altered his bold stand in the matter. To defend Koenig he stabbed his fellow Frenchman to the heart in that dazzling remorseless satire, the *Diatribe of Dr. Akakia.*

This rapier-like pamphet not only cost its author the friendship of the king, but his personal safety in Prussia. As he prudently contrived his exit from the kingdom, the long arm of royal vengeance caught up with him at Frankfort. There Frederick feigning a misinterpretation of his orders subjected his own former idol to forcible arrest and bitter indignities.[90]

Thus in the realm of a royal disciple, Voltaire had proved no more able to survive than he had at Versailles with his own lazy, self-indulgent French king. Of both these rulers he had appeared to be the fawning courtier. Nevertheless, when informed by his niece that while Chamberlain to Prussian Frederick, he might still keep a small pension from French Louis, the recipient replied with much truth and more impudence:

Here I am then serving two masters. He, who said that a man can not serve two masters at a time was certainly right. Therefore, so as not to contradict him, I serve neither one of them.[91]

Free at last of the two royal masters he never really served, Voltaire made his home in the Genevan republic. Yet, and characteristically, he did so only after having knocked in vain at the gates of *la patrie*. Grievances of his own he had against the country of his forefathers. Yet no single action of a long career had more wounded France and angered the French monarch than his transplanting himself to Prussia. So throughout a year the Gentleman-in-Ordinary to His Majesty Louis XV remained in watchful waiting near the frontier, hoping against hope for royal permission to reenter his native land.[92]

Possibility for this permit, in December 1753, had received a setback. The *Essay on the Manners and Minds of Nations* had appeared in print, brought out surreptitiously by Jean Néaulme, a pirate publisher of The Hague. The edition was shamefully incorrect. Yet correct or incorrect his work the author knew would hardly win him the good graces of the French authorities. For exposed in this outline of world history were those ideas and institutions which seemingly had impeded the progress of men and nations. Named first among such forces of darkness were royal ambition and the greed of the Catholic clergy.

Determined to live and work in France, the homesick Frenchman strained his every nerve to placate the authorities of his nation. His actual manuscript he compared with the printed version of the *Essay* and, from two notaries, obtained a formal declaration that the Dutch edition was surreptitious. Yet both Church and State remained unpersuaded. The severe snubbing he received from Cardinal Tencin at Lyons in November 1754 at last convinced him that France, even near the frontier, had no room for a philosopher. So he started life anew on the shores of Lake Leman.

In Geneva, under the comparatively free laws of a republic, Voltaire found new reserves of vitality with which to enter upon his last long battle for justice and tolerance. On Genevan territory, he believed that he had discovered, and this time amidst a people of French language and French descent, a nation as politically reliable as England.[93] "Natural rights" were upheld, so it seemed, by democratic organs of government. Here, far from kings, in a land outside the aegis of the Roman Catholic faith, the author of the *Essay on the Manners and Minds of*

*Nations* could publish in safety a correct, personally supervised edition of his entire collected writings. Here, untroubled by court intrigues and literary cliques, he grew tulips in March and tended his orchards. His youth he had spent in the homes of other people. He had courted Louis XV and tried to live in a gilded cage as the pet of Frederick the Great. In tolerant, clear-thinking Geneva he at last knew peace and independence.[94]

The philosopher was also pleased to behold the confirmation of many of his own theories. For the Genevan republic had become affluent not by war, but by commerce. Her cultured aristocracy understood and appreciated the social value of the merchant. Above all, just as in England, religious tolerance and a fair measure of political freedom had proved compatible with public order and industry.

Far from encountering his usual difficulties with the clergy, the thinker found himself welcomed by the Calvinist ministers as a friend, and almost as an ally. These Swiss Protestant pastors were Christians, yet philosophers. The small Genevan state they ruled over not as oppressors of the people who pursued them for tithes, but as their moral guides and humane councilors.

Thus from his hill-top villa, *Les Délices,* a half-hour's ride from France, Voltaire looked longingly toward his loved home-land. Meanwhile, he schemed to make Geneva serve as the standard-bearer for his ideals for the State.

As a result, the French philosopher soon met with storms in the Helvetian republic. For to the austere city of Calvin he attempted to bring the customs of Paris, while Geneva, he would present to Paris as a concrete fulfillment of his eighteenth-century vision of a "Philosophic Republic."[95] Delighted with the liberal Protestant clergy, he planned to use these men in his effort to free France from that intellectual bondage, inseparable in his age, from revealed religion. With this purpose in view he inspired D'Alembert to write for his *Encyclopedia* the article "Geneva."

Voltaire and his guest, D'Alembert, would shame superstition-

bound France with the knowledge that even a small Swiss republic could boast of an enlightened clergy. Nor had sound
thinking proved disastrous to a respect for Christian teachings.
For here ministers of the Gospel reasoned according to the pure
empiricism of Locke. Nevertheless, the appearance of the *Encyclopedia* article, "Geneva" brought strife to the Swiss community. A formal declaration of protest was the reply of the
ministers of the republic.

Voltaire then felt that in this December of 1757, his friends
the Swiss pastors had failed him as allies. For they refused to
uphold publicly the opinions they had privately expressed to
D'Alembert in the salon of *Les Délices*. He gibed at them for
their intellectual timidity and accused them of a lack of moral
courage. Geneva he now realized could not be counted upon to
wave his party-banner of enlightenment before France and the
world.

The article of D'Alembert, however, had been true in most
essentials. For, as he had stated, the Faith of the Swiss pastors
differed from pure Deism only by a traditional respect for the
Scriptures and for Christ.[96] Still the philosophic Calvinists were
offended. Ministers of the Gospel, they felt, should not allow
themselves to be represented as denying all elements of the
miraculous in their religion. Such an interpretation of their views
would weaken the hold of Christianity upon the people and
thereby undermine public morals. Their policy instead had been
not to reject but to minimize heavenly mysteries.

The Gospel they preached primarily for its humanistic appeal
and civic value. Like Voltaire and D'Alembert, the pastors held
that the supreme criterion for the judgment of human actions
should be the favorable or unfavorable effect on the public
welfare. Yet in their conception of what really contributes to the
public welfare they were in striking disaccord with the self-
styled Hermit of *Les Délices* and his Parisian guest.

This clash was apparent in the issue of the theater. Drama,
whether enacted by amateurs or professional performers, was

rigidly prohibited by the laws of the Genevan Consistory. Spectacles of this kind, the Puritanical pastors believed, excite animal passion and an unholy greed for luxury. Against such temptations to sin, they, as ministers, must protect the community.

To Voltaire this viewpoint was not only alien but incomprehensible. As a classicist and Epicurean, he believed that the disciplinary force of a community should be not austere self-denial, but rational balance, altruistic self-control. He felt scant sympathy for an asceticism artificially imposed by a governing body seeking to regulate by stated taboos the food, drink, and amusements of the citizens. To prohibit the drama was to infringe on the freedom of the individual.

So when native-son Jean-Jacques Rousseau denounced him as an old *polichinelle,* a "master of clowning," and instrument of corruption for pure Spartan Geneva, Voltaire merely laughed derisively. With his French cook, his tinseled entertainments, and the moving sentiments of his dramas he continued to delight whole audiences of Calvinists. For both as an art and as a symbol of a pleasanter way of life, he remained determined to bring drama to the republic.

The Parisian-French thinker bade his adopted country march forward toward new goals of social and cultural progress. Yet after a few enthusiastic steps in this unfamiliar direction, she stopped short and turned back to the ways of her Puritan past. After the controversy provoked by Jean-Jacques Rousseau in his *Letter to D'Alembert on the Theater,* Voltaire found himself the loser. Tired of the continued remonstrances of the Consistory about his play-acting parties, he felt fed up with conditions on the shores of Lake Leman.[97] His answers to Genevan tyranny over manners and customs was the purchase of lands inside France.

So at last Voltaire returned to the soil of *la patrie.* His life at Ferney represents the serene and happy compromise he finally achieved between his love for his native land and his unswerving will to liberate and enlighten Europe.[98] In France, on the stage of his manor-house theater, *Zaïre, Mérope,* and all the creatures of his dramatic fancy could live again unmolested by the prohibitions of the Genevan consistory. Yet while their author acted in his own plays, while he gave marionette shows and provided Parisian entertainment for the notables of Europe, he depended upon Geneva for the protection of his basic rights as an individual.

Thanks to the relatively free press of the republic, the Sage of Ferney could print the truth, as he saw it, and without the consent of his French sovereign. Perched on an obscure wooded boundary of France, he could brave royal orders. Should a warrant of arrest catch up with him, only three and a half miles away were his houses in Switzerland and safety.[99]

Ferney was his real home; Geneva merely his door of exit, his indispensable avenue of escape from the blind autocratic power of Catholic monarchical France. His personal garden he cultivated on home soil. Yet he dared to do so, only because stern, just Switzerland served him as a fortress of refuge in his deadly fight against that sanguinary religious intolerance he called by the name *l'Infâme.*

The time came, however, when not even a remote corner of France would Voltaire accept as his homeland. On July 1, 1766, the powers of Church and State tortured, beheaded, and threw to the flames the nineteen-year-old Chevalier de la Barre. The charge was sacrilege. The authorities of the town of Abbeville had imposed this barbarous penalty. Yet the sentence was inexorably upheld by the Parlement of Paris.

Disheartened at so crushing a defeat for justice and humanity, Voltaire planned to abandon his native country. His war against the "Infamous Thing" he felt should be waged from some more distant base. Among La Barre's possessions were found not only the *Philosophic Thoughts* of Diderot, but the Sage of Ferney's own *Philosophical Dictionary.* Of all his weapons against superstition this last was possibly the deadliest.

Voltaire now acted on his belief that when the State violates the rights of its citizens no man has a homeland. Partly for his own security and partly in horror at a nation which destroyed a youth for a merely foolish act of impiety, the philosopher deserted Ferney. At first he fled to Rolle, Switzerland. Yet even Switzerland he believed too dangerously near the long arm of the Bourbon monarchy and the vengeance of priests and *parlements*. So, to his former philosophic follower, King Frederick, he applied for permission to settle in Cleves.[100]

In his feverish rage at France Voltaire hoped to found on foreign soil a sort of Spartan republic of philosophers. He would take with him a printing press and transport with him his fellow believers in "natural law." In his present mood he considered liberty and upright independence of greater moment than all the charms of France and the amenities of French living.

Beside himself, he wrote to Diderot:

A man like you can only look with horror upon the land where he is so unfortunate as to live. You should go to a country where you would have entire liberty, not only to print what you would wish, but to preach loudly against superstitions as infamous as they are sanguinary. You would not be alone, you would have companions, disciples. You could found there a pulpit which would be the pulpit of truth. Your library could be transported overseas and need be carried no more than four miles over land. At last you would be leaving slavery for liberty.[101]

The so-called skeptic and realist remained captivated by his vision of an academy of philosophers, living and working together in a free country. Under this spell, he did his utmost to win over to his scheme the philosophers of the French capital. He appealed not only to Diderot, but to D'Alembert, to Grimm, Holbach, and Damilaville. His single-minded preoccupation with liberty rendered him forgetful not only of his own interests at Ferney, but of the pleasures and obligations which anchor others to life in their daily environments. To the reluctant Damilaville he wrote heatedly: "I can not understand those who are willing to crawl under the heel of fanaticism in some corner of Paris when elsewhere they have it in their power to crush the monster."[102]

His invitations to the new Republic of Letters, however, found no favor with his friends in Paris. Though bitter critics of the French state, the philosophers remained bound by invincible ties to their mother-country. The salons of Paris and the company of Mlle Volland were the inspiration and nurture of Diderot's impetuous genius. For life in the French capital D'Alembert had refused the presidency of the Berlin Academy and declined a brilliant post at the court of Catherine of Russia. At the frigid response of his friends, Voltaire at last awoke and his air-castle evaporated.[103] His fright and anger with his country now over, he calmly returned to his occupations at Ferney.

Thus by conscious will and well-directed effort he made of Ferney his homeland. Here, like Candide, he cultivated his "garden" and within his small domain placed in triumphant practice his own ideals for the State. Individual happiness he was able to increase. For he removed the tax-burden from the shoulders of the poor to the relatively privileged. When the Genevan republic failed to function as a democracy and trampled on the rights of her neediest citizens, the elderly philosopher came to the rescue. For the Swiss artisans he provided liberty, security, and employment at Ferney. By inducing so many valuable workers to leave Geneva and by his plans for a new French port on Lake Leman to act as a commercial rival to the Calvinist capital, he rebuked the Swiss republic for her political shortcomings and in a manner highly profitable for France.

Also by his colony at Ferney he could prove to his native country that religious tolerance and humanity were not only desirable but practical. His letters glowingly described how Catholics and Huguenots worked and played together like one contented family. The Protestant women made ready with their own hands the little portable altars for the Procession of the

Holy Sacrament, and the priest thanked them publicly in a sermon. At last the "tree of tolerance" was bearing fruit. After his long philosophic struggle the Sage of Ferney could tease his adversaries with the spectacle of his own miniature *patrie* standing firm on "those two pivots of the wealth of the State, be it little or great, freedom of trade and freedom of conscience."[104]

Voltaire continuously insisted that economic health results from the harmonious interplay of agriculture, manufacture, industry, and commerce. A salutary balance between these major forces he managed to achieve at Ferney.

If he dried the swamps, planted twenty-thousand seedlings, grew wheat and raised poultry, he also founded manufactures and industries. His thriving watch factory offered employment and modest comfort to the exiled Genevan artisans, also to many poor French workers of the Gex district. For this manufacture he provided the gold, silver, and jewels and himself bore all the losses. His silk and lace industry and his tile works raised the entire region to a higher economic level, and the sparsely populated hamlet of Ferney soon became a flourishing village.

Commerce he was so far from neglecting that through the aid of Catherine the Great he was able to obtain markets for his Ferney watches in far-off China. Soon he was sending watches not only to China, but to Spain, Italy, Russia, Holland, America, Turkey and Portugal, besides carrying on an enormous trade with Paris.[105]

The commercial success of his products depended to a considerable extent on his skill and ingenuity as a promoter. For the advancement of his silk stocking industry he corresponded coquettishly with the wife of Prime Minister Choiseul and sent her the first pair of silk stockings made by his weavers. To launch his watches at the French Court he even overwhelmed with compliments the reigning mistress, Mme du Barry, and made her the present of an exquisite watch beautifully set with diamonds.

The world of rank and fashion he had sought to conquer in

his youth for reasons of vanity and entertainment. In his mature years, he had courted royalty in order to print what seemed to be the truth and gain protection from the censors. In his eighties, carrying on his philosophic mission in upright independence, he still courted and flattered, though from afar, to win support against concrete wrongs or for the sake of his colony of workers, his "children" at Ferney. His personal evolution was now complete. The witty epicurean poet had become a civilizer, a social reformer, and a humanitarian philosopher.[106]

Paris he now regarded less as a land of personal predilection than a stage for his plays and a proving-ground for his philosophy. Yet his strength he would prove and letters from Paris kept urging him to come and conquer. His virtual exclusion from his native capital inflicted upon him a wound which remained unhealed even through years of happy exile. Louis XV, so he had been warned, did not wish him back, and in this attitude His Majesty remained inflexible. France, though, now had a new young king, and Paris clamored continuously for the return of the banished philosopher.

Voltaire felt seized with an irresistible nostalgia for his native city. As he grew older and the Swiss winters seemed likewise to grow colder and snowier, he longer for the company of his Paris friends and followers, for the Opéra Comique and for the Comédie Française where the creatures of his imagination were triumphantly embodied by the best actors in France. He had no wish to abandon his colony at Ferney. Yet twenty-eight years had passed since he had set foot in his native capital, and he longed to see Paris once more before he died.

At the news of his coming departure for Paris, the Ferney colony felt both alarm and consternation. The so-called Patriarch was their sole protector and support. His responsibilities toward his small community were pressing and, three days before starting off, he all but canceled his journey.[107] He left, however, on February 5, 1778, promising his dejected villagers that he would be with them again in a month and a half. Such was his obvious intention. For he closed the door on Ferney without so much as putting his papers in order. Later in his last illness, he sent back his secretary to complete for him the task.

Paris, however, refused ever again to relinquish her great man of letters. The passionate welcome of the capital soon laid the aged philosopher low. Nevertheless, after his first serious illness, one month before his death, he remembered with remorse his promise to his dependents: "I must leave at once," he wrote to his lifelong friend, d'Argental, "otherwise everything will go to ruin at Ferney"[108]—a fear, which as time proved, was only too well-founded.

Finally he yielded to the persistent entreaties of Mme Denis and on April 27 bought a fine unfinished dwelling on the rue de Richelieu. He would at last take up his rightful position as intellectual leader in the capital and also carry on his practical philanthropies at Ferney. Eight months of the year he would spend in Paris, the remaining four at Ferney. For the four months at Ferney he would leave at once. Only illness and death prevented him from carrying out his plan.

Voltaire's triumphal return to Paris in 1778, after twenty-eight years of absence, and without official right of re-entry gives proof that he had won his life-long battle. At last the liberty and tolerance he demanded of the State were obtainable in Paris, his native homeland and real *patrie*.

He had not dared to brave Louis XV by making an unwelcome appearance in the capital. Now Louis XVI, restrained by public opinion, dared not sentence him to arrest. In the judicial files no official warrant could be found against him. So the new king could only choose to snub and ignore him. Nevertheless, and true to form, even in the last months of his life, the one-time courtier hoped to win from the head of the state some token of acceptance.[109] Yet if Louis XVI would take no steps against his illustrious subject, neither would he honor nor receive him. Over monarchy by "divine right," Voltaire in his lifetime obtained at best a negative victory.

If the State chose to ignore him, the Church threatened and assailed him until his last conscious moment and, indeed, long afterward. Concern for his mortal remains seems to have wrung from him that much disputed statement that he "wished to die in the Catholic Church in which he was born and that he asked pardon of God and the Church if he had offended them." To the "philosopher" party such an act seemed shocking. Yet behind the confession there was more than a grain of sincerity. For Voltaire had never wished to eradicate Catholicism or any religion. By *l'Infâme,* the "Infamous Thing" he meant neither Christianity nor Catholicism, but the brutalizing power of superstition.

The former pupil of the Jesuits vastly preferred Catholicism to any other manifestation of revealed religion. For the Faith of his country he desired no other substitute. Just as the Jesuits had implanted in him the belief that the rules for literary excellence had been established for once and all by the incomparable Ancients, as a formalist, he tended to believe that the sphere of the supernatural had been most effectively marked out by the Catholic religion. On the edge of the tomb he wished to sign a truce not with *l'Infâme,* but with the Church as a French rather than a Christian institution. As a Frenchman he wished to die and be buried in the Faith of *la patrie.*

If in 1778, the king and the Church were forced to tolerate Voltaire, the rest of the nation hysterically acclaimed him. The nobles among whom he numbered many lifelong friends, the bourgeois whose rights and interests he had fought for so fiercely, and the people whom he had defended against the barbarities of the criminal code, all saluted and honored him. From the feverish embrace of the metropolis the so-called Patriarch had no opportunity to recover.

On March 30, 1778, during the sixth performance of *Irene,* the old French philosopher was crowned with laurels, overwhelmed with applause, and literally all but smothered with glory. Yet his triumph, he seems to have sensed, was neither for himself nor for his play. The victory was for Enlightenment, for human emancipation.[110]

Two days later, he wrote in his last letter to Frederick the Great: "It is then true, Sire, that in the end men *will* be enlightened, and those who believe that it pays to blind them will not always be victorious."[111]

France and the eighteenth century had set the seal of approval on a philosophy which invests the individual with rights, dignity and responsibilities. The test of this philosophy in action is a challenge that still goes on.

# The Concept of *La Patrie*

I N THE LATTER HALF of the eighteenth century, French patriots were either conservatives glorying in the France bequeathed to them by history,[1] or else, and more frequently, dissatisfied idealists who expressed their zeal in an effort for national improvement.[2] During the period from 1740 until the outbreak of the Revolution one troubling fact became glaringly apparent. The authority of the State failed to support the interests of the vast majority of the people.[3] Since king and country, *le roi et la patrie,* seemed to exist as mutually antagonistic entities, to feel a love for both became increasingly difficult. Thus bitter perplexity arose as to the true object of patriotic allegiance.

More than any other intellectual leader, except perhaps Rousseau, Voltaire gave clarity and impetus to the growing struggle between traditional patriotism, based on chivalric devotion to a sovereign and his House,[4] and the revival of the classical republican idea of the *patrie*. The territory they called the *patria* the Ancients revered not only as the inherited homeland of the citizens, but as the hearth of their human liberties.[5] Zeal for the *patria* consisted in willingness to defend to the death those stern laws which guaranteed to all members of this free commonwealth the equal possession of their "natural rights."

The author of the *Philosophic Dictionary* dedicated his brains, heart, and genius to the advancement of ideals for human relations by which a string of ill-assorted provinces, held together forcibly by a king, were to fuse into *la patrie* in the revolutionary sense of *la nation*.[6] The mature Voltaire viewed the State as designed originally and ideally for individual human welfare. The purpose of this utilitarian organization was to protect from unjust violation certain prerogatives inseparable from the human status. These "natural rights" or fundamental liberties,[7] which he mentioned throughout his writings, he at last defined in the *Philosophic Dictionary* as liberty of person and property, freedom of speech and press, liberty to worship God in one's own way, trial by jury, and the right of all citizens to stand equal before the laws of the land. Such a concept of the nation presupposes the existence of an implicit social compact.

If the individual and the State honestly fulfill their mutual obligation of protection, on the one side, and support, on the other, the binding force of their political partnership would be not so much the power of the crown or any central authority, but the voluntary adherence of the citizen. Membership in the nation is therefore an act not of fate, but of choice.[8]

These universally applicable principles of justice Voltaire looked upon as the sole rational basis for political unity. If in his earlier poems and plays he treated the sovereign as all-important and identical with the nation, he did so for a practical purpose. The "rights" of the Many, he knew, could not be enforced unless the governing Few fulfill their obligations to the citizens. So instead of arousing the bourgeois and workers to clamor help-lessly for their liberties and interests, he laid his stress on the duties of kings.

A right, though unenforced, is still a right. Monarchs, them-selves, however, decide what they choose to consider their obligations. These last Voltaire tried, for their royal benefit, to define. His preoccupation with statecraft and the use of authority is already discernible in *Oedipus*.

In this classic drama, the first of his works to win fame, the ruler is warned, above all, of the perils of superstition. For such a force of darkness may be used to cheat men of their "natural rights." Philoclete, unjustly accused of the murder of the former king, pleads with Oedipus, his present sovereign, for confidence in honest human judgment. This he must believe rather than the divine oracular sayings that seem to condemn him. Here the future author of the *Treaties on Metaphysics* makes his first appeal for the use of reason:

> Let us trust only in ourselves; judge everything by our own eyes. These let us use as our altars, oracles and gods.[9]

Priests, the young author of *Oedipus* implied, have sworn to advance supernatural rather than earthly interests. These spokesmen for an invisible power can deceive and exploit the people: "Our priests are not oracles, as a frivolous populace believe. Their so-called power and wisdom is founded on our credulity."[10]

*Oedipus* as an enlightened ruler is receptive to these arguments. If the gods need a victim, he, the head of the State, and not Philoclète, should be chosen: "To die for his country is the duty of a King. 'Tis an honor too great to be yielded over to a subject. I would have laid down my life in the defense of yours."[11]

Here is patriotism in the Corneille tradition, a conventionally noble sentiment enjoyed by "well-born souls," a matter for tirades and togas. However when asked his aims as a ruler Oedipus replies: "To be useful to mortals."[12]

The keynote of the new century was now heard. Foreshadowed in these words was that mid-eighteenth-century *bienfaisance* widely preached by Diderot and so well formulated by the aging Voltaire in his *Philosophic Dictionary*.[13] The theatrical grease paint on the face of patriotism was disappearing as this passion changed from a *beau sentiment* to a merely *bon sentiment*.

Patriotic actions, however, were "good" or "useful" only if the ruler himself strove for justice and humane dealings. In the early eighteenth century the king was the nation incarnate. He alone could make of his kingdom either a vast territorial prison or a free secure homeland worthy to be called by his subjects *la patrie*.

Since all depended on the monarch, Voltaire would educate

and enlighten him. So at the outset of his career he strove to be, in his writings, a tutor to kings.

*Télémaque* he may have read at the Lycée Louis-le-Grand. Yet no proof of Fénelon's influence can be found in his works until 1731, when in the eighth of the *Philosophic Letters* he borrows verbatim from the text of *Télémaque* a definition of royal authority.[14] The source and implication of this definition will be discussed later. Still, the interesting fact remains that with or without Fénelon's influence, young Arouet set out to compile maxims for kingly conduct. This ambition is evident in his *Letter to the Prince de Conti,* but above all in the *Henriade's* censored dedication to young Louis XV.

The dauphin was told by the author that his chance to rule France was given him only because Henri IV, the founder of his line, was a great man. Later, as king, he should follow in the footsteps of this illustrious ancestor. Then came some observations of a character most censorable:

Shameful indeed for kings is this surprise we all feel when they love sincerely the happiness of their people. . . . May you some day accustom us to regard this virtue as an ornament inseparable from your crown.[15]

In the *Letter to the Prince de Conti,* written contemporaneously with the production of *Oedipus,* young Arouet drew a miniature of the type of ruler he considered patriotic. Admiration he professed neither for a flattered fop nor an arrogant conqueror. Most desirable was a royal defender of his nation, supremely able to discover ability, foster the arts, and enlighten his followers. Tact forbade the poet to preach noble qualities to a personage who was supposed to inherit them with his rank. So he adroitly credited the prince with these essential virtues:

You whom honor leads and for whom justice lights the path. Who knows how to be both a prince and a citizen.[16]

This last line reads less as a congratulation than as a challenge on the part of the new century. Here Voltaire urged upon the

Prince de Conti the role of that enlightened and benevolent despot whose happy kingdom existed only in the imagination of eighteenth-century philosophers. The essence of such a monarch was his assured understanding of how to be at the same time a "prince and a citizen." As a prince he would remain his country's absolute master; as a citizen he would act as an incorruptible guardian of the nation's laws, and as an unselfish protector of the common interests. This citizen-prince, the author assumed, would prefer advancement and prosperity within home confines to military conquests beyond the frontiers. Between the realities of justice and the mythical benefits of armed aggression, the future Voltaire had already made his choice:

> A just and sincere heart wins our esteem far more
> Than all those conquerors looked up to as gods.[17]

The power of monarchs for good or ill concerned him still more personally when he wrote the *Henriade*. Unjustly imprisoned in the Bastille by a selfish, corrupt ruler, young Arouet found consolation and escape in composing an epic poem. This he signed with his newly chosen name, Voltaire.

In anger at France as a political organization, he would raise an artistic monument to *la patrie* as a cultural entity. Molded in the classical tradition, he had been taught to regard the epic poem as the noblest form of literary art. Homer gave Greece the *Iliad* and Virgil had bestowed upon Rome the *Aeneid*. Modern France had no such literary ornament. So with the fervor of true inspiration he took up that task at which Ronsard, Chapelain, and other literary patriots had failed.[18] He sought to endow his country with a national epic poem. Yet in this poem he would also celebrate the temporary establishment within French boundaries of some of the universal rights of all men.[19]

The epic, as designed and executed by Voltaire, was according to accepted eighteenth-century standards impeccably patriotic. For the subject of the poem was the founder of the ruling dynasty, his military triumphs and the audacity of his leadership.

Yet the author glorified his hero not as a king or a Frenchman, but as the leader who won for his compatriots the world-wide principle of freedom of worship. With Henri IV both as his example and excuse, the poet dared point to the brief though successful realization of those policies of religious toleration and humanity which the Edict of Nantes enunciated. This critical approach, strikingly out of keeping with the sweep and fire associated with epic poetry, is evident in the coolly judicious opening lines:

> I celebrate this hero who ruled in France,
> By right of conquest, and of birth, a King
> Who through long misfortunes learned how to govern.[20]

Though conventional in form, the *Henriade* has nevertheless some revolutionary implications. For no conscious glorification of France is to be found. Instead, such patriotism as the poem expresses, consists in a new and deeper significance attached to the word *patrie*.

In the early eighteenth century before such works as Boling-broke's treatise entitled *The Patriot King* (1749),[21] and Abbé Coyer's *Dissertation on the Ancient Word 'Patrie,'*[22] (1755) this term meant to most Frenchmen the locality or even the actual place where a man was born. The word had an antique classical connotation and was used almost exclusively in poetry. In feudal France, loyalty to the king had superseded devotion to a given locality, its laws, and its people. So love of *la patrie* was regarded as a passion burning only in the hearts of those heroic ancients who lived in the small city states of Rome and Greece. Such patriotism was a classical theme most effective in drama and a fertile subject for schoolboy oratory.

Before the end of the first quarter of a century, however, Voltaire was applying the term *patrie* to France as a political unit, to all the varied peoples held together by the French monarchy. When in the *Henriade,* published in 1723, Richelieu and Mazarin are judged as "useful to their king, cruel to their country,"[23] the author was already making a distinction between service to a king and devotion to that body of citizens, united in their interests, who made up the nation.[24]

Henri IV emerges in the poem as the king who identified himself with the French nation and its citizens. The importance of this first of the Bourbons is that he served his country well. The Duc de Guise was in the employ of Spain, Henry III inept, and Catherine de Medici serving a celestial authority which, as she fancied, demanded men's massacre. Allegiance to any of these princes of the ruling house, so the people discovered, had absolutely no bearing on their interests as Frenchmen. Therefore patriotism, as the poet demonstrates, became identified less with the dynastic claim of a sovereign than with that sovereign's political policies. Those of Henri IV were capable of uniting France and securing justice and peace.

Indeed the first of the Bourbon kings defeated the League by making the advancement of the entire nation his political platform. In the *Henriade,* Henri IV appears as a Protector of the French people, a man whose passion for *la patric* overcame party warfare and religious opposition. The much criticized conversion of the ruler to Catholicism the author presents as no mere political opportunism, but as an unselfish concession to the will of the majority of his subjects. For the sake of national unity, he was willing to sacrifice his own religious preferences. For the same temporal goal, he also secured for his people the inalicnable human right to worship God in their own way. By this act, the Edict of Nantes, which Louis XIV later condemned and in 1685 revoked, Henri IV spared France untold misery and bloodshed.

Here the epic hero as depicted by Voltaire rises to his full height as a humanitarian patriot.[25] The granting of religious toleration, the author broadly hints, was a major victory for reason and enlightenment, a victory still attainable because once briefly achieved, and by a great French king, within the boundaries of the monarchy. Unlike other patriotic epics, the *Henriade* contains no blind worship of royal authority apart from the value of the sovereign to the people of the nation. Henri IV, the poet implies, earned his crown when he led France from anarchy to reconstruction.

Three years after the publication of the *Henriade,* when banished to England, Voltaire enlarged his conception of the role of the monarch. Instead of a personal Protector of the people, like Henri IV, his imagination became fired with the idea of a king as legal guardian of a constitution. Guaranteed in the constitution of England were the fundamental liberties of all Britons.

To these rights and liberties, the monarch himself was subservient. The British king ruled not by any arbitrary whim, but by a fixed body of laws as the First Magistrate of his people. This constitution and its human fundamentals Voltaire sought to make known in the *Philosophic Letters.*[26] Under the spell of the same ideas, he wrote a drama on republican patriotism.

His tragedy *Brutus* was begun in England and finished in 1730 when he returned to his French homeland. The dedication to Lord Bolingbroke includes an admission that the poet had started his play in English, while staying at the home of his friend, Falkener. Bolingbroke, it seems, had inspected an early draft of the drama. So the author thanks the noble Englishman for having offered him encouragement in a work "capable of inspiring such fine sentiments."[27]

Such a statement implies that, as a routine theatrical property, the poet meant to make full use of patriotism. This antique emotion, however, he thoughtfully reexamined in the light of English liberal theories.

In *Brutus* Voltaire revived the ancient classical idea of the *patria* and gave it import for his century. His hero he portrayed as a stern republican patriot whose primary devotion was to the laws of his homeland. This body of laws in their prestige and rigidity are reminiscent of the British constitution. Informed

that his son's love of *la patrie* ensures his loyalty to Rome, Brutus
replies uncompromisingly:

> . . . but first of all he should love the laws
> He should be their slave; indeed give them full support.
> He who desires their violation does not love his country.[28]

Such patriotism is essentially political. Brutus loves Rome
not so much as the land of his forefathers, nor as the country of
his personal predilection, but Rome to him is glorious as the
guardian of man's civic liberties. To him love of *la patrie* means
a resolution to defend to the death the rights of Roman citizens
as they are defined by the laws of the immortal city. For these
republican principles are active. Their purpose is to bestow both
liberty and happiness upon a population which the mother-
country just passively nurtures.

Though in 1731 *Brutus* could command a public for fifteen
performances, this play was revived and received with tumultuous
applause during the French Revolution.[29] A hero who viewed
*la patrie* as centered in universal abstract principles was more
than acceptable to an audience who passionately revered the
Declaration of the Rights of Man. For the patriots of these
stirring times, like Voltaire's Brutus, looked upon the nation as
a free association. To this association they owed not their
national character, but the assurance of their individual liberties
as citizens.

Aside from political allegiance, the author also proves his
comprehension of the inescapable bond of nationality. In Titus,
son of Brutus, he portrayed a love of country more profound
and unreasoning than any conscious devotion to the laws of a
republic. This attitude is well expressed when Titus surmounts
his hatred of the Senate and declares his willingness to defend
Rome:

> Roman I am and Roman I wish to be
> Either through greatness, virtue or prejudice, perhaps,
> Born among the Romans, I shall perish with them.[30]

In explaining loyalty to *la patrie* as a phenomenon that occurs "either through greatness, virtue or *prejudice, perhaps,*" (the italics are the writer's) the skeptical, critical temper of the eighteenth century is revealed through all the conventional heroics of the French classic theater. These words in a tragedy of 1730 are already prophetic of the author's mature challenge in his *Thoughts on Government* of 1752:

What is love of country? A composite of self-love and prejudice which society for the sake of its own protection has raised to the status of a great virtue. It is essential that this vague word 'the public' should make a profound impression.[31]

England convinced Voltaire that patriotism could find sound expression only in the devotion of all classes to the public welfare. The greatness of Britain he explained by the successful social cooperation that existed between the nobility and the middle class, trade and religion, the king and the legal representatives of the people. To promote these conditions in his native France he wrote the *Philosophic Letters*.

Whether in art, manners, or politics, the countries of the world should learn from each other. For false patriotic pride, the author of the *Essay on Epic Poetry* pointed out, is nothing more or less than "stupid self-love," while "true and responsible love of country consists in doing good to one's nation and contributing to its liberty as much as possible."[32]

In the king of England, Voltaire beheld a ruler who combined the force and initiative of a sovereign with the stalwart loyalty to human rights characteristic of a republican patriot. In the eighth "philosophic letter" he thus described to his own countrymen the power of the king of Britain: "He has absolute power to do good, yet to do ill, his hands are tied."[33]

In these words he appropriated almost verbatim the definition of royal authority voiced to Mentor by the inhabitants of Crete in Book V of Fénelon's *Télémaque*.[34] Again, years later he reproduced almost textually whole passages from this popular classic in *Zadig* and to a lesser extent in *Micromégas*.[35] Yet the above quoted sentence of 1731 stands as the first incontestable proof of Fénelon's influence on Voltaire. The date 1731 is too late to have any bearing on the brilliant *History of Charles XII,* a biography already completed in 1729. Nevertheless it seems more than likely that, while on British soil, the banished Frenchman either read or reread that guide to kingly conduct, *Télémaque.* For in the judging of monarchs, England had provided him with a new standard.

Kings he now estimated according to their success or failure in upholding the liberal principles set forth in the British constitution. For the so-called British liberties were the claims not only of Britons but of all members of the human species. The monarch who identified himself with these world-wide claims and enforced them within the confines of a nation would be both serving humanity and acting as a national patriot. He would earn thereby the voluntary adherence of his subjects.

For the acceptance of these theories, Voltaire tried in the *Philosophic Letters* to win over the public. In his *History of Charles XII* he made his appeal directly to the king.

With royal absolutism everywhere prevalent, he still looked upon the enlightenment of the sovereign as the safest, surest, and most practical means toward national improvement. To further this purpose he wrote his many detailed and keenly critical accounts of the careers of past princes. His lifelong aim was to win for French citizens more liberty and security. Yet this change he hoped to bring about gradually, painlessly, with the approval of even such a monarch as Louis XV. He stood for a reform that came from the top of the social order rather than the rank and file at the bottom of it.

To the biographer of Charles XII and Peter I, the sovereign was important not only as a ruler, but also as an arbiter of manners, as a symbolic embodiment of the State who, in a patriarchal sense, imposed his own standard of mores on the country as a whole. Such an idea of the king, Voltaire expressed when he described Sweden under the leadership of Charles XII:

"The nation was born war-like and every people unconsciously assumes the type of genius of its king."[36]

Throughout his works he spoke not vaguely of any "glory that was Rome," but of the "Age of Augustus." The seventeenth century, he referred to neither as the epoch of Racine nor the era of France in her supremacy. This period he celebrated as the Age of, or rather, the Century of Louis XIV. Seldom, if ever, did the author of the *Essay on the Manners and Minds of Nations* view the sovereign as molded by those historical forces which the nineteenth century was to classify as the "race," the "environment," and the "epoch."[37] The head of state seemed to him a free agent who needed only to be instructed and uplifted. Therefore to further progress within the nation he endeavored to persuade the monarch to encourage certain actions and policies as socially useful and to frown upon other types of enterprise as harmful or unprofitable. With this aim in mind, he wrote the life of the warrior-king of Sweden.

Charles XII, he hoped, would serve monarchs as an example of the futility of military conquest. For, as the author challenged his possible royal readers:

. . . where is the sovereign who can say: 'I have more courage and more virtue, a braver spirit, a more robust body; I understand war better; I have better troops than Charles XII'?[38]

The fact remained that with all these moral and material resources, the Swedish king met with ultimate disaster. Almost mockingly the author demanded: "What should other princes hope for, who have the same ambition, though fewer talents and resources?"[39]

Charles XII failed his people by dedicating himself to the sterile art of destruction. Though stressing this truth, the historian portrayed the ruler as a hero of unequalled greatness of soul. Indeed, the passion of the Swedish king for warfare was above the material plane, where through political strategy, a conqueror seeks to preserve both territorial gains and economic advantages.

The Charles XII Voltaire depicted seems driven to conquest by some strange inner compulsion.[40] He pursued his enemy, the former King Augustus, in Saxony without a thought of recapturing Ingria from Russia. After the battle of Pultava, which obliterated any results from his previous conquests, Charles still refused peace from the czar and fled to Turkey. Thus with a hero on the throne, the kingdom of Sweden was led to neglect and ruin. The courage, the abstinence, the self-sacrifice of Charles XII all proved powerless to "do good to men" which to Voltaire was the essence of all virtues and greater than any one virtue.[41]

In contrast to Charles XII, Voltaire stressed the tremendous social utility of Peter I, Czar of Russia. In his foreword to the life of the famous czar, written thirty years after his *History of Charles XII,* he is even more emphatic in his praise of Peter at the expense of Charles: "Judged to-day, Charles deserves to be the first soldier of Peter the Great. One left only ruins, the other was a builder in every way."[42]

The author granted that the czar of Russia lacked the disinterestedness, the personal integrity that characterized the Swedish monarch. Nevertheless Peter rescued his half-frozen kingdom from semi-barbarism. He modernized manners, he built up industry and commerce, and he established intellectual cooperation with men of art and science in other nations.

Czar Peter waged war only with a definite and patriotic end in view. As a conscientious tutor to kings, Voltaire pointed out how the Russian ruler consented to help Augustus of Poland only on condition that Livonia be ceded to Russia. In both the *History of Charles XII* and in the later biography of Peter I he praised the skill of the latter monarch in maintaining a safe balance of power for his nation.[43] For the fame of the czar was not the dazzling though ephemeral fame of the soldier. Unlike Charles XII, the glory of Peter the Great was based on his achievements as legislator, as statesman, as organizer, and as innovator.

The final victory of Peter over his rival at Pultava Voltaire regarded as the one military victory that had ever accomplished anything for the good of all humanity. For the outcome of the battle had brought thousands of backward people under the czar's progressive rule. If Charles XII had fallen, there would be in Europe one less hero. Yet had Peter the Great perished on the battlefield of Pultava, the largest empire in the world would have sunk back to the barbarism from which it had recently emerged.[44]

Above all, Voltaire valued a monarch whose achievements were of human benefit rather than of profit merely to the advancement of his kingdom. As he forcefully asserted in his *Discourse on the History of Charles XII,* preface to the second edition of his royal biography: "The princes most worthy of immortality are those who have done some good to men."[45]

The use of the general term "men" or "mankind" rather than "subjects" or even "compatriots" is typical of his consistently humanistic outlook. This regard for humanity in general is reaffirmed even more positively in his letter to the Maréchal of Schullembourg of 1740. Here he stated that the ideal prince would abstain from conquest and political warfare neither from desire to conserve the lives of his national subjects, nor for the sake of his own kingdom's prosperity. Such a prince who, as he expressed it, "loves peace because he loves men" would make humanity his cardinal virtue.[46]

His highest praise went therefore to Henri IV, who not only spared his country bloodshed, but won briefly for Frenchmen the universal right of freedom of worship. In his philosophic disciple Frederick of Prussia he had hoped to behold a champion of enlightenment, eager to bring about humane reforms and more equitable social standards. Then from Prussia the light would spread.

A somewhat lesser rank Voltaire assigned to Peter I and

Louis XIV. These kings he considered admirable organizers of human talent, who masterfully directed all activities within the countries they ruled. Remorseless oppressors of other nations, they nevertheless raised the material and intellectual level of their own respective kingdoms and in so doing made, almost against their wishes, a lasting contribution to European civilization.

The growth of Voltaire's sense of the duties a monarch owes to his subjects is nowhere more strikingly illustrated than in his account of the Patkul affair in his *History of Peter I, Emperor of Russia,* 1759 (Part I) as compared with his brief mention of this incident in the *History of Charles XII of Sweden.* In his biography of 1731 he seems to have mentioned the torture and execution of Patkul merely as an example of the fantastic extremes of loftiness and barbarity revealed in the character of the Swedish king.[47]

In his *History of Peter I, Emperor of Russia,* however, the author treated the Patkul affair less as an instance of personal injustice than as an intellectual issue. The career of the unhappy individual, Patkul, offered him a clear illustration of a clash between the "natural rights" of the individual and the political claims of kings upon their subjects. The case kindled his indignation. For he believed the man to have been the victim not only of two violations of "natural rights," but of an infringement of international law as well.[48]

A Livonian gentleman, Patkul, had been exiled by the father of Charles XII of Sweden. His crime? Only that of representing his country according to its laws. Some much needed rights and privileges he had respectfully requested for the citizens of Livonia, a land under Swedish rule.

His later execution as a rebellious Swedish subject had therefore, so Voltaire believed, no ethical sanction. For this man, when captured, was serving not Charles XII but the czar. His adopted country was Russia.

His unjust exile had absolved him of any obligations to his

native homeland. Banishment, so said the French philosopher, had "placed him in a position to reclaim the natural right of all men to choose for themselves a country."[49]

Both in this statement of 1759 and in the *Questions on the Encyclopedia* of 1770 the author implied that freedom to choose and adopt *la patrie* is included in that primitive "natural right" known as the "pursuit of happiness." Charles XII, by willfully destroying a former Swedish subject, had thereupon betrayed the purpose which Voltaire believed should underlie all organized society. For this purpose, which should be dear to monarchs, was the promotion of human welfare through safeguarding the basic rights of man.

The same practical humanitarian insistence on the duties which the nation owes the citizen prevented the French philosopher from ever succumbing to any blind worship of France as an abstract entity. Nor did he ever show any mystical tendency to identify his country symbolically with any individual present or past. No patriotic enthusiasm for either Saint Louis, Jeanne d'Arc, Henri IV, or Louis XIV induced him to judge these national figures except according to their contributions to the earthly well-being of the French people.

In Saint Louis, whom most Frenchmen revered as France's guardian angel, Voltaire beheld a well-meaning, though superstitious, sovereign. While in his *Essay on the Manners and Minds of Nations* he credited this king with a personal excellence that amounted to sainthood, he likewise deplored the social ineffectiveness of these same virtues. As a historian Voltaire pointed out that though a saint, Louis IX left unfulfilled his earthly obligations to his subjects. Through ruinous Crusades to the Holy Land in behalf of other-worldly interests, he often failed a people who claimed him as their protector here on earth.

Similarly, in Jeanne d'Arc, whom Chapelain had celebrated in an epic poem, and whom the twentieth century was to adopt as France's official national heroine, Voltaire recognized both a tool and a victim of the corrupt forces of Church and State. He praised the courage of the Maid and condemned the hypocrisy of her ecclesiastical accusers. Yet he found neither beauty nor inspiration in her story. For Jeanne d'Arc, he believed, had served not only among the legions of France, but in the dark and formidable army of superstition. Therefore in his bawdy poem, *The Maid,* he covered her with burlesque ridicule.

In the *Century of Louis XIV,* Voltaire glorified France as a cultural entity, even though he remained coolly critical of Louis XIV as a ruler. He honored the Grand Monarch for the encouragement this king offered all types of noble enterprises, for his heroic nonmaterial love of glory. Nevertheless the historian condemned the extravagance of Louis XIV and also his intolerance and callous indifference to the security and well-being of the vast majority of his subjects. By a detailed account of the greatness and weaknesses of the great Louis, he hoped to guide the halting footsteps of his successor to the path of national and world progress.

The conscious statements of Voltaire on patriotism show no real inconsistency. True, in those plays, in which he clothed his favorite ideas in fancy dress for the enlightenment of the public, love of country is voiced in tones both literary and oratorical. Such was the expression this sentiment called forth in the first third of the eighteenth century. Even as late as 1760, in *Tancrède,* he proved that he could still make dramatic capital of patriotism.[50]

More rarely as in *Adélaïde du Guesclin* and in *Mahomet* he stressed the unconscious attachment of individuals to their homeland.[51] Yet the notable fact remains that neither in plays, poems, indeed in none of his writings did he ever exalt patriotism in any other form than zeal for the public welfare. When in the *Temple of Glory* of 1745 he wrote:

> Fortune presides over combats, ravages,
> Glory is in good deeds.[52]

he was reasserting in language, understood by Versailles and acceptable to Louis XV, the same convictions he had proclaimed in his *History of Charles XII* and was later to voice in his "life" of Peter the Great.

A new variation on the theme of patriotism he essayed in *Rome Saved,* a drama of 1759. Discreetly he placed before the public the idea that the general good of the nation is more important than any governmental machinery designed for that purpose. As the Cicero of his drama counsels republican patriots:

> The most sacred duty, the dearest law
> Is to forget the law to save the country.[53]

In his *Poem on Fontenoy* of 1745, Voltaire seems to have reverted to patriotism in the traditional form of personal service to a monarch. Yet his stand is amply explained. At this period in his life he was serving Louis XV as Royal Historiographer. With a position at court he hoped to act as guide to a ruler not only on the printed page, but also in person. A military victory inspired by the royal presence he, a poet, would make the most of. When asked to celebrate the occasion in verse he responded grandiloquently.

His song of victory, though, the philosopher feared, might foment hatred for other European nations. To offset any such narrow overly patriotic impression he published a *Discourse*. Of the seventh edition of his original poem, this work, also of 1745, served as preface.

The poet here took occasion to state that while glorifying his king he had no intention to shame or disparage the defeated countries.[54] Though France had shown high courage on the battlefield, so also had her adversaries. Since throughout Europe the education and training of officers remained much the same, these men all shared the same good qualities.[55] Indeed, the French, the English, and the Austrians were all children of a common European heritage of laws, customs, and ethical standards. Therefore wars between these nations, the poet implied, were an insane sort of fratricide.

After an unsuccessful attempt to guide Louis XV at Versailles and an even greater failure with Frederick the Great at Potsdam, Voltaire addressed his message less to a king than to all thinking beings. During the first part of his life he had laid his emphasis on the obligations of the monarch. After 1753 he insisted primarily on the rights of the citizen. In such works as *Republican Ideas* of 1762 he discussed the terms of the basic agreement between the individual and the nation. However in his discussion of *patrie* in the *Philosophic Dictionary* and in his later contributions to this subject in *Questions on the Encyclopedia* nearly all his earlier thoughts and tentative opinions became finally crystallized.

In his essay of 1764, Voltaire's concept of the origin and meaning of *la patrie* was unsentimental and wholly practical. *La patrie,* he believed, originally consisted in a group of families, who all inhabited a given area.[56] This primitive society was gradually organized so as to form a State or "nation." Such a startling change in the pattern of life was brought about by common needs and dangers. As the author of the *Philosophic Dictionary* explained:

Everyone wishes to be able to lie down in his own home without another man claiming for himself the power to make him lie elsewhere. Everyone wants to be sure of his life and fortune.[57]

He here admitted that organized society or that portion of it called the nation was devised so as to protect human life and property. Of all the so-called "natural rights" this last was the most fundamental. Furthermore, by contributions and services to the communal life of the State the individual had been able to gain within this social framework certain material benefits. The primitive necessity for the first social contract the French philosopher thus described:

A few families first assembled against the bears and the wolves; the family which had only grain exchanged this product with the family which had only wood.[58]

Such human interdependence and cooperation led to the formation of an economic system and a State in which membership could actively contribute to the welfare of more and more citizens. The citizen was thus enabled to carry on more effectively his individual "pursuit of happiness." The laws of the first community were for the permanent security of all, and man was free in as much as he fulfilled his engagement with society.[59]

Thus, as judged by Voltaire, the nation, *la patrie,* had been formed solely to uphold and maintain the "natural rights" of countless individuals, all sharing the pleasures and dangers of a given locality.[60] Such primary rights the French thinker had long recognized. Yet, as previously mentioned, their precise political expression he defined only in the *Philosophic Dictionary* in his section on the British constitution.[61] Restated concisely and in the most general terms possible, the basic liberties he consistently cherished were the right to life and property, liberty in conformance with the Golden Rule, and the right to pursue as much individual happiness as is compatible with the common welfare.

The nation, he believed, was organized not only to protect man but man's earthly possessions. So his conception of *la patrie* was rooted in private property.

What does it mean to have a country? Does it not mean, perchance, a good field, about which the owner, lodged comfortably in a well-kept house, is able to say: "This field which I cultivate, this house which I have built are mine. I live here under the protection of laws no tyrant may infringe upon."[62]

"Natural law" decrees that the individual has the right to the fruits of his labor. Man should then be able to claim the territory, however small, his care and toil have made fertile. The ownership of land or, more generally, any portion of the nation's resources binds the citizen to his country both economically and socially. He becomes in this way a shareholder in the holdings of the community and thereby of the nation. For by cultivating the land entrusted to him he has improved his share of the raw materials that lie within the national jurisdiction.

A voice should then be granted him in the affairs of the community, of the sovereignty. The author of the *Philosophic Dictionary* believed that the State can serve humanity effectively only as an association of free men seeking together the common good and for the sake of this good willing to reconcile their conflicting interests. Only as the member of such an organization can an individual be rightfully said to have a *patrie*.[63]

So Voltaire was at one with Euripides in the belief that one's homeland is "wherever one feels happy and at ease,"[64] or more precisely, where the individual knows liberty and security. For national affection depends on the treatment a person receives in his native land and on the strength of his human ties there. Is it then strange, challenges the French thinker, that a Jew lacks passion for his homeland, if born at Coimbre and hounded by bloodthirsty Inquisitors who would burn him alive for his culinary tastes and inherited opinions. Of such a person is Palestine the country?

Vaguely he has heard that, in other times, his ancestors, whoever they were, inhabited this stony sterile land, surrounded by an abominable desert; and that today the same little country, which yields them almost nothing, is owned by the Turks. Jerusalem is not his homeland. In fact, he has none. Not a square foot of the earth's surface belongs to him.[65]

Also, in Paris, what could a baker's boy reply if asked if he had a country? Indeed, that he has no homeland; none other than the stove to which he owes his bare subsistence. "A thinker who heard this conversation concluded that in a land of considerable size there are often several million men who have no country at all."[66]

Thus, as estimated by Voltaire, the persecuted, the destitute, and the enslaved have no *patrie,* nor can they love the country they inhabit. Toward these men, deprived of their natural rights, the State has failed to keep the implicit social contract which underlies all government. The reverse, the French philosopher held, is true in regard to hired soldiers and intriguers. For such adventurers have failed to make the contributions and sacrifices which their pact with the native land demands of them. Have characters of this type a country? "Even less so than a bird of prey which returns nightly to the maternal nest in a hole in the rock."[67]

Nor have monks in their monasteries an earthly country. Their holdings are in the Kingdom of Heaven.[68] All these classes of men Voltaire viewed as alike in that they have no stake in the communal life of the nation. Through misfortune, personal greed, or other-worldly interests, they were unable to contribute to the welfare of their fellow-men within or without the national organization. In cases like these he considered the bond with *la patrie* as materially broken.[69]

Since the origin of the State, in his opinion, was wholly practical, national sentiment seemed to Voltaire neither sacred nor obligatory. Passion for the native land was to the author of the *Philosophic Dictionary* nothing more than an extension of the *amour-propre* of the individual. Attachment to *la patrie* he regarded as fondness for a congenial way of life, familiar scenes, and old friends. The saying of Euripides so triumphantly quoted in the *Questions on the Encyclopedia,* he expressed with only slight variation in his correspondence as early as 1734. In a letter to Thiriot in English he told his friend that he would have been contented to settle permanently in England except for ties of friendship which bound him to France and "where friendship is there is our native land."[70]

Each man has the right to choose his own country. Nevertheless Voltaire conceded that unless the government was corrupt or tyrannical, the native land would inevitably be where the individual was happiest. When a Parisian spoke of his profound attachment to his country, this man was referring not to a national abstraction. His devotion, the French thinker asserted, was to the comforts, society, and amusements that Paris afforded him.[71] So patriotism, in the realistic estimation of Voltaire, was natural rather than noble.

Personal love of *la patrie,* however, should not be confused with the ethical obligation on the part of the State and the citizen to fulfill their social contract. National affection the French philosopher regarded as the sure concomitant of a just government and a cultured civilization. Yet, in his opinion, this individual patriotic feeling was important only as it inspired the citizen to aid justice, serve freedom, and use his talents to perfect conditions of life within his native land.

"Virtue," the author of the *Philosophic Dictionary* redefined as *bienfaisance envers le prochain,*[72] the "doing of good deeds to one's neighbor." Thus love of country seemed to him virtuous when actions prompted by this emotion were humane and could be ethically sanctioned. Passion for the native land expressed in the form of military aggression and contempt for other nations he unfailingly condemned as harmful to the world-wide fraternity of reason, or in Christian phraseology, to the Brotherhood of Man. Indeed so perverted a use of one's natural preference for the homeland defeated the fundamental purpose of organized society, and, in his opinion, this purpose was enlightened self-interest.

Hope, nevertheless, is held out in the article "Patrie" that the law of enlightened self-interest which led to the formation of sovereign states, might also govern dealings between nations. For Voltaire liked to look upon nations as members of a great world society, seeking their own well-being, yet respectful of each other's interests. The necessary rivalry their statehood had brought about, he even regarded as a force of progress. For such vigorous competition, when applied to the arts of peace, had spurred these countries on to achievements unknown when all Europe was cast in the Roman mold.[73]

In the eighteenth-century world, however, cosmopolitan humanitarian feeling was difficult to reconcile with national loyalty.

For peace on the European continent was largely dependent on that equal distribution of hostile forces known as the balance of power. As the French thinker summed up the problem:

Sad it is, that often in order to be a good patriot one becomes the enemy of the rest of mankind. . . . To be a good patriot means to wish that one's home city or country may grow prosperous through commerce and powerful by force of arms. It is clear that one country can not gain without another losing. Nor can it conquer without making men in other lands unhappy.[74]

Faced with the still unsolvable problem of conflicting national interests, a philosopher, a world citizen, has, according to Voltaire, just one answer. He can only wish that the size and strength of his homeland be such as to tip the European scales on the side not of war and bloodshed, but of peace and international harmony.[75]

# La Patrie and the Principles
# of Democracy

V OLTAIRE'S CONCEPT of *la patrie* is based on liberal principles, and may be judged democratic in essence. For throughout his writings he clung resolutely to the conviction that the State exists for the individual, as opposed to the authoritarian dictum that the individual exists for the State.[1] His practical, non-sentimental view of the nation was part of that intense humanism which characterized his entire outlook on life and destiny.

In a Christianity that sanctioned religious persecution and the evils of monarchy by "divine right," he felt that his con-temporaries were being enslaved to a myth of their own creation. In such works as the *Commentary on the Thoughts of Pascal* and the *Sermon for Fifty People,* he aimed to free humanity from all subservience to supernatural authority, and to prove to his century that man's best friend should be man.

As a humanist, Voltaire placed the dignity of the human being above any class or nationalist abstraction whatever. That men could call upon a mere classification, based on convenience, to inspire each other to uphold their honor seemed to him both absurd and superfluous. Instead of appealing to a magistrate to be worthy of the cloth or to a soldier to maintain the honor of the regiment from Champagne, he would substitute the pre-cept: "Remember your dignity as a man."[2]

This attitude is decidedly realistic. For he refused to consider a nation or institution as any greater or nobler than the individuals, weak or strong, who happen to compose it. Indeed, the entire philosophic system of Leibnitz seemed to him an absurdity merely because the "all is well" explanation of the universe had no meaning for the individual. In this "best of all possible worlds," man suffered hunger, privation, oppression, and disease. In the *Philosophic Dictionary* he wittily pointed out that a person whose bodily organs had become diseased was martyred by the immutable physical laws of the universe,[3] and died in torture by a marvelously ingenious interplay of natural forces.

Therefore, he looked upon the individual as the only possible unit of social organization. Such a view is evident in his fancied portrayal of that primitive and natural society which time ripened into *la patrie*. This early human association he imagined as a group of men who, with their families and their possessions, had banded together for the sake of mutual material benefits and for protection against certain common dangers.[4]

In a patriarchal community, thus organized, equality, he asserted, was "natural." It was natural and therefore just for every father of a family to be master in his own home. It was indeed unnatural and contrary to all laws of justice for this same man to hold authority over any household other than his own. The only way to ensure to all men the equal exercise of this "natural right" of liberty of person and property was for each head of a family to have a voice in the direction of communal affairs. As Voltaire stated in the *Republican Ideas* of 1762:

A society being made up of several houses and the several lands adjoining them, it is contrary to nature that any one man should be the master of these lands and these houses, and it is in harmony with nature that each master should have his say concerning them for the welfare of society as a whole.[5]

This same insistence that the individual, his rights and his well-being, form the sole "reason-for-being" of the nation, he repeated in the article "Patrie" of the *Philosophic Dictionary*.

In the following terms his theoretical citizen of a country deserving to be called *la patrie* defines his accepted prerogatives:

When those who own, as I do, fields and houses gather together to discuss their common interests, I have a voice in this assembly. I am a part of the whole, a part of the community, a part of the sovereignty; there is my country. Anything other than this habitation of free men, is it not oftentimes a stable of horses under the command of a groom who kicks them at his pleasure? One has a country under a good King; none under a bad ruler.[6]

Apart from all considerations of the method of government, the country Voltaire would recognize as a true homeland must create for its citizens an atmosphere of freedom. In such articles of the *Philosophic Dictionary* as "Laws," "States," and "Equality," he as much as admitted that a wholesome mental and moral climate can exist only under a political regime able to foster a feeling of liberty, of equality, in the sense of respect for the inviolability of human personality—and lastly, of a unity of social purpose conducive to a spirit of fraternity.[7]

Love for these three great abstractions which were to become the war-cry of French democracy is evident in most of his major writings. Yet to him the amount of liberty, as well as the amount of fraternity, attainable for a nation is primarily dependent on that central concept of equality. So he spent much of his life attempting to elucidate this troublesome *égalité* and its meaning in relation to society.

To Voltaire all men were equal in the sense that all men were equally human beings.[8] By this he meant that from Paris to Peking all men had five senses, sought pleasure, avoided pain, and possessed the tremendously important faculty of reason. They were born in pain and they died in pain. They were alike in all their physical functions. This "natural equality," insisted upon by both Voltaire and Rousseau,[9] refers first to these universal and basic conditions of life, and secondly, to the primitive and equal claim of each individual to the pursuit of happiness.

On man alone the Supreme Being has conferred the gift of

reason. Therefore man alone of all creatures has an ethical responsibility toward his choices in life. The sense of justice and love for fellow members of mankind inherent in the human species inevitably drew men together within an organized society.[10] This same justice and sympathy prompted them to demand for themselves and their fellows certain natural and inalienable rights.[11]

These primary rights politically expressed, for example, in the British constitution uphold still further the idea of man as a moral personality. For liberty of person and property implies that the individual is worthy to be his own master. The right to express religious beliefs and political opinions, as well as the right to assemble to discuss the government, presupposes a conception of man as intellectually and ethically mature. Such civic responsibilities are founded on the assumption that the human being is capable of effecting a harmonious relationship between his own particular interest and the common good.

Since all men share equally the human status, Voltaire believed that each and every one was equally entitled to the rights and privileges of man's estate. In his *Thoughts on Government* of 1752 he declared in praise of the liberal government of Holland: "A citizen of Amsterdam is a man; a citizen at a few degrees of longitude beyond it is a domestic animal."[12] Nevertheless, the French thinker makes clear that primitive equality and the natural fundamental rights this condition confers upon the individual implies neither equality of ability nor social equality:

Such equality does not imply the absence of subordination. We are all equally men, but not equal members of society. All the natural rights belong equally to the Sultan and to a man of the Bostangi tribe. The one and the other should have the self-same liberty of person, family and property.[13]

Social inequality, however, was the outcome of man's painful struggle for survival. In the *Philosophic Dictionary,* Voltaire asserted that social equality could exist only in a world where all men were free from both wants and needs. If the earth provided ample and salutary sustenance for all human creatures, each and everyone could live unto himself alone. Amidst the abundance of nature's bounties, servitude would be be unknown. For why seek servants when no services are needed?

These happy conditions, however, have always been contrary to reality. So the reason inherent in the human species universally recognized the inescapable fact of man's dependence on man. The result was subordination.[14] Thus of the immemorial demands of men for equality the French philosopher remarked paradoxically: "Equality is therefore the condition most natural and at the same time the most chimerical."[15]

In his article "Equality" he gave a striking illustration of how at the dawn of society one large family and two small ones responded to their vital and immediate need for a relationship with each other. For, as he pointed out, it was impossible for two small families who tilled a rocky barren field to subsist alongside of the larger industrious family who cultivated an excellent plot of soil. Thus, of the two impoverished families, one offered service in exchange for bread; the other attempted to rob and murder the prosperous household and was thereupon subjugated. Voltaire concluded: "The family that gave service is the origin of domestic-workers and field-laborers. The subdued, beaten family is the origin of slaves."[16]

Of two possible solutions of the problem of man's dependence, one was founded on justice and reason. Enlightened self-interest accounts for the initial agreement between master and servant, just as it explains any other satisfactory civic relationship.

On the other hand, the dealings of the subsequently enslaved family with their affluent neighbors began with violence and ended with violence. In this last case, the exercise of the evil "right of the strongest" by both parties violated the inalienable rights of human beings and, in so doing, violated the commands of "natural law." By violation of "natural law," the French philosopher meant failure to act in accordance with the ethical

insight man has received as a gift from his creator.[17] Since subservience is the price of earthly survival, reason and respect for
human personality require that this condition be regulated so
that, as far as possible, both the men serving and those served
might equally profit by their relationship.

To Voltaire, the imponderable task of all government is to
restore man to his primary equality in a world where servitude
is inevitable. In his opinion, despotic rule, arbitrary social conventions and the brutalizing power of superstition all represent
attempts to solve the problem of man's dependence by the unjust
"right of the strongest." These abuses, he believed, have no
rational basis. For they trespass on the equal claim of each
individual to the pursuit of happiness.

The State should recognize that all citizens are equally human
beings, even though the insufficiency of the earth's products and
the inequality of mind and character assign these men to different roles in society.[18] Laws should therefore be established to
preserve and fulfill for individuals in every walk of life the just,
inviolable rights to which all are equally entitled as members
of the human species. Since social and economic inequalities
seemed to him inescapable,[19] Voltaire unceasingly advocated the
only kind of equality he judged practical and possible. This was
legal equality. The belief that all men should be equal before
the law, the French philosopher voiced in many of his most
significant writings.

In his chapter on medieval Switzerland in the *Essay on the
Manners and Minds of Nations,* he clearly defined this useful
type of equality, as enjoyed by the Swiss republic.

This word does not mean the absurd and impossible equality by
which the servant and the master, the laborer and the magistrate are
lumped together on the same level; but the equality of the citizen
before laws he can count upon to defend the liberty of the weak
against the ambition of the strong.[20]

Again in his *Thoughts on Government* he asserted: "The

best government would seem to be one under which all classes of men are equally protected by law."[21] This strict equality, upheld for instance by the British constitution, explains his admiration for the English government.

He failed, however, to realize that laws designed to ensure the "natural rights" of each individual in his social sphere could not be enforced in the Bourbon monarchy. For the privilege of wealth and aristocracy was all-powerful. Laws existed to protect a French citizen from an unprovoked attack by his neighbor. Yet when the attacker's name was Rohan and the attacked was a mere Arouet, this ruling became invalid. Theoretically, all individuals charged with a civil or criminal offense were entitled to a fair trial by jury. Yet when legal satisfaction could be obtained only by costly journeys to a local parlement which held jurisdiction over a wide area of the countryside, the fulfilment of this "natural right" became for many persons financially prohibitive. The further necessity of paying for expensive presents called *épices* to judges whose offices were bought and sold not only caused justice to miscarry, but barred the impoverished majority of Frenchmen from any semblance of civil equality.

These abuses Voltaire fought bitterly. Still, as he made his strong plea for a uniform code of law before which all citizens stood as equal, he scarcely realized that this end could not be attained without an almost revolutionary reform of other inequalities which he himself judged inescapable.

The democratic way of life rests on the belief that the primitive equality of men as members of the human species should find the fullest possible social expression. If, as Voltaire consistently maintained, *la patrie* exists for the individual, a government should not merely file respectfully in the archives of the State the just though unenforceable claims of the citizen. In order to carry out the terms of the basic social agreement, the State should endeavor to bring about as far as possible an equal opportunity of self-realization for each member of the national commonwealth. The question is to what extent the author of the *Philosophic Dictionary* esteemed desirable and practicable these ideal aims of true democracy.

As the social critic Harold Laski summarizes democratic philosophy in the *Encyclopedia of Social Sciences*:

The notion of equality points the way to the essence of the democratic idea—the effort of men to affirm their own essence and to remove all barriers to that affirmation. All differentials by which other men exercise authority or influence they do not themselves possess hinder their own self-realization. To give these differentials the protection of the legal order is to prevent the realization of the wishes and interests of the mass of men. The basis of democratic development is therefore the demand for equality, the demand that the system of power be erected upon the similarities and not the differences between men. Of the permanence of this demand there can be no doubt; at the very dawn of political science Aristotle insisted that its denial was the main cause of revolutions. Just as the history of the state can perhaps be most effectively written in terms of the expanding claims of the common man upon the results of its effort, so the development of the realization of equality is the clue to the problem of democracy.[22]

Voltaire was wholeheartedly in sympathy with this fundamental purpose of democracy. In his *A, B, C* dialogue of 1768, a work in which he discussed with incomparable brilliance some of the most baffling questions of all time, *B*, the interlocutor who acts most often as a spokesman for the author, declares in the section on government:

To be free, to have only equals is living the real life, the life of man in his natural state; any other life is an unworthy artifice, a bad comedy in which one person plays the master, another the slave, another the parasite and another the go-between. You will admit that man can have descended from the natural state only through cowardice and stupidity.[23]

The successful republic continually represented to him the incarnation of his ideal for the State. For such a self-governing nation gave concrete and triumphant expression to the basic equality of all individuals as members of the human family.

In *Republican Ideas* he conceded that a perfect government had never existed because men had passions and that without passions men would have no need of government, nevertheless: "The most tolerable of them all is undoubtedly the republican form of government because this form brings men nearest to the condition of natural equality."[24]

The citizens of a republic owed allegiance not to any one man and his clique but to the just impartial laws of the State. These ensured the natural and equal prerogatives of mankind such as liberty of person and property, religious freedom, the right to discuss the government and to have a voice in its policies. Under a rule of this kind, the artificial obstacles to individual self-realization like religion and social rank would be nonexistent. The absence of functionless privilege would lead the way to an economic leveling which would bring to the average citizen far-reaching material and intellectual benefits. Ability in men of all classes and creeds would be given the opportunity to develop, and all citizens would contribute, as far as they were able, to the advancement of the commonwealth.

Voltaire felt confident that the nation which accordingly put in practice these democratic principles would prosper. A republic, as the perfect and complete fusion of particular interest with the general public welfare, would win the loyalty and devotion of all its members. As he realistically asserted: "A republican is always more devoted to his homeland than is a royal subject, for the simple reason that one prefers one's own goods to those of one's master."[25]

If property was made individual and inviolable and ability encouraged and rewarded, the citizens would strive toward new goals of attainment. "In a real republic, each man being sure of the ownership of his goods and his person, works for himself with confidence, and in bettering his own condition he betters that of the public."[26]

Unlike any aggrandizement of the nation brought about by the enslavement of the multitude, the greatness of the republic would be actual and organic. Such greatness would be achieved by the exhuberant health of all the cells in the body politic. Yet, while he fought one by one the battles of democracy, Voltaire resigned himself to the knowledge that his ideal republic existed only in Utopia. Nor did he entertain any hope that its basic principles could be successfully fulfilled through the political technique of democratic government.

The fact remained that either by "cowardice" or "stupidity" men have fallen from that pure state of nature in which they had lived freely and independently as equal hedonistic units. The individual might therefore reclaim as much of his primitive birthright of liberty and equality as could be safely attained in a complex civilization in which all human beings were desperately and inextricably interdependent. The supreme social purpose the French philosopher recognized as the establishment of conditions which would enable each individual to fulfill his maximum potentialities for service and enjoyment. Yet he still felt regretfully persuaded that for the work of the world to be done, as the ransom of survival in organized society, a vast army of poor workers was necessary.

In the article "Equality" in the *Philosophic Dictionary* he declared:

The human race, such as it is, can hardly subsist without an infinite number of useful men who own nothing at all; for certainly no man in easy circumstances will leave his own land to come to work for you on yours, and if you need a pair of shoes, a Master of Petitions will not be the one to make them for you.[27]

These opinions he also expressed in the *Century of Louis XIV* and in his correspondence.[28]

He had contended that all human associations were originally founded on justice and sympathy. Yet he remained equally convinced that only under the pressure of material needs could man overcome his natural taste for idleness and maintain that industry upon which the social structure depended. The various contradictions and faltering inconsistencies inherent in Voltaire's plea for the advancement of the common man are all explained by his inability to find any real *modus vivendi* between the unattainable ideal of democratic equality and the seeming need of society for economic inequality. The failure of the French philosopher to advocate or foresee any complete economic liberation of the peasants and workers has caused his ultimate democratic aims to be underestimated.

Harold Laski has declared in the *Rise of European Liberalism*: "In any essential sense, Voltaire has no use for equality. Equal property is a mere chimera; it could only be attained by unjust spoliation."[29] Mr. Laski seems here to infer that equality in "any essential sense" is primarily economic. Such a concept, it is true, was profoundly alien to the creator of *Candide*.

Since to Voltaire the individual was ever the unit of social organization, economic equality would have seemed to him meaningless. For equality of this type disregards the individual as a moral and intellectual entity. According to the terms of the original social agreement between the State and the citizen, property, so the eighteenth-century thinker believed, should be the just recompense for talent and industry. The unequal contributions of the citizens to the national welfare must be necessarily rewarded by unequal material assets. This idea Voltaire accepted as an inevitable law of life.

That he worked for the economic and political advancement of the bourgeois was unquestionable. The interests of this class were nearly identical with his own. Yet in a civilization dominated by the clergy and the nobility, when the third estate had barely attained any measure of political influence, no such realist as Voltaire could confidently preach the economic liberation of the illiterate mass of the people. The mere thought of all three estates and the "people" existing on a common material level would have seemed to him insanely grotesque, even if such a condition could have been brought about without the overthrow of society.

In the half-feudal eighteenth century, and innocent of the

doctrine of Karl Marx, he dedicated his life to the shaping of conditions which pointed the way to a nearer fulfillment of the ideal of equality of opportunity. This equality, as Mr. Laski himself has stated, is the essence of modern democracy.

Though Voltaire's ultimate goal was democratic, his method of approach was that of the true liberal. If democracy means the realization of equality, "liberalism" has been defined authoritatively as:

. . . a belief in the value of human personality, and a conviction that the source of all progress lies in the free exercise of individual energy; it produces an eagerness to emancipate all individuals or groups so that they may freely exercise their powers, so far as this is done without injury to others; and it therefore involves a readiness to use the power of the State for the purpose of creating the conditions within which individual energy can thrive, of preventing all abuses of power, of affording to every citizen the means of acquiring mastery of his own capacity, and establishing a real equality of opportunity for all.[30]

In the *Encyclopedia of Social Sciences* Guido de Ruggiero shows the difference in emphasis between democracy and liberalism, those two closely related branches of the same humanistic tree:

Whereas liberty involves differentiation and division, equality entails leveling and centralization. Liberty and equality which find their embodiment respectively in liberalism and democracy are thus complementary and at the same time antithetical: complementary, in as much as absence of equality, at least equality of opportunity degrades liberty to the level of exclusive and therefore oppressive privilege; antithetical in as much as equality is conducive to indiscriminate leveling and indirectly to excessive centralization.[31]

Thus equality of opportunity may be reached either by the direct route of democracy or by the longer more roundabout path of liberalism. Voltaire chose the latter. In his eyes the paramount aim of the nation should be the attainment of a society in which individual ability could develop freely, unhindered by irrational or arbitrary restrictions. In this way the talents of each citizen could contribute most effectively to the common good and raise the level of civilization within the State as a whole. Therefore, unlike Rousseau, he placed his stress less on equality than on human development and accomplishment, and on the freedom which would make this individual self-realization possible.

To Voltaire the English middle-class motto of "Liberty and Property" expressed the goal which the State should make attainable to the citizen.[32] In a sound political order property should represent the tangible reward of socially valuable services regardless of their sphere of origin. Thus ownership by an increasing number of individuals throughout the nation would mean the successful functioning of the social contract. For, according to the implicit pact he envisioned, both the State and the citizen maintain their relationship by a constant mutual interchange of benefits and services.

Amidst the decadent feudalism of the eighteenth century, the first step toward the gradual liberation and enlightenment of the majority of Frenchmen must necessarily be the abolishment of feudal privilege. In the opinion of Voltaire, the rich advantages conferred by the social order upon the clergy and the nobility had no longer any relation to usefulness to the nation. Ardently he inspired and abetted those attempts of Turgot to force these two classes to relinquish some of their unearned benefits and share the economic burdens of the kingdom in a measure befitting their wealth and influence.

The Sage of Ferney called Boncerf's much disputed pamphlet, *The Disadvantages of Feudal Dues,* "the wisest and most patriotic book I have ever read."[33] For this treatise was written to prepare the public for the efforts of Turgot toward something like fiscal equality. In place of the hated *corvée* the author would substitute a property tax to be paid by well-to-do landowners. Also *banalités,* those industrial monopolies run by nobles to the financial detriment of whole communities, Boncerf desired abolished, though not without adequate compensation to their owners for so sudden a loss of income. He attacked such immemorial abuses of the *ancien régime* as duties on the sale of land, hunting privileges, and other feudal exactions, large and small, which the first two estates wrung from the miserable peasantry.

The Patriarch of Ferney looked upon this pamphlet as dictated by a patriotism of reason. Love of country enlightened by reason made it clear that the expenses of life in an organized society such as the nation must be allotted to the citizens best able to bear them.

The French Philosopher felt anger at the brutal exploitation of the poor and weak by those highly privileged classes whose Christian and civic duty commanded them to protect such unfortunate groupings. The not so distant shadow of the guillotine may be glimpsed in the searing words which he, Voltaire, the godson of Châteauneuf and the one-time pet of Chaulieu, addressed to the wealthy though functionless order of *"abbé,"* the same ecclesiastical order which had implanted in him its own hedonism and religious skepticism:

You are right, Gentlemen, take over the earth; it belongs to the strong or to the clever who take possession of it; you have profited by times of ignorance, superstition and folly to strip us of our inheritance and to trample us under foot, so that you can fatten yourselves on the substance of the unhappy: tremble lest the day of reason and reckoning should come.[34]

Mr. Laski asserts that the destruction of feudal privilege in France merely resulted in a transfer of political and economic power from the nobles and clergy into the hands of the rising, acquisitive bourgeoisie.[35] This eventual historical outcome should not be confused with the original aim of the leveling movement. For the actual and immediate purpose in view was to relieve the peasants and workers of certain specific burdens which had become well-nigh unbearable.

In the worst of these, the *corvée,* Voltaire beheld a form of slavery which robbed the peasants and workers of the "natural right" of liberty of person and property. This tax violated the liberty of person of the agricultural laborer in that it condemned him to two weeks of back-breaking labor on the roads without pay. It violated property rights. For working power constituted the sole property of the worker and remained his only recourse against slow starvation. Lastly, since the toiler has ownership only of his individual manpower, it logically follows that the natural and inalienable prerogative of the laboring classes is to choose their conditions of labor.[36]

Voltaire felt convinced that those sensational new edicts, fought for by Turgot in the early months of 1776, would protect working-class rights and lead to the economic betterment of a vast section of the population.[37] One of these measures substituted for the *corvée* a money levy to be paid by prosperous landowners, while the remaining land tax was to be the personal responsibility of the monarch. The other almost equally revolutionary edict would liberate the industrial worker from those guilds and corporations which so long had exploited him.

The Sage of Ferney beheld a second step toward relieving the miseries of laborers in the abolishment of serfdom. Both the State and the individual, he maintained, would be better served when each peasant became a proprietor who cultivated his personal plot of land with a zeal inspired by ownership.[38] Then, the soil of France would reach new goals of productiveness, while at the same time a large class of the French people would attain the initiative over their own destiny conferred upon them by property.

Without this initiative to think and act freely, no individual, Voltaire believed, was ripe to share, in any democratic sense, the civic responsibilities of government. His statement in *Republican Ideas* and in the *Philosophic Dictionary* that the right to regulate communal affairs should belong chiefly to owners of landed property was based on sound observation.[39] The mass of the peasantry, whose only possessions consisted in their physical energy and manual skill were completely illiterate. What instruction they received, if any, was limited to a few lessons in the catechism.[40] The same unhappy ignorance prevailed among the equally propertyless artisans.[41] At the age of ten they generally began their years of apprenticeship to a master who more often than not was little better than any slave-driver. Their mode of living was miserable and like the peasant-laborers they had neither time nor strength to learn anything outside their trade.

In *Republican Ideas* the French philosopher declared that citizens who possess neither lands nor houses have no more right to a voice in public affairs than have hired clerks the right to direct the business of their employers. Nevertheless, and the following adjoinder is typical of his unfailingly progressive outlook: ". . . they can have the status of associate, either by rendering special services or by paying for their association."[42] In his opinion, useful service and an economic stake, however small, in the common national enterprise should bring its political reward.

Therefore when in *The Rise of European Liberalism,* Harold Laski asserts that Voltaire had for the common people a "profound contempt"; that he judged the *canaille* as unworthy of enlightenment,[43] such statements seem remarkably unfair. Realism, not arrogance governed the eighteenth-century thinker's attitude toward the working classes. If he failed to advocate the education of the French masses, his reason was not that he deemed them "unworthy." Under existing conditions, he doubted the efficacy of this approach to their betterment.

The laboring classes, he felt persuaded, could be granted neither political expression nor enlightenment until their daily terms of living had been made more bearable. To countless needy toilers crushed by the economic millstone of the existing tax system he failed to see how learning could prove of any great or lasting benefit. Scholarly pursuits would make the people failures at those inescapable occupations upon which they depended for their livelihoods. Honest laborers would desert the countryside and flock to the cities in order to knock at the doors of professions which must remain inexorably closed to them.[44] Starvation and unemployment would await them and, as a result, the common good would suffer.

For these reasons in 1763, Voltaire approved the exclusion of laborers from any share in the new plan of national education sponsored by La Chalotais.[45] Three years later he wrote lightly to Damilaville that no lord of a large manor-house could wish for a staff of servants whose weighty erudition distracted them from their menial tasks.[46]

Unable to solve the problem of dependence and servitude in a manner other than his century and, at the same time, convinced of the irrational unsatisfactory nature of this solution, he concluded in this letter of 1766: "When the populace take it upon themselves to reason all will be lost."[47]

Nevertheless, his own views on working-class education were continually subject to modification in the light of new evidence. In Geneva firsthand observation revealed to him that the instruction of the workers proved compatible with the public welfare. He knew Genevan watchmakers desirous and capable of learning. The enlightenment they acquired contributed to their general efficiency and the mental improvement of so large a class raised the level of society as a whole. In a letter to Linguet of 1767 he remarked:

But Parisians would be astonished to see, in many cities of Switzerland and above all in Geneva, almost all industrial workers spend at reading the time left over from their work. No, monsieur, all is not lost when the people are placed in a position to realize that they have a mind. All, on the contrary, is lost when they are treated like a herd of bulls, for sooner or later they will gore you with their horns.[48]

In Geneva, Voltaire championed working-class demands for political expression. For here the artisans already possessed a fair degree of enlightenment and lived under conditions which made self-improvement possible.

Geneva was theoretically a republic. Yet neither by constitution nor by actual rule could this government conceivably be called democratic or in any true sense liberal. The ruling class consisted of the General Council, the Little Council of Twenty-five, and the Consistory of the Clergy. The General Council, made up of "citizens" and bourgeois, voted the laws, levied taxes, and decided upon the issues of war and peace. Yet despite this technique of democratic government all the political power was concentrated in the hands of the members of the Little Council of Twenty-five. The offices of these magistrates tended increasingly to become hereditary; while members of the other councils had finally obtained the privilege of being irremovable. The result was a system of co-optation which created a close monopoly of political offices in the hands of a few leading families. Geneva was an oligarchy and the people were not represented at all.[49]

In Geneva Voltaire had hoped to witness the successful operation of his ideal republic. Yet here as elsewhere the few governed the many. Three-fourths of the population consisted of those industrious watchmakers whose skill sent Genevan watches to the far markets of the world. To this large class Geneva owed her wealth and fame. These enlightened artisans however were not only deprived of all political rights, but trade and commerce, military service, and the liberal professions all remained rigorously closed to them. They were not even allowed to petition the Councils, a right which, aided by the Lord of Ferney, the bourgeois had only with the greatest difficulty obtained.[50]

If Voltaire had supported the bourgeois in their fight for representation, with even more tireless ingenuity he sought to win some measure of civil and commercial equality for the artisans. He conferred with their leaders at Ferney. He offered them excellent advice on how to hold their own against two such powerful and hostile political parties as the magistrates and the bourgeois.[51] To the statement which the Genevan watchmakers had prepared for the French mediator, he himself added an introductory letter.

When this step failed the workers received from him *Petition to the Mediators,* a document written under the veil of anonymity and clearly listing their claims and grievances. His *Petition,* however, the cautious *Natifs* considered too radical. So the philosopher patiently set to work to soften the requests therein stated.[52] The appeal momentarily found favor with the plenipotentiaries of Berne and Zurich. Yet owing to the jealousy of the bourgeois who blackened the *Natifs* in the opinion of the authorities, these efforts toward working-class emancipation merely ended in failure.[53]

Though for Geneva Voltaire had hoped to win some measure of democracy, on the political and intellectual advancement of French workers he remained relatively conservative. In 1768 he assured D'Alembert that he had no desire to bring to the working-class a schooling which might upset the religious convictions of shoemakers and servant girls.[54]

In Catholic, monarchical France any sudden or wide-scale enlightenment for the laborers and artisans might prove dangerous. For the masses of the population had no intellectual foundation upon which to build a finely reasoned philosophy of man's duty to man. The possible loss of religious faith by so large a group, he believed, might result in moral vacuum. Discontent, unemployment, and rebellion might spread among the workers, and after such an upheaval, even more stringent conditions for the people.[55]

The socially indispensable labor of the workers condemns them to ignorance and in turn their profound ignorance fits them only for unremitting toil. This is the *impasse* beyond which Voltaire's social theorizing rarely penetrates. In practice, however, far more than in theory, he fought for the mental and material improvement of the peasant and artisan. Despite his seeming lack of enthusiasm about peasant-education, he founded at Ferney a school for the children of laborers.[56]

Continually he combatted the unjust distribution of taxes, that flagrant source of mass poverty. In Gex, his home community, he waged a long and bitter war on the salt tax, a grossly unfair levy, collected by an official little better than any modern racketeer. At last, with the aid of Turgot, he achieved a reform, which in the France of the *ancien régime,* remained without precedent. The more privileged forty percent of the population paid the entire tax, and the remaining sixty percent of impoverished citizens were completely exempted.

Unable to change the social and financial position of the workers, Voltaire improved their condition, whenever he could, by private philanthropy.[57] His watch factory, silk works, and textile mills offered countless poor artisans the opportunity to earn a livelihood.

When the Genevan watchmakers finally lost the battle for political expression, Voltaire, unlike Rousseau,[58] assumed full responsibility for his leadership. As the more rebellious watchmakers were exiled from the city, he attempted to install them at Ferney and at Versoix, a new French port, which, with the aid of Choiseul, he hoped to open on Lake Geneva. The Versoix settlement, however, was not ready for the accommodation of so many families and the eclipse of Choiseul soon ruined all chances for the completion of the project. So the remnant of this colony he housed, at his own expense, at Ferney. For the employment of the exiled artisans he soon established, on his own premises, a thriving watch factory, an ancestor of the one which made Besançon famous.

The democratic goal of equality of opportunity, the author of *Candide* believed, could be best fulfilled through the progressive liberation of social classes from ignorance and economic bondage. While seeking to free the workers from the many barriers to their self-realization, he made his strongest plea for the education of the bourgeois. In his eyes, the third estate was the pivotal class in the social structure, and the only one among whom the primitive social agreement between the individual and the State was in active operation.[59]

If the clergy and nobility possessed without serving, the people served without possessing. The *bourgeoisie* both possessed and served. Their active participation in the life of the nation placed them in a position to be consulted by the ruling class on social and economic issues affecting the welfare of all Frenchmen. In close touch with the proletariat, an intelligent, educated *bourgeoisie* could act as a cohesive force in French society. For they could influence the ruling class to adopt policies that conformed with the interests of the countless lower ranks of the people.

As he concluded his aforementioned letter to Damilaville of 1766: "One must educate not the hand-laborer, but the good *bourgeois*, the city-dweller, this enterprise is great and ambitious enough."[60]

To Voltaire, enlightenment was a movement which should proceed from the sovereign. It should be put in practice by the aristocracy, gain impetus from the *bourgeoisie* and finally tame the fanatical fierceness of the benighted proletariat. The enlightenment of the third estate was the first step toward the enlightenment of the masses. The *bourgeoisie* was on the rung of the social ladder immediately above the people. The example of a humane and tolerant bourgeois class could, he believed, prove of inestimable value in preparing the way for a new type of society unfettered by superstition.

His sense of progress is evident in one concise paragraph in the article "Superstition" of the *Philosophic Dictionary*:

These magistrates will then prevent the superstition of the people from becoming dangerous. The example of these magistrates will not enlighten the rabble, but the bourgeois leaders will restrain them. There has perhaps not been a single riot, a single religious outrage, in which the bourgeois of former times have not been implicated, because those bourgeois were rabble; but reason and time will have changed them. Their gentler ways will soften the manners of the vilest and most ferocious populace: of that we have striking examples in more than one country. In a word, the less superstition, the less fanaticism; and the less fanaticism, the less unhappiness.[61]

Like a physician Voltaire was anxious to determine how much

enlightenment could safely be injected into the body of society without subjecting it to serious convulsions. For after a long series of treatments he looked forward to a drastic and overpowering effect upon the patient. Still, his letter to the Marquis de Chauvelin casts considerable doubt upon what Harold Laski speaks of as Voltaire's "profound respect for the established order, whose principles he is not willing to jeopardize by too drastic or wide a scrutiny."[62]

In 1764 the Philosopher of Ferney penned the following eagerly prophetic words:

Everywhere I see scattered the seeds of a revolution which will come inevitably and which I myself will not have the pleasure to witness. The French arrive late at everything, but they get there at last. The light has so spread from place to place that it will burst out on the first occasion, and there will be a splendid noise. Young people are fortunate; they will see fine things.[63]

He kept before his eyes the vision of a self-governing people's state, in which men could rise to positions of civic responsibility through sheer brilliance and capability.[64] Yet unlike most idealists, he was well aware of the distance which separated him from his remote and difficult goal. Of all political organizations the republic accorded to the individual the most power over his own destiny. At the same time, in order to preserve such advantages as liberty and security, the State demanded of the individual much integrity and self-discipline.

Though Voltaire had held that the republican form of government should be conducive to prosperity, he also conceded that such an organization rarely remains both rich and a republic. A republic is the government of a society on the rise and ignorant of outside perils.[65] In his opinion, the harmony of social purpose essential to democracy is most likely to exist in small frugal states. For there the citizens are united by strong common interests and a fairly low standard of living forces upon an enlightened people habits uniformly sober and industrious.[66]

These conditions, however, were conspicuously absent in eighteenth-century France.

Rather than the form or method of government, Voltaire concentrated on the results he demanded of the governing process. He heartily approved of government "for the people" in the sense of a ruling policy which aimed to achieve the greatest good of the greatest number. Yet, in a country made up of a disjointed group of provinces, inhabited by countless human beings whose only common bond was their illiteracy and subjection, any talk of government "of the people" or "by the people" he would have rejected as Utopian nonsense.

Instead of crusading directly for an unattainable democratic equality, he fought for the triumph of certain concrete and attainable liberal principles. These principles he looked upon as the political expression of "natural rights," and he believed that they could be best upheld and enforced by constitutional monarchy.

The same universal ideas of social justice reached triumphant expression as much in the American Constitution as in the French Declaration of the Rights of Man.[67] To Voltaire, to the American Founding Fathers, to the French patriots of 1789, the function of the nation, *la patrie*, was not to bestow upon a man his national character, but to assure him of his fundamental liberties as a human individual.[68] Such a conception of the nation was the natural outgrowth of a cosmopolitan, humanitarian philosophy.

According to thinking of this kind, the cornerstone of the duties which the State owed to the individual was the maintenance of a strict legal equality. This much of the primordial equality of men, Voltaire, as previously stated, believed could and should find concrete expression in the laws of the land. Social distinctions and economic privileges, he likewise insisted, should represent the commensurate reward of those who served loyally and effectively the public welfare.

In *Republican Ideas* of 1762 the French philosopher allowed his theoretical citizen of an ideal republic to state boldly:

Never at all have we known this odious and humiliating distinction between nobles and plebeians which traced to its source means nothing more than lords and slaves. Born equal we thus remain equal and dignities, that is to say public responsibilities, we have given to those who have appeared best qualified to bear them.[69]

The recognition and utilization of talent invariably brought to a nation both material and intellectual progress. The glory of Louis XIV and the great accomplishments of Peter I of Russia he explained by the willingness of these two sovereigns to make use of the brains, technical skills, artistic genius, and financial ability of men of plebeian or even humble origin. Though he quibbled with Rousseau about marrying off a dauphin to the executioner's daughter on the grounds of compatibility alone,[70] he nevertheless approved the union of Peter the Great with a young commoner of rare merit.[71] Posterity, he observed, now commends this action. Such a change in public opinion he attributed to the spread of enlightenment.

. . . this wholesome philosophy which has made so much progress in the course of forty years; philosophy, sublime and circumspect, which teaches that only outer marks of respect should be shown toward every kind of grandeur and power, while real respect should be reserved for talents and for service rendered.[72]

These ideas reached their final condensation in Article I of the *Declaration of the Rights of Man* of 1789: "Men are born and remain free and equal in the possession of their rights before the law. Social distinctions can only be founded on usefulness to the public."[73] Indeed, legal equality is thus defined in Article VI of this famous document:

It [the law] should be the same for everyone whether it protects or whether it punishes. All citizens, being equal in the eyes of the law,

are equally eligible for all dignities, positions and public employment, according to their capacity, and without other distinctions than
those of their virtues and their talents.[74]

Nevertheless, unlike the leaders of the French Revolution,
Voltaire believed that the laws of a nation should uphold the
common good rather than the common will. The *volonté
generalé* so exalted in both the manifestos of 1789 and 1793 would
have appeared in his eyes far too unenlightened.[75] He sought to
get to the root of the whole problem of civic relations by pleading
for laws that were in conformity with "natural law" or the
Divine Reason which governs the universe. "Natural law," he
insisted, is grounded in the innermost nature of man and society,
and therefore is above and beyond convention, arbitrary acts of
legislation, or any other institutional devices. The prime dictate
of this great law and the one from which all others stem is "Men
must help each other."[76]

In a hostile world, in the face of an unbountiful nature, the
first moral obligation of man is to aid and befriend man. The
rules laid down in the Ten Commandments and the other ethical
contributions of ancient Israel the French thinker recognized as
manifestations of "natural law." In his eyes, Moses was a pious
fraud who had imposed himself on his people by proclaiming
that the Deity had revealed to him alone and in private the moral
precepts which the Supreme Being had enabled all men to discover through the use of "reason,"[77] a simplified term for free
inquiry or free examination.

"Natural law" commanded that human beings deal with each
other in accordance with the Golden Rule.[78] Laws which conformed with this ideal norm would therefore preserve the liberty, security, and property of each individual. Rulings such as
these would indeed be the "common will" if all men could speak
with courage and clarity.[79] To Voltaire no rank, however elevated, or even the highest office in the land, exempted a human
being from respectfully upholding these basic prerogatives.

Though the application of reason might yield results that varied widely according to time and place, universal reason remained ever the same. The wise statesman should accordingly strip from the legal code of the State those frivolous, irrational, parasitic corruptions of law engendered by outworn utility or by the "right of the strongest."[80] The more a government served the people, the more the rulings of the State were in close harmony with "natural law." As he concluded his discussion of past governments in the *A, B, C* dialogue: "The more man-made law conforms to natural law the more bearable life becomes."[81]

Convinced that the nation's laws should be designed to protect the terrestrial interests of the citizen, Voltaire unfailingly championed a clear-cut separation of the powers of Church and State. The object of the State was primarily the advancement of the temporal happiness and well-being of the people. The Church, on the other hand, aimed at the salvation of man's soul in a celestial kingdom beyond the tomb. A set of rulings superimposed on the canons of state by agents of a supernatural authority and contemptuous of earthly improvement, the French thinker refused to countenance. Such ecclesiastical laws, acting as parasites on the legal system, could only breed confusion and discord.

These ideas Voltaire expressed in nearly all of the writings in which he discussed government. The most concise statement of his entire point of view he summed up in *Republican Ideas*:

It is an insult to reason and the laws to pronounce the words "civil and ecclesiastical government." One should say "civil government and ecclesiastical rulings"; and none of these rulings should be made except by the civil power.[82]

The real *patrie* of the clergy was the Kingdom of Heaven. Therefore he deemed it only reasonable for them to renounce all attempts to govern the kingdoms of the earth. Accordingly, in this same section Voltaire urged that marriage be placed under civil law, that magistrates regulate the number of days laborers may set aside for devotional purposes, and that no foreign potentate should receive the first year of revenue from a piece of land that the people had granted to a priest who was also their compatriot and fellow-citizen.[83] All these matters which concerned the earthly dealings of the citizens with each other should fall under the sole jurisdiction of the State.

Similarly, the French thinker argued that education should be taken out of the hands of the clergy and placed as far as possible in the control of laymen. The purpose of education, he believed, is to provide the young with instruction and training which would fit them for full useful lives as members of society. This civilizing task, he insisted, could not be most effectively carried out by men who, for the sake of other-worldly interests, were sworn to poverty, celibacy, and idleness—all conditions directly opposed to success in the temporal world.[84]

In the past when the first estate had been the only class which possessed any learning, schooling by churchmen had been necessary and unavoidable. Now in the latter half of the eighteenth century, the laity was also enlightened. When the Jesuit order was abolished in France, there arose a widespread desire among thinking Frenchmen to free schools and colleges from ecclesiastical domination and bring the instruction of youth under the aegis of the State. This movement Voltaire furthered. Eagerly he heralded the plans for national education proposed by Guyton de Morveau and La Chalotais. Like these men he believed that youth should be trained for citizenship by learned laymen who alone could instill in them the necessary civic virtues.

The type of education he himself had received at the Lycée Louis-le-Grand he now repudiated for the younger generation. These young people should be taught not to become wits and polished versifiers, but to be citizens. Instead of concentrating exclusively on the mythology, oratory, and poetry of a bygone culture, they should learn modern languages, physics, and mathematics. English, German, and Italian would prove of inestimable value in the field of diplomacy, and a knowledge of French history would acquaint young Frenchmen with the interests of France and the great traditions of *la patrie*. Schooling of this socially useful type should be made to reach as many people as possible.

In 1764 Voltaire wrote enthusiastically to Guyton de Morveau whose plan for national education had the approval of the entire philosophic party:

Your plan, Monsieur, is a service to the country. It is to be hoped that Frenchmen will learn much and even become acquainted with public law which here in France has never been taught. I hope that all such educational assistance will form men of a new type of ability. I am ending my career, but I take consolation in the hope that the new generation will be better than the one I have known and seen.[85]

Indeed the clergy, Voltaire stated in the *Philosophic Dictionary* and many other works, has no more right to regulate matters of state than a tutor dwelling in a noble household has the right to full authority over the lives of his charges.[86] Since all men were subjects of the State, the sovereign ought to determine under exactly what conditions an individual should be allowed to preach or enter monastic orders. The first allegiance of a cleric should be to the civil power. If an ecclesiastical order happened to be dissolved by the sovereign as incompatible with the public welfare, the vows of its members should become invalid. For this oath was necessarily antedated and outruled by the implicit social compact which bound the individual to the State and to society.[87]

In his *Poem on Natural Law* of 1756, which is perhaps the most beautifully worded summary of his whole philosophy, he stated that the merchant, the workman, the priest, and the soldier were all royal subjects and members of the State.[88] Consistently he regarded the clergy as so many royal employees pensioned by the king and therefore on a common political level with the comedians and ballet girls they believed it their duty to damn.

As public servants among other public servants, he maintained that the clergy also should contribute financially to the support of the kingdom. Therefore he declared in the *Philosophic Dictionary*: "Magistrates, laborers and priests have an equal duty to pay taxes to the State because they all stand equal as members of State."[89]

In the *Voice of the Sage and the People* his relentless insistence that the first estate should be taxed had virtually ruined him in his native land and forced him to accept the hospitality of King Frederick.

Unlike Montesquieu,[90] Voltaire did not view the Church as a means of tempering the power of absolutism. The Christian religion with its stress on individual human personality and its insistence on the equal importance of all souls before God was unquestionably both liberal and pacifistic. Yet Voltaire was less interested in the latent implications of this faith than in the influence exerted by the higher clergy in the eighteenth century.

In regard to literary censorship, taxation reform, and the vexatious matter of "notes of confession" he beheld the Church usurping the function of the civil authority. Since he admitted only one law, the civil law, it is clear that he viewed the ecclesiastical power as subservient to the temporal power. The Church he regarded as an important adjunct of the State, a sort of moral police force whose role was to hold in check the antisocial desires of the populace. While the government made laws to prevent the outward acts of the citizens from conflicting with the common good, the function of the Church was to control the thoughts and the inner attitude of the people. The clergy, by invoking an invisible higher power and by preaching that after death the individual was for his earthly actions rewarded or punished, inspired fear in the masses and held them to their duties. Just as the State could perform its duties best when independent of ecclesiastical rule, so could the Church best fulfill its high mission when unsullied and uncorrupted by the intrigues of the temporal power.

On the social value of religion Voltaire thus expressed himself in *God and Men*:

What other check can be found for greed, for secret and unpunished misdeeds than the idea of an eternal master who sees us and who judges even our inmost thoughts? We do not know who first taught this doctrine. If I knew him and was sure that he would not misuse it, that he would not corrupt the medicine he is offering mankind I myself would build him an altar.[91]

Though the separation of the spiritual and temporal powers was not yet possible within the nation Voltaire felt persuaded that subservience to Rome was the first religious shackle from which his countrymen might free themselves.[92] While Gallicanism was not in itself liberal, it nevertheless represented a primitive step in the direction of a more liberal lay policy. Consequently he adhered to the ideas set down in Bossuet's famous Declaration of the French Clergy of 1682. The most important of these postulates held that the temporal sovereignty of kings is independent of the pope, that a general council is above this potentate, that the ancient liberties of the Gallican Church are sacred, and last, but not least, that the infallible teaching authority of the Church belongs to pope and bishops jointly.

A French Catholic Church, independent of the domination of the Vatican, meant a break with the medieval idea of a politically united Christendom. Indeed, the association of Gallicanism with the whole movement of eighteenth-century Enlightenment was made manifest in the latter reaffirmation of Bossuet's doctrine of Gallican liberties in the Civil Constitution of the Clergy of 1790. Such a concept of religious matters implies the exaltation of national interests in preference to ecclesiastical demands that drained the state of its wealth and resources.

On the whole the liberal principle to which Voltaire devoted the major efforts of his lifework was liberty of conscience. His first appeal for religious toleration he made in the *Henriade,* an epic poem glorifying the French king who, even though briefly, placed this important principle successfully in action. In the

*Philosophic Letters* he proclaimed to his dubious compatriots the social benefits of independence of worship as put in practice in the flourishing civilization across the channel. The *Essay on the Manners and Minds of Nations* and nearly all his other histories attempt to prove that the violation of the individual's right to seek, in his own way, an answer to the imponderable questions of the universe has caused bloody warfare between nations and seditions and crimes within national boundaries. This also was his message in his innumerable letters to sovereigns. The freedom to profess in peace the religion of one's choice he ever regarded as one of the inalienable rights of all human beings, and indeed as a cornerstone of civilization.

Convinced that tolerance should come first on the long list of man's duties toward man he declared in the *Philosophic Dictionary*: "What is tolerance? It is an adjunct of humanity. We are all of us made up of errors and weaknesses; let us forgive each other our blunders; this is the first law of nature."[93]

Far from fomenting dissensions within the nations the multiplicity of religious sects made for peace and social concord. This conviction which, after his contact with England, he had first voiced in the *Philosophic Letters* he reasserted in the *Treatise on Tolerance* of 1763.[94] The coexistence in the state of several religions obviously necessitated a spirit of diplomatic restraint and intelligent conciliation on the part of these sects toward each other. In their common struggle for influence, they would preserve between them an inevitable balance of power much like the one needed to keep the peace between nations.[95]

Therefore Voltaire viewed with some alarm the destruction of the Jesuit order in 1764. For he had maintained that "Jesuit foxes were essential to combat Jansenist wolves though both breeds were actually wolves in the pack of superstition."[96] Indeed, a large number of divergent cults, each with an exclusive claim to divine origin, inevitably acted in itself as a strong argument for tolerance. The customs and ambitious pretensions of these various sects would present an unfavorable contrast with the harmony and uniformity of a natural religion founded on "natural law." Tolerance would then lead to sanity in regard to religion. Religious persecution, on the other hand, excited that fanatical zeal for martyrdom so fatal to earthly welfare.

Much as he crusaded for freedom of thought and worship, the French philosopher nevertheless held that a certain degree of enlightenment must exist before toleration can even be considered a safe policy. In his *Treatise on Tolerance* of 1763 he made the unequivocal pronouncement:

If a government is to give up the right to punish human errors, those errors must not be crimes; crimes, they are when they bring discord into society and they bring discord when they inspire fanaticism. Men must therefore begin by not being fanatical in order to deserve tolerance.[97]

He placed the good of the nation, of humanity, above exclusive devotion even to an abstract principle he cherished as much as freedom of worship. As long as religion remained a mere attempt on the part of groups or individuals to interpret, in their own terms, the imponderable immensity of the universe, faith belonged outside the sphere of civic affairs and should accordingly be tolerated. However, when a given cult inspired or abetted antisocial acts or sedition, the practice of tolerance became contrary to the public well-being and under these circumstances, he maintained, should be restricted. A similar restriction is found in the *Declaration of the Rights of Man* of 1789: "No one should be called to account about his opinions, even religious ones, so long as their manifestation does not upset public order as established by the law."[98]

His personal life and the bulk of his writings prove that the ideal closest to Voltaire's heart was liberty of conscience in the fullest sense. Yet on this issue, as on other social problems, he stands revealed as a cautious liberal rather than a radical egalitarian. The democratic concept of the equality of all religions before the law he never expressly advocated. As a realist and a practical reformer he knew well that a religious equality both legal and social could not be attained in an age when, with hardly any semblance of justice, Protestants still were hanged.

In his *Treatise on Tolerance* he made his most pressing appeal for the merely liberal principle of the toleration of all religious sects within the confines of the state.[99] When according to these terms he argued for religious freedom he felt confident that he was preaching a theory which had already been tried and tested by reality. England presented the spectacle of many sects existing peaceably within the strongest and best governed state in Europe. Though toleration was placed in effect, public honors and important positions were closed to all those who were not of the Anglican religion. This material condition, he merrily pointed out in the *Philosophic Letters,* acted as proof of the sanctity of the official religion and created innumerable proselytes.[100] Rather than weaken his case with a plea for absolute tolerance, he brought his demands into conformity with the halting progress of enlightenment in his century. So for France, he fought long and fiercely to obtain at least the same amount of liberty of conscience that he had seen successfully practiced in England.[101]

Another fundamental liberty which Voltaire unfailingly championed was freedom of speech and press. Contrary to the opinion of Emile Faguet, there is an overwhelming weight of evidence to prove that the eighteenth-century thinker was clearly and emphatically in favor of this liberal principle.

In *A Comparison of the Politics of Montesquieu, Rousseau and Voltaire,* Faguet makes the following pronouncement:

About liberty to think, speak and write, Voltaire is always of three opinions; first, that such a liberty is an excellent thing, secondly that it should be confined within very narrow limits; thirdly that it should be absolutely denied to those who do not think as he does. The result in practice would be a liberty so restricted as to amount to nothing.[102]

This statement of Faguet is based chiefly on a passage from the *A, B, C* dialogue of 1768. *B* who is supposed to be a Frenchman and who most frequently represents his author thus defines intellectual subjugation or "slavery of the mind":

I mean this prevalent custom of molding the minds of our children as Carib women mold the skulls of their children . . . to establish laws which prevent men from writing, speaking or even thinking, just as in the comedy, Arnolphe wants to own the only ink-pot in the house, and make of Agnes an ignoramus so he can do with her whatever he pleases.[103]

*A* who is an Englishman replies that if such laws existed in England, he would flee after setting fire to his island. Thereupon *C* answers:

However it is fortunate that everyone does not say what he thinks. One should insult neither in writing nor in speech the ruling powers and laws under whose protection one enjoys one's fortune, liberty and all the pleasant things of life.[104]

In his quotation of this passage Faguet gives undue importance to the opinions of *C* by his failure to quote more than one line of their refutation by *A*. In this way he completely misrepresents the thought of Voltaire on so important an issue. For *A* does more than question whether a free man should be abolished just because rash revolutionaries tend to make ill use of this right. In the section not quoted by Faguet *A* replies with the ring of his author:

I would as soon order you struck dumb in order to stop you from uttering bad arguments. Thieving takes place in the streets. For such a reason, should walking there be forbidden? Stupidities and insults are said. For any such reason should speaking be forbidden? In our land each and every man may write what he thinks *at his own risk and peril*. There is no other way to address the nation. If in the opinion of the nation you have spoken ridiculously you will be hissed, seditiously, you will be punished; if, however, you have spoken wisely and nobly, you will be loved and rewarded. . . . No liberty at all exists among men without the freedom to express thoughts.[105]

In these lines, which Faguet fails to mention, Voltaire makes his stand for a free press. Yet, at the same time, he holds the individual severely accountable for his use of this essential liberty. Overt appeals for a violent overthrow of the government, he maintained, are and should be punished. Otherwise, as the individual has the right to address the public through the medium of the printed page, so is the public equally entitled to bestow approval or disapproval on the opinions therein stated. For liberty of thought can have no reality apart from liberty of expression.[106] When the French philosopher seemed in numerous instances to belittle books and their influence,[107] he had a two-fold purpose. First of all, he was making a sly appeal to the censors to relax their vigilance. Secondly, he was attempting to prove to the authorities that revolutions did not spring from that extremely small class which made up the reading public. Unswervingly he clung to the opinion that tyranny of the mind debases man to the level of beasts.[108] These same ideas, upheld in his article "Liberty of the Press," in the *Letter to Christian VII* and throughout his correspondence, are in harmony with principles both democratic and liberal.

Again Faguet is vague when he speaks of Voltaire's request for liberty of the press restricted by penal measures.[109] In *Republican Ideas,* the eighteenth-century thinker remarked that while a free press was a "natural right," "written misdeeds should be punished just as are those committed by word of mouth."[110] In this provision the author was only making clear the duty of any government to formulate laws against libel and slander, a point upon which he had also insisted in the above-mentioned *A, B, C* dialogue of 1768.

Thus, any impartial estimate reveals that Voltaire advocated as much liberty of thought and expression as proved compatible with laws designed to preserve the good of the national community. If, as he consistently maintained, the State exists to promote the welfare of the citizens, the individual must indeed be free to criticize the government and voice his opinions on all matters which vitally concern his interests, whether through the mouths of delegates or on the printed page.[111] This was the essential distinction between a nation of free men and a kingdom of slaves.[112] Still, he also insisted that as the individual has the right to seek protection by law from malicious libel, so is the government justified in defending itself against attempts at sedition made manifest on the printed page. Some such restrictions upon the freedom of the press have been accepted as necessary in all forms of government. Indeed, Article XI of the *Declaration of the Rights of Man* of 1789 makes the following provision: ". . . every citizen may speak, write, and print freely. Yet he must also answer for any abuse of this liberty in specific cases determined by law."[113]

The effort of Voltaire to free individuals and groups from those irrational fetters imposed either by tradition or by the evil "right of the strongest," was also applied to economics. He was a staunch advocate of free trade in general, and, in particular, of free trade within national boundaries. In spite of his admiration for Colbert, he blamed this great minister for refusing to allow the free circulation of grain within the provinces of the realm. In the *Century of Louis XIV* he passes the following judgment:

This is the only stain on his administration; a bad one; but what excuses it, what proves how difficult it is to destroy prejudices in French administration, and also the difficulty of doing good, is that this mistake, observed by all thoughtful citizens, has not been remedied by any minister for a hundred years, not until the memorable epoch of 1764 when a more enlightened *contrôleur général* rescued France from profound misery by granting free trade in grain, or at least, free, except for a few restrictions similar to those in force in England.[114]

If he spoke thus warmly of the experiment in free trade brought about by Contrôleur Général Terray, he had even more enthusiasm for those radical steps toward economic liberalism later sponsored by Turgot. This minister of finance was the most brilliant exponent of the physiocratic school of economics. Though Voltaire dismissed as absurd the inordinate stress these econ-

omists placed on agriculture, their theories still seemed to him
a courageous attempt on the part of mankind to work out a
"natural system" of economics. For the Physiocrats wished to
apply reason and "natural law" to monetary forces.[115]

Indeed, the rationalism which bound Voltaire to the Physiocrats was nothing more than a practical application of that deductive method of Descartes which a great popularizer like
Fontenelle had made accessible to the reading public. To Voltaire
and the Physiocrats "reason" or the capacity to think was a sort
of divine searchlight. This gift the Supreme Being had bestowed
upon mortals so that the laws of the universe might become
discernible to each individual. The laws that govern all living
things, the leader of eighteenth-century Enlightenment believed,
are self-interest and interdependence. In the economic sphere
the harmonious interplay of these constant human factors could
be expressed only in the unrestricted action of supply and
demand.

Consequently, when in the decree of September 13, 1774,
Turgot removed from the grain trade practically all duties and
authorized the importation of foreign cereals, Voltaire was jubi-
lant. Ecstatically he wrote to D'Alembert: "I have just read the
master-piece of M. Turgot. We seem to be facing new Heavens
and new earths."[116] He consistently applauded the campaign of
the minister of finance to extend the principle of free commerce
to wine and other food products.

Since free trade seemed a corollary to "natural law," any
extension of this principle Voltaire looked upon as progress. At
the same time he was well aware that in the eighteenth century
free markets between nations or even tariff reduction were impossible of realization. For these measures, to be placed safely
in effect, would require an agreement on the part of other powers
to pursue a similar policy.

Though in the opinion of Voltaire the time had not come to
remove all trade barriers, a plea for greater economic freedom is
implicit in most of his writings. In the *Summary of the Century*

*of Louis XV* he made the emphatic comment: "Commerce should be the bond between nations. It should console the earth and not lead to the earth's devastation."[117]

High competitive tariffs are glaringly out of keeping with the whole Voltairean outlook on commercial relations between sovereign states. Commerce, he believed, could be used as an important means of *rapprochement* between nations and, better still, as a deterrent to hostility and aggression.

Thus, the key to individual self-realization within the framework of the nation the French thinker beheld in certain specific applications of a liberal philosophy. These were the free interchange of commodities, the separation of Church and State, liberty of conscience, freedom of speech and press, the rewarding of merit regardless of rank, and the lessening of economic inequality. On these liberal principles modern democracy is founded.

Only the political order established by "natural rights" and by the major liberal principles could, he believed, justify its existence and by common consent endure through the centuries. In his own day and age he saw these rules for human relations most effectively upheld by the British Constitution. In the article "Government" of the *Philosophic Dictionary* he made about the constitutional monarchy of England the following prediction: "It is believable that a constitution which has affixed the rights of the King, the nobles and the people, and under whose rulings everyone finds his security, will endure as long as anything human can endure."[118]

Though the English had bought with blood their fundamental liberties, he felt certain that they had nevertheless won a major moral victory, and a victory of inestimable importance to their whole life as a sovereign nation. For a state not founded on a belief in the dignity and importance of the individual was predestined to revolution as soon as the oppressed had the power or the opportunity. Liberty, as the greatest and rarest of blessings, must ever be the one most bitterly fought for.

England, so Voltaire believed, combined the fierce devotion

to man's rights characteristic of a republic with the force and authority of hereditary monarchy. In the land across the channel he beheld a monarch who ruled as the guardian and administrator of laws which reclaimed for all citizens a fair measure of their natural freedom. The constitution was supreme, and the king merely the First Magistrate of his people. If as first executive he violated the rules of the kingdom or sought to impose his authority by unconstitutional means, though he occupied the throne, he alone was a rebel.

Voltaire felt persuaded that England, unlike France, possessed a technique of government through which the liberal concept of human personality could be made politically effective. The two houses of Parliament represented the nobles and the people respectively. Under the impartial guidance of the sovereign these classes learned to reconcile their divergent interests for the sake of the public welfare. The House of Commons theoretically expressed the wishes and claims of the average citizen, and since upon the fulfillment of these wishes and claims the public welfare was in such a large part dependent, the House of Commons, though second in rank, came first in influence.[119]

The French philosopher, nevertheless, failed to realize that as practically carried out the English system of government was neither democratic nor wholly liberal. The two houses of Parliament limited the power of the sovereign and formed a forcible organ for public opinion. Even so, the organization of the House of Commons was not based on any democratic scheme of popular representation.[120] Stringent property restrictions on the franchise, and an unequal proportioning of representatives throughout the boroughs of the land, were wide-scale abuses in the eighteenth century. Worse still, seats in Parliament were often bought and sold to the highest bidder. As a result the House of Commons represented less the wishes of the people than the interests of rich landowners and closed corporations.[121]

In Britain, as in Geneva, Voltaire fancied that he had glimpsed the realization of his ideals for the State. Yet England, like Geneva, was ruled by an oligarchy. The English government was liberal not in the technique of its administration, but in the tenets of liberal philosophy embodied in its constitution. Nevertheless, in British constitutional monarchy, the French thinker perceived an effective compromise between the apparently unattainable ideal of democracy and the prevalent reality of royal absolutism.

About the French *Parlement,* however, Voltaire had no illusions. This corrupt, inefficient body, he believed, obstructed without really tempering the rule of the monarchy.[122] Through their time-honored right of issuing remonstrances the *corps* of magistrates were supposed to convey to the sovereign the desires and wishes of the majority of his people. While the French philosopher admitted that the issuing of remonstrances was sanctioned by "natural right,"[123] he still insisted that these judicial courts labeled *Parlement* had never represented the nation and that they continued not to do so in the eighteenth century. Admission to *Parlement* was barred to all save members of the nobility and parliamentary offices had been a marketable commodity since the days of Francis I.[124]

In their refusal to register any royal edict these exalted members of the legal profession had long been swayed not only by a blind *esprit de corps* but by the most selfish class feeling. Never was this more apparent than in their determined opposition to the six tax reform edicts of 1776.[125]

In that prerevolutionary dispute over the "rights of man" headed by Turgot and *Parlement* respectively, Voltaire was more than willing that the king should trample on the claims of *Parlement.* For liberal and democratic principles, he believed, were being upheld by Louis XVI and his minister of finance. The king stood for measures which freed the majority of Frenchmen from an unfair, crippling system of taxation and defended the "rights" of the worker. *Parlement,* on the other hand, was on the side of oppressive privilege.

Therefore, if, for France, he even favored for a time the

rule of a benevolent despot, he did so only in order that the French kingdom might be made safe for a daring new policy which protected as never before the welfare of the individual, a policy which upheld not the interests of class but the interests of the nation.

To Voltaire, the first duty of all patriots was to help establish within their native land a trustworthy State. In his eyes, a reliable national organization would be one founded on "natural rights" and on their political expression through the major liberal principles. "Liberty," to the leader of eighteenth-century Enlightenment, would mean "liberty" in accordance with the Golden Rule and laws designed to safeguard the common welfare. "Equality," in its most elementary stage, he viewed as the right of all men to stand as equal before these rulings to which they owe their freedom. "Fraternity," he would have recognized as the united effort of the people to improve the earthly lot of their fellowmen. For the goal to be reached was equality of opportunity, and the safest path toward it lay in gradually freeing individuals and groups of all irrational obstacles to their self-realization.

Democracy, however, implies that the individual is the sole unit of social organization. Yet in the eighteenth century the average citizen had neither the freedom nor the "enlightenment" required to take over the civic responsibilities of government. Of this unhappy fact Voltaire was well aware.

So instead of a self-governing republic, he desired a strong state which would use its power to apply democratic principles to human relations and thus enable the greatest number of citizens to attain a mastery of their capacities. Then the betterment of the individual citizen, he felt persuaded, would result in the betterment of the State. For the nation, like all other man-made institutions, can be neither greater nor stronger than the individuals who give it life and being.

# The State as a Dominant Power:
## Part 1

### THE WAY OF MILITARY CONQUEST

F
EW EIGHTEENTH-CENTURY PHILOSOPHERS recognized more clearly than Voltaire the stabilizing force evoked by such abstractions as "God," "king" and "country." Yet these same terms he subjected to relentless analysis, whenever the emotions involved in their blind acceptance proved incompatible with humanity, and with reason, socially expressed in enlightened self-interest.

To Voltaire, patriotism, or devotion to king and country, should mean that the individual was ready to serve courageously the common interests, and fight for them, whenever the need should arise.[1] Unfailingly the French thinker rejected any idea of the nation as a sacred entity with a mystical importance of its own above and beyond those human beings who live within its boundaries. The State, in his eyes, existed only as a haven within which a fair amount of freedom and security was made attainable for the individual.[2] The sovereign, he viewed, not as the unimpeachable embodiment of *la patrie,* but as a chief executive and social leader. As head of the nation, the ruler could have no glory or significance apart from his value to his subjects.

When the king failed to maintain a sound State organization or trampled on the rights of his subjects, Voltaire called him by the name he merited by his actions. In his *Thoughts on Government,* he thus defined the malevolent despot:

A prince who, without justice or due form of justice, imprisons or executes his subjects, is nothing but a highway-robber of the breed they call "Your Majesty."[3]

Deeds, not exalted theoretical claims, imposed respect upon the philosopher. Whenever the dignities attached to monarchy far outweigh the worth of its actual services, this or any other institution becomes a myth as deceptive as enslaving.

Therefore to advance the national interests would mean in the opinion of Voltaire to serve the nation through the living reality of the people. Wars of aggression he deemed powerless to achieve this end. The formative period of his life had been spent in the early eighteenth century, when France, drained of vitality, had been lead to the verge of bankruptcy by the wars of Louis XIV. As a youth in Paris he had met with ample opportunity to observe the wretchedness and semistarvation so prevalent among the lower ranks of the population. These early, firsthand impressions no doubt nourished in him the lifelong conviction, finally voiced in the *Philosophic Dictionary*, that war is the epitome of all evils and the scourge of civilization.[4] Whatever the outcome of these struggles which so long had devastated Europe, the people of all contending nations were inevitably the losers. As he declared in the *Century of Louis XIV*: "In Christian monarchies, the nations as a whole have no personal interest or stake in the wars of their sovereigns."[5]

Noteworthy here is the fact that Voltaire makes an almost revolutionary distinction between the "nation" as expressed through its people and the State as a "Christian" monarchy sanctioned by "divine right." This same distinction was later to inflame the patriots of 1793.

Indeed, in the article "War" of the *Philosophic Dictionary* he summed up the political war as caused by royal ambition. The prize was, as often as not, a strip of sand on a disputed frontier, and the excuse some vague dynastic claim for long centuries forgotten.[6] The annexation of territory seized by military violence could offer the citizens of the nation no practical or pecuniary advantages. Frequently the author of the *Philosophic Dictionary* pointed out that war in the modern world differs from war in the Roman world. For the rulers of "Christian" states have neither the means nor the expectation of appropriating the wealth of the nations they subjugate in so unchristian a manner.[7]

In the wars waged by their ambitious sovereigns, the rewards of the people are death, famine, poverty, and pestilence. These, the writer of the article "War" asserts, might be endured as "gifts of Providence." Yet how much more unendurable such calamities become when visited upon the population by mere human embodiments of Providence like kings and their ministers.[8]

Louis XIV, however, Voltaire admired. The late Sun King had briefly fulfilled one abiding dream of eighteenth-century Enlightenment. For, under his rule, France had attained a civilization which combined artistic and intellectual supremacy with material prosperity. Yet this great achievement the monarch himself had compromised. Louis XIV had been led astray by his passion for military glory.

As historian, Voltaire described in the *Century of Louis XIV* how the wars of the Grand Monarch depleted the national treasury. Indeed the king, by his stubborn continuance of the conflict, rendered financially ruinous those artistic and architectural masterpieces that stood as lasting monuments to the greatness of his age. During his long struggle against the League of Augsburg the curtailment of luxury at last became imperative. The manufacture of de luxe objects was a source as well as an indication of the wealth of the realm. To lessen the production of goods, the quality and workmanship of which were internationally famous, meant not only loss of national prestige, but an actual threat to the economic health of France.[9]

As the warfare continued, no other recourse remained than to alter the currency. For the mere survival of this operation the historian praised his country's vitality.[10] Obliged to resort to such ruinous expedients, Louis remained powerless to provide for his subjects the protection and security he owed them as head of the state.

In the far-flung dynastic pretensions of this king, Voltaire saw mere excuses for bold acts of usurpation.[11] Apart from the validity of such royal claims, the uniting of France and Spain under the Bourbon crown was judged by the historian as neither possible nor desirable. For the momentary acceptance of such French dictation by the king and people of Spain had been brought about merely by the "right of the strongest."

The *Century of Louis XIV* contains no express statement of disapproval. Yet the annexation of another nation by force was contrary to the author's whole philosophy. In the *Philosophic Dictionary* he dismissed all such dynastic pretexts for aggression and maintained that "in order to make laws for a people their consent is necessary."[12]

In the *Essay on the Manners and Minds of Nations,* he showed how material conquest could drain the victor nation of both energy and resources. For these must necessarily be expended in efforts to quell the repeated insurrections of the conquered. Preoccupation with the internal affairs of the newly acquired territory would then lead to a neglect of the homeland, and of home industries, agriculture, and manufactures—all that constitutes the true prosperity of the realm.

Nor did widened boundaries tend to increase in the citizens any vital sense of national devotion. As Voltaire observed in the article "Patrie" of the *Philosophic Dictionary*: "The larger this country becomes, the less it is loved, for a love shared with others grows weak. It is impossible to love tenderly a large family one scarcely knows."[13] He remained convinced that with every unjustified expansion the inner quality of the nation inevitably deteriorates.

For this reason the designs of the Grand Monarch for national aggrandizement were seen by his historian as not only unethical, unprofitable, but foredoomed to failure. This king, blinded by a passion for "grandeur" both for himself and his dynasty, failed to reckon with a Europe in which all nations strove to maintain the balance of power.[14] His unquenchable ambition served only to provoke the powerful coalition of other states against him. This led to wars of such increasing scope and magnitude that even with the most brilliant armies of his age, defeat was unavoidable.

The historian stressed how the early campaigns of Louis XIV in Franche-Comté and in the Spanish Netherlands brought him into conflict with the Triple Alliance or the combined forces of England, Holland, and Sweden. His aggressions in the Palatinate provoked the vigorous opposition of the League of Augsburg, while at the end of his reign, the War of the Spanish Succession involved France in a hopeless struggle against nearly all the major powers of the day. This general European warfare finally resulted in clashes between colonies, so that a wave of destruction spread to the far corners of the earth.

The threat to humanity in an ever expanding theater of war, Voltaire viewed with genuine alarm:

One result of both the industry and the fury of men is that for two centuries the desolation of war has not been limited to our Europe. We exhaust ourselves in money and man power so that we can go to destroy each other at the extremities of Asia and America. The East Indians upon whom we have imposed our settlements by force and the American natives whose continent we have ravished and destroyed, look upon us as the enemies of human nature. For we have hastened forth from the far corners of the globe to butcher them only to destroy ourselves in the end.[15]

He judged alarming not only the extended geographical area covered by modern warfare, but also the invention and use of ever more deadly implements of slaughter. He spoke prophetic words about the French invention of a bombing cannon, a notable contribution of the age of Louis XIV to the art of combat. Concerning the use of this weapon against a pirate-infested port of Algeria he declared:

One part of the city was crushed and consumed; but this art [of gunpowder] soon introduced into other nations served no other end than to multiply human calamities, and more than once proved dreadful to France, the land of its invention.[16]

In the art of warfare the establishment of a cruel precedent made cruelty competitive. Therefore, despite his horror at the burning of the Palatinate, Voltaire partially excused Louis XIV for annihilating all remnants of the German army stationed near the French boundary. The Sun King's own armies had shown the world the menace of these troop movements along the frontier. So fear of enemy retaliation seemed not without foundation. The historian even foresaw peril in the competitive arming of these two nations against each other, and added ominously that if Germany lacked money the discipline and endurance of her soldiers were excellent.[17]

The wars of Louis XIV proved that the use of force could only be met by more force until the resultant wreckage became universal, for Louis XIV had made France the enemy of Europe and the world. Well might he have armies unsurpassed in skill and equipment. His country was trapped in an ever widening circle of armed opposition. Thus, the results of his long efforts were not conquest, but lost colonial territory, while his much-heralded military supremacy passed over to the enemy.

As a bourgeois critic of Louis XIV, Voltaire blamed this king for ruining his country in wars as devoid of purpose as without concrete accomplishment. Louis had chosen to exalt France by the doubtful means of conquest. Yet behind his theoretical aggressions there was evidently no coherent plan.

He wrested Franche-Comté from Spain, but accepted by treaty a few towns in the Spanish Netherlands. He marched off amidst a fanfare of triumph to annihilate Holland but was bought off by permission to annex Franche-Comté.[18] He captured Lorraine and restored it to its ruler. His troops laid waste by fire and sword the whole Palatinate region. The outcome of these desultory atrocities was the Treaty of Ryswick, which from the standpoint of boundaries accomplished next to nothing.

His generals had ravaged the greater part of Europe. Yet the king agreed to peace terms as disadvantageous as if he himself were vanquished. Nor at the Peace of Ryswick (1697) did he set forth his claim to the Spanish Succession, a cause to which he was to devote the remainder of his career.[19] Still, despite these failures, the Grand Monarch had achieved the one war aim for which he had so steadfastly striven. Throughout his long series of losing battles Louis XIV had pursued and attained *la gloire,* or glory.[20]

The historian of France in the era of her greatest flowering did not fail to appreciate this nonmaterial triumph. Glory he viewed not in the Anglo-Saxon sense of a worldly reputation for outstanding accomplishments. To the author of the *Century of Louis XIV,* "glory," as applied to military affairs, meant not so much fame, as the spontaneous *frisson* or "thrill" inspired by the beauty of heroic action. According to this truly French conception, the glory of great deeds exists apart from the success of their outcome and independent of their value toward a given objective. Never is this attitude more apparent than when Voltaire told how Louis XIV formed the plan of a hazardous attack on the British Isles. The War of the Spanish Succession had practically ruined his nation. Yet Louis wished to join Scottish supporters of the Stuarts in an invasion of England. Such a project, the historian remarked with elation, astounded Europe. For, as he made clear: "Success was doubtful, but Louis saw a certain glory in the enterprise alone. He said himself that this motive determined him as much as political interest."[21]

Toward "glory" in the sense of "grandeur" the author of the *Century of Louis XIV* displayed a similar weakness. The arrogant ill humor of princes in their dealings with each other, he believed, often precipitated warfare. Nevertheless he praised Louis XIV for insisting on the *préséance* of the French crown above that of all other nations. Indeed Voltaire seems to honor in Louis XIV of France a preoccupation with glory which he had deemed reprehensible in Charles XII of Sweden. The intrepid exploits of the Swedish king he had attributed to desire for vengeance, military genius, and personal eccentricity. Yet the author of the *Century of Louis XIV* inclined to the opinion that the disastrous wars of Louis XIV sprang from his love of all great enterprises, whether in the realm of art, science, or military affairs.[22]

The glory of Charles XII was merely individual. All France, however, contributed to the glory of Louis XIV. The magnificent armies of the Sun King, the valor and skill of his generals, their bold undertakings, so indomitably conducted—all were typical of the nation's supremacy in every line of activity. As Corneille and Racine made French literature illustrious, so Condé and Turenne endowed their native land with that poetry of heroic action known as "glory." This nonmaterial asset, Voltaire believed, had beauty much like one of the fine arts.

Nevertheless, as a historian, he unfailingly stressed the vanity and sterility of just such military glory. The attempted destruction of Holland by Louis XIV he looked upon as contrary to the true interests of humanity. For European civilization was, in his eyes, a splendid cooperative enterprise, and Holland a useful member of the family of nations. The heroic flooding of the dikes by the Dutch managed to check the invading armies and save the flourishing republic, thus depriving Louis XIV of what Voltaire described as the "deplorable glory of having destroyed the strangest and finest endeavor ever brought about by the industry of mankind."[23]

Again he lacked enthusiasm for the triumphant campaign of Turenne against the Palatinate.[24] This great general he honored less as a national hero than as an individual of rare courage and foresight. At the same time he held him responsible for the ruin of a whole innocent population, and censored him for atrocities accountable only by the competitive cruelty of warfare.[25]

Once again the author of the *Century of Louis XIV* returned to his central idea that throughout a war the people are ever sacrificed. The nation was bled white and drained of vital material resources merely so Louis XIV could render French arms immortal.

Indeed, the following conclusion of the *History of Charles XII* could be applied with equal fitness to the career of the Sun King: "His life should teach kings how much a peaceful and successful government is to be preferred to such an amount of glory."[26]

On the whole Voltaire condemned war as immoral and unprofitable. In many cases he attacked aggressive warfare with merely practical arguments. These last, he knew, would have most influence on the ruling class he was addressing. Yet in the *Essay on the Manner and Minds of Nations,* while admitting that in Roman times military exploits actually contributed to national prosperity, his attitude as a historian remained condemnatory. As he wrote of Rome in the days of Sylla:

In the midst of brigandage, patriotism was the dominant force until the time of Sylla. Throughout more than four hundred years this love of country consisted in bringing back to the communal mob what one stole from other nations. This is a virtue in thieves. To love one's country meant to kill and plunder other men.[27]

Patriotism he valued only according to whether its outer expression was helpful to mankind in general. Wars of aggression and pillage certainly were not. In the *Philosophic Dictionary,* in which so many of his ideas reached their final crystallization, he again threw aside materialistic considerations and denounced "this scourge, this crime of warfare which includes all scourges and all crimes."[28] A military campaign was, in his opinion, nothing more than a wave of organized crime that offered the greatest possible scope for all manner of individual crimes. His moral, intellectual, and almost physical horror of war may be discerned in the somewhat emotional statement that follows: "All the vices, collected from all times and all places, will never equal the evils brought about by a single campaign."[29]

That the so-called moral leaders of his country never once raised their voices against these campaigns of murder and plunder provoked in Voltaire a flood of indignation. The humanitarian and epicurean in him looked with contempt upon a clergy that thundered against harmless things that made life pleasant and said nothing against this sinful scourge that ravaged Europe. With a cry from his innermost nature he thus challenged the so-called guardians of conscience:

Wretched doctors of the soul, you wail throughout an hour and a quarter about a few pinpricks, and you say nothing about the sickness which tears us in a thousand pieces! Philosophers, moralists, burn your books. So long as the stubborn caprice of a few persons can bring about the slaughter of our fellow men, the fraction of the human race dedicated to heroism will be the most frightful element in all of nature.[30]

As high priest of "natural law," Voltaire set for himself the task that the spokesmen for official revealed religion had so callously neglected. War he condemned as contrary both to the Christian brotherhood of man and to what philosophers call the "world-wide fraternity of reason." For reason also indicates that all thinking beings are brothers, and that unconsciously they revere a universal morality based on order and mutual consideration.[31]

Accordingly, the aggrandizement of the homeland at the expense of other nations was in profound contradiction with the whole scheme of Voltairean thought and ethics. To Voltaire, ethics consisted in the achieving of an exquisite balance between the spirit of altruism and man's fundamental egotism. By a return to the natural, to the primitive, he meant the triumphant fulfillment of those progressive instincts inherent in human nature.

The difference between his point of view and that of Rousseau and other primitivists is made clear in the *A, B, C* dialogue of 1768. When *B* tells *A* that prerogatives and parliamentary procedure are contrary to the pure law of nature, *A* retorts: "And, if I tell you that savages corrupt the law of nature, whereas we follow it?"[32] *A* therefore states in admirably concise form the ideas his author has already expounded at length in the articles "Men" and "Instinct" of the *Philosophic Dictionary*:

Is it not true that instinct and judgment those two eldest sons of nature teach us to seek in everything our own good and also the well-being of others, above all when their well-being and ours are evidently so inseparable?[33]

Since all persons are inescapably interdependent, the law of human nature and therefore of earthly progress is "Help each other." Voltaire, like the writers of the American Declaration of Independence, believed that the aim of man is the "pursuit of happiness." "Happiness" as such might take the form of either material prosperity or intellectual and artistic enjoyment. The spiritual or ethical aspect of existence lies in the will and capacity of man to act so that an ever larger number of his fellow beings can also pursue and enjoy "happiness." Whosoever succeeds in doing this for his fellows places himself in harmony with the "divine reason" or "natural order" which rules the universe. As the author of the *A, B, C* dialogue asserts:

Those persons who contribute the most to society will then be the ones who are following nature most closely. Those who invent the arts (which are a great gift of God), those who propose laws (to do which is infinitely easier) will then be the persons who have complied most fully with "natural law."[34]

The nation considered politically and therefore unsentimentally should be a complex and wide-scale expression of the principle, "Help each other." The same principle of enlightened self-interest the French philosopher wished logically to extend to relations between nations. Just as robbery and murder are harmful on the individual scale, so are the attempts of rival states to loot and devastate each other. To Voltaire, wars of aggression were immoral because they were unreasonable. For the word "reason," to his way of thinking, had ethical implications.

Since the dictates of "natural law" are as difficult to apply as true Christian principles, he considered war as well-nigh inevitable. The 1764 version of his article "War" of the *Philosophic Dictionary* he concluded with the following admission: "Worse still, war is an inevitable scourge. One may note that men have always adored Mars. Sabaoth is the Jewish god of arms, but in Homer, Mars is called by Minerva a furious, insane and infernal god."[35]

This same conviction he restated with even more force and persuasiveness in a new opening paragraph to the essay in the 1771 version of the *Questions on the Encyclopedia.* Here he asserted that not only human life, but all of nature, is given over to mortal and everlasting struggle. With a remarkable feeling for the oneness of everything organic he declared in these incisive words: "All animals are perpetually engaged in warfare, each species is born to devour another species. There are none, even to sheep and doves, that have not gobbled up a prodigious number of imperceptible animals."[36]

Such conclusions, however, failed to drive him to defeatism. Instead, he found in these same arguments a spur to progress. Man, he insisted, possesses neither horns nor claws but the gift of reason. The human being is compelled by no instinct to suck the blood of his fellow creatures. On the contrary, he feels drawn toward them by pity and sympathy, except when under the pressure of conflicting interests.

Whenever man fails to use reason in solving the problem of these conflicting interests, war as well as every other social disorder follows. As passion and greed stifle and falsify the dictates of reason, the human species sinks back into primitive chaos. As Voltaire describes this subhuman condition:

When reason is perverted man becomes of necessity a brute. Society then amounts to nothing more than a hodgepodge of beasts who devour each other in turn, and monkeys who judge wolves and foxes. Do you want to change these beasts into men? Then begin by allowing them to be reasonable.[37]

Consequently he despised war as the crudest and most inconclusive way of solving national or social problems. The aggrandizement of the nation by means of conquest he considered as nothing less than international highway robbery. Yet throughout history mobs of unsettled men have been gathered together and in the name of patriotism sent forth on this false and inhumane mission. Thus the Patriarch of Ferney sneered at the national ideal of glory: "He [the King] dresses them in a coarse blue cloth at one hundred and ten cents a yard, edges their hats with coarse white thread, turns them to the right and to the left, then marches them off to glory."[38]

With even more contempt, Voltaire viewed wars of religion. Tirelessly he pointed out the flagrant contradiction involved in using force to gain adherents to a religion of peace, nonresistance, and brotherhood. Christianity had a wide humanistic appeal and should inspire a love for humanity. Instead, such Christianity as he saw practiced evidently inspired manifold acts of inhumanity. This wide divergence between theory and practice, taken for granted by most men, seemed revolting to a mind of fearless and unequalled integrity.

Furthermore, in the past, when crusading warriors had combined material greed with superstitious fanaticism, the result was the most hideous massacre. This pious masquerade Voltaire exposed in the *Essay on the Manners and Minds of Nations.* Charlemagne he portrayed not as a high-minded "defender of the faith," but as a pious brigand, for Charlemagne had robbed and slaughtered the Saxons in the name of his God.[39]

The same hatred of physical coercion and bloodshed led Voltaire as a historian to despise civil war as an instrument of progress. Those much admired British liberties, he had to agree, were won by revolution.[40] Nevertheless, while admitting this fact, in the *Essay on the Manners and Minds of Nations,* he seemed almost wilfully blind to the abstract issues at stake in the clash between Charles I and Parliament. In refusing to grant the king his illegal demands for funds, the House of Commons was actually enforcing the principles of constitutional monarchy. Yet this refusal the historian treats not as an epoch-making decision, but as an act of insubordination prompted by pride and avarice.[41]

The only type of war Voltaire viewed as compatible with the public welfare was a defensive war. By the successful conduct of this military operation, a sovereign truly served the nation through the medium of the people. For he thus provided them with the protection and security that was their due as members of the State.

The attitude of an ideal prince toward warfare the French thinker expressed in a casual statement about Fénelon's royal pupil, the Duc de Bourgogne: "Skilled in the art of warfare, he looked upon this art as the scourge of the human race and as an unhappy necessity rather than as a source of true glory."[42]

Since wars appeared inevitable, Voltaire would preserve peace through military preparedness. To preserve the peace meant to ensure the continuation of the fruitful processes of human co-operation as expressed in art, science, industry, and commerce—indeed all those enterprises which directly affect the happiness of the individual. Considered in this light, the training and equipment of armies was not destructive but constructive, and an aspect of national life scarcely less important than agriculture.

In the spring of 1757, during the Seven Years' War, Voltaire made a personal contribution to the art of warfare. The selfsame philosopher, so alert to the danger to mankind in increasingly formidable weapons of destruction, himself invented a military supply car. Designed and modeled upon the ancient Assyrian war-chariot, his implement had, as history proves, both a past and a future. Indeed, the Voltairean invention, which clearly foreshadows the modern tank,[43] was well thought of by Louis XV's minister of war. Though the inventor was a poet, a philosopher, and an advocate of peace, no agreement to maintain a European equilibrium, he believed, would hold without the means to enforce it. So he paid a reluctant tribute to Mars as well as to Apollo.

While any defensive military effort Voltaire respected as just, and in the best sense patriotic, he placed his finger on the fundamental intellectual dishonesty in the preventive war, as counselled by Montesquieu. The author of the *Spirit of Laws* had declared that the protection of *la patrie* occasionally requires an attack on a neighboring nation. For during a semblance of peace this state might be building up for itself a more favorable position from which to take the offensive.[44]

To these arguments Voltaire replied: "If ever there was a war obviously unjust, it is the one you propose; it is to march off to kill your neighbor for fear that your neighbor (who is making no attack on you) will yet be in a position to attack you."[45]

Proof would be needed to show that this foreign nation was planning the ruin of the homeland. The only possible evidence of such a move would consist in visibly hostile preparations.

If such were the case, and his own country, without direct tangible provocation, declared war on the suspect state, then, insisted Voltaire, the native land would be the aggressor and the war waged by the homeland would be aggressive, not preventive.

As this critic of Montesquieu now challenged: "You mean that you must chance the ruin of your own land in the hope of ruining, without reason, the land of your neighbor? This is surely neither honest nor useful, for one can never be certain of success, you know it well."[46]

Thus the only just war, Voltaire believed, was a struggle for national survival in the face of direct attack. His response to this problem well represents the positive constructive character of much of his thinking. He urged not a "preventive war," but that his nation imitate the military, diplomatic, and social methods by which the neighboring state across the frontier had become so formidable.[47] The result could then mean not mutual destruction but salutary competition, and the diagnosis and cure of many a national weakness.

For the extending of national domination, the author of *Candide* saw only two desirable expedients. These were economic power and intellectual leadership. To rule by such vital forces, the homeland must be preserved from the crime of offensive war and from the misfortune of defensive war.[48] The answer of Voltaire to the ever-present menace of military assault was in extensive arming and in maintaining as far as possible the balance of power.

According to this ancient political axiom, the states of Europe made up a sort of federal community, the essential prerequisite of which was the preservation of a just political equilibrium, or a condition such that no one sovereign state or ruler could absolutely predominate or dictate terms to the rest. Each and all remain vitally concerned in the permanence of this arrangement. So when any one power threatens the balance of power on the continent, every member of the international community is obliged by duty and by self-interest to stop the aggressor nation by armed might.[49]

The whole balance of power theory Voltaire looked upon as a political truism, and in his *Diatribe of Dr. Akakia,* he used this truism with strikingly comic effect.

Akakia can scarcely find a patron for his engineering exploit to the earth's mysterious center. As his difficulties are explained: No ruler will wish to take charge of our hole because the opening would be a little too large, and it would be necessary to dig up at least all of Germany, which would prove notably prejudicial to the European Balance of Power.[50]

Indeed, the steadfast determination of the French philosopher to work for a continental balance of power explains a stand, during the Seven Years' War, which some critics have considered well-nigh treasonable. Yet, safe in liberal Switzerland

and entirely his own master, the "hermit of the Alps" was serving the true interests of France and Europe.

In the summer of 1757 he saw his country being sucked down ever deeper in a struggle which was ruining France and uselessly devastating all the contenders.[51] For after the battle of Kolin on June 18, the aggressive military might of Frederick the Great which had brought on the war, was, for all practical purposes, broken. Stubbornly as the warrior-monarch refused to admit defeat, his surrender seemed inevitable. Yet the Austrian empress was sacrificing France and draining the blood of Europe in a fanatical effort to regain her former supremacy in the German empire. She was not only striving to win back her lost province of Silesia; her ultimate goal was the total destruction of Prussia. To the pursuit of this objective she had hopelessly committed her French ally by the terms of the Austro-French offensive and defensive alliance contracted at Versailles on May 1, 1757.

Voltaire looked upon the annihilation of the Prussian kingdom as incompatible both with the security of his own nation and with the welfare of Europe.[52] The disappearance of Prussia would destroy all chances of establishing a balance of power in Europe, and in maintaining this imperfect and perilous equilibrium between hostile forces, the French thinker saw the sole hope of peace.

A strong Prussia was at once a French and a European necessity. By fighting to crush Prussia, France was draining herself of vitality only to strengthen immeasurably her ancient foe, Austria. Since the expansion of the French nation had historically tended toward that natural frontier formed by the river Rhine, the interests of France and Austria had continually conflicted. If in the present struggle France brought about the ruin of the Prussian state she exposed herself to the aggression of a natural enemy, which the skill of a long line of the greatest French generals and statesmen had only recently managed to restrain.

With remarkable disinterestedness Voltaire strove behind the scenes for the peace he considered so imperative for his nation.

To bring this about, he tried out the Duc de Richelieu and Cardinal Tencin, a friend and an enemy, though both were high-ranking favorites at court. In 1759, fearful lest his former connection with the Prussian monarch might prove prejudicial to any agreement of his making, he took upon himself the role of an anonymous address, a bureau through which King Frederick's peace-feelers reached the eye of Choiseul. His attempts, however, failed.

It became increasingly clear, and even to some government officials, that the foreign policy of the State as represented by Louis XV and his flatterers was not supporting the interests of French citizens. As Voltaire wrote to François Tronchin of Lyons on December 8, 1757: "I know for a fact that Versailles is given over to Austrian interests and that it is very difficult to bring about any negotiations which would offend persons powerfully committed to a policy of unreasoning assistance to Vienna."[53]

Many of Voltaire's contemporaries, and not a few of his later critics, have felt that by secretly working for a peaceful understanding between France and Prussia, the French philosopher was frustrating the efforts of his nation to crush a menacing aggressor. They accused him of indifference to his country's glory and of an unpatriotic sympathy for an enemy-monarch. These opinions were based on those intimate, almost affectionate letters he wrote to Frederick all through the conflict; also on certain mocking gibes at French military ineptitude contained in his correspondence.

Nevertheless any impartial examination of his words and actions during the Seven Years' War proves beyond a doubt that Voltaire remained truly French in his sentiments and was devoted to French interests. The slight versified "treasons" which he occasionally penned to Frederick were merely part of the detached, disinterested pose assumed by D'Alembert, Buffon, and other literary men in the cosmopolitan eighteenth century.

The crushing military defeat of the French at Rossbach on

November 5, 1757, shook the "hermit of the Alps" into revealing his true feelings. Beside himself with sorrow and indignation at so great a humiliation of France by Prussia, he wrote d'Argental that he wished to leave Switzerland, that he could hardly endure in a foreign country the shame of *la patrie*.[54]

His concern for his native country took the form not only of words but of actions. Immediately after the battle of Rossbach he wrote to his banker in Berlin, ordering that his funds be placed at the disposal of French prisoners. For many of these men were suffering and without ready money.

Once, a secondary object of his private peace overtures might have been to offer his former royal disciple an alternative to ruin. Yet after the French defeat at Rossbach, Voltaire viewed the survival of Frederick merely in terms of that political algebra dictated by the balance of power.[55]

In 1759, on the occasion of his third attempt to arrange a peaceful settlement between France and Prussia, he wrote cold-bloodedly in a letter destined for the eye of Choiseul: "Luc [Frederick] is a scamp, I know, but must one ruin oneself in order to annihilate a scamp whose existence is necessary?"[56]

From his retreat in Switzerland, the French thinker saw an exhausted France weighed down with subsidies and fighting two wars, while her colonies lay imperiled. For Louis XV insisted on rigidly adhering to the unfavorable terms of his treaty with Austria. As a result, the French nation was too hopelessly weakened to carry on effectively her maritime struggle with England, and the Prussian enemy was given an opportunity to recover. From such a bloody impasse Voltaire beheld for his country no other escape than a prompt cessation of hostilities with Prussia.

Today competent historians agree with him.[57] Her hopeless involvement in a war without strategic object cost France her major colonies and left her position in Europe irremediably weakened.[58]

Thus, in the eighteenth-century world, Voltaire could think of no better means of national defense or brighter hope of respite from war than in maintaining the balance of power in Europe. Yet this precarious balance could offer, he knew, only negative benefits. To conserve on the continent an equal distribution of jealous, opposing forces, even for any length of time, was practically impossible. Nevertheless adherence to this principle could preserve intact the identity of *la patrie*.[59]

Furthermore, the seeking of mutual protection through alliances and coalitions, the French thinker believed, was conducive to progress. For each country would wish to become desirable as an ally. Therefore each country would be spurred on to a maximum development of genius and national individuality.

Voltaire regarded a respect for the international equilibrium both as sound statesmanship and as a rudimentary expression of enlightened self-interest between nations. He censured Louis XIV for flouting so fundamental a rule of politics, and he praised Peter the Great for using it as a weapon of national defense. Louis XV he discreetly criticized for pursuing a policy which would hand over the balance of power to a natural enemy. At best the mere existence of alliances and coalitions served to discourage, and without recourse to arms, those encroachments sanctioned only by the "right of the strongest."

Throughout his writings the French philosopher tried to discredit force and violence as a method for solving either national or international problems. These he would see solved instead by reason, clemency, cooperation.

Since this utopian day seemed so remote, Voltaire accepted the time-honored doctrine of the balance of power as the best available means of safeguarding the nation from outside perils— a means sufficiently imperfect as to be well in keeping with this "best of all possible worlds."

# The State as a Dominant Power: *Part 2*

## THE WAY OF ECONOMIC AND CULTURAL SUPREMACY

To the leader of eighteenth-century Enlightenment the success or failure of the nation depended on the effectiveness of the State as an organization formed to serve the public welfare. French influence he would extend only if such national domination could be attained by peaceful means and at the profit of the individual citizens. The annexation of territory seized by military conquest resulted, he believed, in the external aggrandizement of a political organization which had become an internal failure. For the price of such expansion was usually the people's well-being.[1]

The extended influence of his nation through economic power, he viewed, on the contrary, as the consequence of the inner strength of the political organization.[2] Indeed, the eminence gained through material prosperity was the product of that superabundance of national vitality arising from the skilled coordination of agriculture, manufacture, industry, and commerce. These arts had little to do with either celestial happiness or the perpetuation of a myth of national glory. Yet, as a believer in terrestrial values, Voltaire saw in the flourishing of these vital and practical aspects of the life of *la patrie* the surest means of making the Here and Now agreeable. For what matters, he declared, is that our poor human species should be the least miserable as is possible.[3]

Both the Epicureanism of Voltaire, and his love of bourgeois comfort, found expression in his conviction that in the modern world, the greatness of a nation is achieved not through war but through commerce. As early as in the *Philosophic Letters*,[4] he remarked on how often the fortunes of war are decided by money. Indeed, those nations like Holland, which had gained power by commerce found conquest unnecessary. Rarely, though, does a warrior-nation retire on its laurels to seek command through trade.

England had proved to this last rule a notable exception. For Britain, at her period of military supremacy, was a poor and sparsely populated agrarian nation. Yet ever since the reign of Elizabeth when the English devoted themselves to commercial rather than military enterprises, their kingdom had attained a wealth and eminence unknown when half of France was under British rule.[5] Voltaire held that a national superiority won through commerce was equivalent to the most wide-scale promotion of the public welfare. Such an ambition was therefore humane and in the highest sense patriotic.

In his economic ideas, the author of *Candide* stands revealed as a cultural and humanitarian patriot. Yet because of certain inconsistencies in his theories about industry and commerce, his writings fail to set forth a clearly defined economic policy. Like many thinkers of the late eighteenth century, he was faced with the opposing views of two schools of political economy. The first was a continuation of the seventeenth-century mercantilist school of protective economics, whose most brilliant exponent had been Colbert. The second consisted of the Physiocrats,[6] daring advocates of a system of "natural economics" who were attempting to apply "reason" and "natural law" to monetary forces. Both schools held principles on which Voltaire based much of his philosophy.

The Physiocrats founded their doctrines upon those natural laws which the author of the *Essay on the Manners and Minds of Nations* had stated were graven on the hearts of all men from France to the islands of Japan.[7] The rationalism common to both Voltaire and the Physiocrats was merely a practical application of that deductive method of Descartes which had reached eighteenth-century philosophers through the intermediary of such writers as Fontenelle. To Voltaire and the Physiocrats "reason" was an impartial thinking process which enabled an individual to deduce certain laws of the universe.[8] With these laws man must place himself in harmony. "Reason" taught Gournay and his school that all human beings were impelled by nature to seek their self-interest, and that in the economic sphere this self-interest found tangible expression in private property. Thus the ruling force in the economic order was private property, above all property in land.[9]

The key concept of the Physiocrats was the primacy of agriculture. These eighteenth-century economists insisted that agriculture alone was productive. For all riches are necessarily derived from the soil. As compared with agriculture, they viewed industry and commerce as "sterile." The materials extracted from the earth are merely given new form by the manufacturer. The increased value of the object after it has passed through his hands represents only the quantity of natural resources and materials used and consumed in its elaboration. Commerce likewise is "unproductive," amounting as it does to nothing more than a transfer of existing wealth.

The Physiocrats argued that to increase the wealth of the nation meant to add to the quantity of raw materials available for consumption. Upon the annual excess of the mass of agricultural products (including metals!) over their production cost, national prosperity depends. The State revenue which must be derived from this net-product should therefore be raised in the manner simplest and most "natural," namely a single levy in the form of a land-tax.

If the Physiocrats judged landed property as all important, they also placed high value on property in the form of movable goods. The cultivation of the soil would yield only insignificant returns were it not accompanied by the assurance of free disposal of the produce, as well as of the essential working capital. Similarly, property in the form of an individual's working-power was given by these economists a high and independent status. Every worker, they believed, should be entitled to sell his services freely and at his own terms.

In fact, the various liberties preached by the Physiocrats were mere corollaries of the right of private property. Free trade, for instance, is primarily the unquestioned freedom of the landlord to produce whatever he wishes and to market his product unhampered by restrictions. Such absolute individualism leads logically to complete cosmopolitanism. For the inalienable rights of the producer-seller recognize no political boundaries and therefore have precedence over all international conventions.

Society, the Physiocrats maintained, should be governed by private self-interest, the born servant of the general interest. In their opinion, free competition, "the mainspring of human perfectibility," was conducive to justice. For such a system bestowed upon each individual an equal right to follow his self-interest. The social organization should be constructed so that enlightened self-interest would be the individual's surest policy for securing happiness. Thus to preserve the "natural rights" of all, the freedom of each member of the group should be limited as soon as that freedom becomes inconsistent with the rights of others. Judged from such a point of view, government is an indispensable evil, existing only to guarantee from artificial interference the free operation of natural forces. For freedom of exchange should be encouraged, competition allowed to flourish, and monopolies or privileges done away with.

Voltaire looked upon the Physiocrats as his fellow-workers in the Enlightenment movement. In their acceptance of earthly values, their faith in "reason" and enlightened self-interest, they were in accord not only with his own philosophy but with the major liberal tendencies of the late eighteenth century. Still, he never adopted *en bloc* the entire creed of these economists. Their belief in land as the sole source of the wealth of the State appeared to him as particularly absurd. The fallacy in their talk of the "sterility" of manufactures and industry was demonstrated to him by his everyday experience in the lumber country of Gex. The single land-tax he attacked in the *Man with Forty Crowns*,[10] wittily puncturing for all thinking people the Physiocratic argument that only landlords should pay taxes, since all riches spring necessarily from the soil.[10]

Free trade Voltaire upheld. Yet he did so only because this Physiocratic article of faith was part of his own philosophy of progress.[11] Free interchange, as the purest expression of enlightened self-interest he felt, would result in a new friendly *"rapprochement"* between nations. The world is united by luxury he had stated in the *Worldling*.[12] Indeed, a simple cup of coffee stirred his imagination with thoughts of a happy collaboration between Arabia, China, and the forests of America.[13] The bounties of nature in some regions of the earth make up for her deficiencies in others, while the differing needs of mankind would unfailingly ensure a profitable exchange of products. Thus the efforts of the various nations would be directed not at mutual destruction, but toward helping each other to secure those commodities which render life more pleasant, comfortable, or aesthetic. Then converts would be won over to "reason" and gentle Epicureanism, the cause of Enlightenment would prosper, and the stage remain set for future progress.

Though the Physiocrats advocated international free trade, they hardly expected to apply this principle immediately. Under existing conditions the world market was highly competitive. Tariffs and other protective measures could be safely set aside only if and when rival powers agreed to adopt a similar policy.[14]

Instead, Turgot and the Physiocrats campaigned for the free

interchange of goods within the French kingdom, a measure long argued for by Voltaire. In 1751, in his *Dialogue between a Philosopher and a Comptroller of Finance,* the French philosopher had stated that to render Guienne and Brittany enemies through high customs duties was as ridiculous as for the master of a household to permit menials to devour in an antechamber half the dinner they were to serve him.[15] For insistence on such trade restrictions he criticized Colbert.

True to these convictions, in the last quarter of the century the Sage of Ferney gave his wholehearted support to the efforts of Turgot to establish the free circulation of grain and other food products within the French kingdom. With sardonic pamphlets the aged philosopher fought side by side the radical minister of finance in his struggle with king and *Parlement* in behalf of these reforms.[16]

A gradualist, Voltaire felt that the success of free trade within the kingdom would mark an important first step toward the extension of this principle to commercial dealings with other countries. Like Turgot and the Physiocrats he looked forward to a happy eventuality when between foreign powers the laws of supply and demand could operate as freely and unrestrictedly as seemingly decreed by nature. Once conditions were ripe for this great benefit there would dawn an era of peace and cooperation between nations.

Since this utopian day, he knew, was remote, Voltaire held on to some old-fashioned mercantilistic opinions. Exports, to his way of thinking, should exceed imports, and imports should be severely taxed.[17] For the exportation of money to foreign powers is an economic factor which tends to impoverish the nation.

In the *Century of Louis XIV* and the *Man with Forty Crowns* he advocated a curtailment of luxury expenditure whenever the securing of such articles involved large shipments of precious metals to foreign countries. In the *Man with Forty Crowns* he declared:

Another cause of our poverty is in our new-found wants and needs. We must pay our neighbors 4 millions worth for one article and five or six for another, merely to stuff up our noses a malodorous powder from America; coffee, tea, chocolate, cochenila, indigo, the spices are costing us more than 60 millions a year.[18]

He shared, however, neither the mercantilist conviction that a nation's wealth consists primarily in the sum total of precious metals in circulation,[19] nor the physiocratic belief that agriculture alone is productive. To Voltaire, what constituted the nation's capital was population, industry, skill in utilizing ability.[20] Spain, he pointed out, though rich in metal, was one of the poorest countries in Europe. For this nation had neglected manufactures, failed to organize industry intelligently, and allowed countless men and women to rot away in monasteries and convents, idle and, in all senses of the word, unproductive. The American gold owned by Spain and Portugal flowed, therefore, to England with whom she traded. Meanwhile, despite this hard-won metal treasure, the proud Spanish and Portuguese kingdoms remained quite as impoverished as before.[21]

Equally unrealistic to Voltaire seemed the physiocratic notion that agriculture alone can achieve prosperity. Such a point of view wholly overlooks the enhanced value lent agricultural products by industry and manufacture. The French philosopher held, on the contrary, that agriculture, manufacture, industry, and commerce were all vital forces in the economic life of the State. Their harmonious interplay corresponds to that perfect chemical balance of elements which, in the human body, makes for robust health. So closely related were these four aspects of national existence that no one of them could thrive or prosper independently of the other. The progress of viticulture gave rise to the discovery of champagne, which commanded a high market value in prosperous cities. The commerce of the city flourished, thanks to this product of the surrounding country, and the wine-growers in turn became enriched.[22]

In his *Dialogue Between a Philosopher and a Comptroller of*

*Finance* the author concludes: "The real wealth of a kingdom is not in gold and silver; it is in the abundance of all commodities, in industry and in labor."[23]

He dreamed of the State as a vast machine directed by a genius picked by the aristocracy with man power as the necessary cogwheels and property as the animating force. For even such wealth as arose from industry and the labor of human hands was useless without a "directing spirit,"[24] a king, or, better still, a progressive-minded minister of finance. Such a competent leader would strive for the general economic interests. He would offer financial encouragement for an increase in population, and establish a sound banking system, even permitting the use of paper money, so long as these bank notes never exceeded in value the metal funds they represented.[25] So the author challenged with a conviction bred of his middle-class origin: "Do you know that a minister of finance can do more good and consequently be a greater man than twenty marshals of France?"[26]

In Turgot, Voltaire beheld the man of action ready to put in practice the humanitarian principles which he himself, a writer and a thinker, had already voiced in the *Philosophic Dictionary*. His plea in the article "Taxes" that high social rank should not entail tax-exemption, his insistence in "Property" that the sole property of the workers consisted in his right to sell his labor at the most favorable terms possible, his lifelong wish to save the integrity of the law-courts by prohibiting the sale of judgeships——all found expression in Turgot's sensational edicts of 1776.[27]

Nevertheless, the author of the *Philosophic Dictionary* paid equal or even greater tribute to that directing genius who, in the illiberal past century, had helped win France a position of cultural supremacy. This master-organizer was Louis XIV's minister of finance, Colbert.

To Voltaire, the age of Louis XIV represented all the world could ever show of artistic and intellectual greatness, outward magnificence, and elegance of life and manners.[28] Cultural

supremacy, along with successful promotion of the public welfare, he looked upon as the noblest type of glory attainable. For
a great culture, even while national in achievement, enriches the
human mind and thus contributes to world civilization. As early
as 1733 he had insisted:

Above all, do not believe that this empire of the mind and this honor
of being the intellectual model for other peoples is a frivolous type
of glory. These are the infallible signs of greatness in a nation.
Always and under the greatest princes the arts have flourished and
artistic decadence is sometimes a symptom of the decline of the
State.[29]

The century of Louis XIV had witnessed, Voltaire believed,
the complete realization of the genius of the French nation.
Indeed the cultural glory won by France had surpassed that of
Rome or any ancient empire. For the nation, ruled by Louis
XIV, had triumphed artistically and intellectually in competition
with other European powers most of which were highly
civilized.

In France, artists and writers had always depended for their
support on the patronage of the mighty. So for the full blooming
of genius, enthusiasm and generosity seemed needed on the part
of the aristocracy. To his own age, the author of the *Century of
Louis XIV* never wearied of pointing out that "nature" invariably
forms an abundance of gifted individuals blessed with every
class and description of talents. Society should nurture these
talents with money and prestige. Otherwise the fine "trees
planted by Louis XIV might perish from neglect."[30]

The national garden was designed by Louis XIV. Yet its
cultivation and upkeep was the work of his minister of finance.
Voltaire honored Colbert as an instrument of French greatness.
Not only did this master-organizer assist and encourage French
genius. He summoned to France men of talent from all corners
of Europe. The Italian architect, Bernini, was richly paid to
come to Paris to work on the Louvre. The Belgian artist Vander
Meulen was granted a pension to record His Majesty's campaigns

on canvas and embellish with his skilled brush the "Furniture of the Crown." Despite the extreme religious intolerance of the age, Louis XIV on the recommendation of Colbert, even welcomed to his court the Protestant scientists Huygens and Roemer.

This active collaboration of the nations of Europe in order to create beauty, their partnership in science, their united effort to apply the facts they had discovered to the welfare of mankind, all made up Voltaire's vision of peace and world progress. The seeming fulfillment of his personal ideal for Europe, he thus commemorated in the *Century of Louis XIV*:

We have seen gradually established in Europe a republic of letters. All the sciences, all the arts have thus received mutual aid. Academies have formed this republic. Italy and Russia have been united by letters. The Englishman, the German and the Frenchman go to study at Leyden. The celebrated physician, Boerhaave, was consulted both by the Pope and by the Czar. His greatest pupils have thus attracted foreigners and have become in a way international physicians. True scholars in every line have strengthened the bonds of this great society of minds which knows no frontiers and is everywhere independent. The communication still lasts; it remains one consolation for the evils that ambition and politics spread throughout the earth.[31]

Cultural supremacy Colbert helped win France, though in ways inimical to this cosmopolitan vision. French artists might study in Rome. Yet severe penalties would have been imposed upon them had they attempted to settle, or enrich with their talents the art of Italy. The design of Colbert was not cultural interchange, but the appropriation by France of all that was rare and excellent beyond the boundaries.[32] Louis XIV's minister of finance was not, as his historian liked to think, a devotee of European civilization. His aims instead were ruthlessly nationalistic.

Similarly Colbert served Voltaire as proof that with skilled organization a state could be enriched by luxury. His theory of the close relationship between luxury and progress, the eighteenth-century thinker had compounded in part from the economic ideas of such Englishmen as Petty, North, and Mandeville;[33] also from Pierre Bayle and French *libertin* philosophy. Tangible expressions of magnificence Voltaire continually associated with culture and the fine arts. For according to his extremely French conception of the aesthetic, beauty was a nobler more general term for elegance, and the fine arts, exquisite furniture, and elegant manners, all varying but almost equally important expressions of the beautiful. Thus as artist and Epicurean, he gloried in the establishment of the manufacture of such timeless art objects as Gobelin and Beauvais tapestries; also the organization at Lyon of lace and brocade industries to clothe suitably the most polite society Europe had ever known.

In these acts of Colbert, Voltaire saw the happy means to a happy end. For the luxury or magnificence of the few had brought about the gainful employment of the many.[34] The author of the *Century of Louis XIV* saw no sense in the renunciation of life's pleasures. His epicurean ideal was the enjoyment and control of them.

Nevertheless the French philosopher was well aware of the relative nature of the vague term "luxury." As he defined it in his *Observations on M. M. Jean Lass, Melon and Dutôt* of 1738:

What is luxury? It is a word we use with no more thought of a precise meaning than when we speak of the climates of the orient and the occident. There is in actuality no point on earth above which the sun rises and sets, or if you wish, each and all points are orient and occident. The same is true about luxury. There is none, or it is everywhere.[35]

To Voltaire, luxury was closely indicative of material and social betterment. Since a higher standard of living often causes the "luxury" of yesterday to become the commonplace of today the pleasant superfluities accessible to the wealthy increase in quantity while they improve in quality. To avoid the ambiguity contained in any hard and fast definition, Voltaire described luxury as the "expenditure of a rich man." "To be rich," he declared, "means to enjoy." Accordingly, a simple eighteenth-century squire was richer than Hugh Capet. For this medieval monarch could enjoy only those crude and imperfect commodities made available by an age devoid of industrial development and skilled labor.[36] In the same way, with the gold treasure of the Indies, a man could still be poor if his needs were unsatisfied. An absence of coffee on his own breakfast table, said Voltaire, would be due not to a lean purse, but to the backwardness of his country in affairs of commerce.[37]

He also recognized that an increase in the amount of precious metal in circulation does not necessarily entail a parallel development of consumable luxury commodities. The purchasing power of money diminishes by any sudden influx of gold into the national treasury, and the gold metal itself is incapable of procuring direct enjoyments.

Luxury articles, though, are products of man's industry and ingenuity. In a state founded on property and therefore inequality, the multiplication of luxuries represents the productive power of the people directed toward the realization of the agreeable and the aesthetic. The resultant prosperity arises not from the accumulation of inorganic metal, but from the expert utilization of man's varying abilities, and from the well-balanced functioning of all the economic forces of the nation. Such organic enrichment brings with it an improved standard of living.[38]

Voltaire praised Colbert as a friend of peace who helped France to achieve domination through such peaceful means as economic power and cultural supremacy. On French manufactures the minister of finance imposed and enforced rigorous standards of excellence. French goods no less dazzling than the Sun King's armies he sent forth to the world market to capture from foreign countries large supplies of their gold.

As a man of his century, Colbert held that "there is only one fixed sum of money that circulates through Europe"—that this amount of money almost never varies and that the consumption of goods in all countries is static. Since prosperity is determined by the influx of precious metals into the state treasury, one nation can not gain without another losing. Consequently, in the words of the great mercantilist, commerce is a "money war."[39]

As a historian, Voltaire failed to note how provocative of actual military war was Colbert's economic protectivism. Quite oblivious of this essential factor, he blamed the clash with Holland and the interminable struggle with the League of Augsburg on the insatiable ambition of Louis XIV. He neglected to show how the tariff of 1667 waged an economic war on England and Holland, or that on Dutch goods the duty was raised from forty to eighty pounds per piece. Dutch commerce the minister of finance had set out to ruin. In order to protect French sugar refineries he went so far as to refuse to sell Holland raw sugar from the Antilles.[40]

The author of the *Century of Louis XIV* seems almost wilfully blind to the fact that the king's struggle with Holland was half caused by Dutch economic reprisals. These excluded by prohibitive tariffs French textiles, wines, and *eaux de vie*.[41] The ensuing conflict, the historian viewed as motivated solely by enemy efforts to maintain the balance of power in Europe. Yet Holland, economically crippled by Colbert, was urged on by the need to retaliate. As Voltaire thus described the Peace of Ryswick:

Peace occurred as a result of lassitude with war, and this war had been almost without object: at least on the side of the enemy-alliance it amounted to nothing more than the vague plan to diminish the glory of Louis XIV, and on the part of this monarch himself, merely the consequence of the same greatness which had not wished to yield.[42]

In the achievement of Colbert, Voltaire beheld an example of how courtly magnificence could be made to serve the public welfare and national culture contribute to world culture. His seeming endorsement of this Minister's war-provoking mercantilistic policies amounted, however, to no essential departure from his humanitarian view of international relations. As a French-

man, and as a historian, he remained dazzled and even somewhat blinded by all Louis XIV and Colbert had accomplished
for the greatness and glory of France.

In general, however, Voltaire preferred a stable international
peace and the well-being of French citizens to any form of
national aggrandizement. Typical of this point of view was his
attitude toward colonial possessions. Unmoved by any overseas
glorification of France as an abstract entity, he valued colonies
only when they helped the individual inhabitant of the mother
country to prosper. For this reason alone his policy was mercantilistic.[43]

Colonies in his opinion were so many farms whose chief
function was to supply the mother country with raw materials
and commodities which the State would otherwise be forced
to purchase from foreigners.

As a modern historian expresses this mercantilism conception,
the mother country was the entrepôt for all colonial staples:

Imports and exports were to be a monopoly of the merchant marine.
The last monopoly of the carrying trade was designed not only to
support the shipping-interests of the parent-country, but to prevent
the fraudulent introduction into the colonies of foreign merchandise
and the exportation of colonial commodities to other countries. The
whole scheme of a self-sufficing economic empire, which this system
envisaged, had the supreme object of procuring that favorable balance
of trade for the mother-country which was the final objective of all
colonial powers.[44]

The French East India Company Voltaire consequently
viewed as an effective answer to the economic challenge offered
France by the Dutch trade monopoly with the Indies. Since from
the Dutch East India Company Frenchmen persisted in purchasing tea and spices, Colbert made these luxuries available to
his countrymen through a Far Eastern company of their own.[45]

Though a believer in luxury as a valuable stimulus to progress, Voltaire saw only two occasions when luxury expenditure
harmed a nation: first, when money spent for these commodities

exceeds the industrial resources of the State, as is often the case with small countries; secondly, when indulgence in pleasant superfluities entails the export of metal to foreign nations. This last circumstance was a threat not only to France, but to all nations which engaged in the hazardous Far Eastern trade.[46]

Increasing public demand, however, had changed the exotic spices of India from luxuries to necessities. Thus, Voltaire declared, the only way for France to hold her own in competition with other countries was to be "ruined" through her own trade monopoly rather than through the commercial companies of her rivals. Any loss of precious metal through exportation, he believed, could be well made up for by the earning power of France as a nation, by that agricultural and industrial superiority which enabled French crops and manufactured products to win from wealthy Spain large stores of American gold. He had the vision to perceive that only nations capable of creating at home a vigorous, expansive industrial organization could successfully extend their power and influence overseas.

To Voltaire, each colony was a business venture, profitable or unprofitable, as the case might be. Tropical and subtropical dependencies he considered by far the most valuable:[47] first, because they could supply France with exotic commodities and raw materials unobtainable in her temperate climate; secondly, because such colonial possessions were vitally dependent on the various products shipped them by the mother country.

Colonies in the temperate zone failed to provide any such opportunity for the favorable exchange of dissimilar products. Many French statesmen regarded these dependencies as relatively useless, for they tended to become mere replicas of the mother country, producing the same crops and providing in part for their own manufacturing needs.

Thus, in 1758, when Voltaire dismissed Canada as a "few acres of snow" and wrote that he wished this colony "at the bottom of the Arctic Sea,"[48] he was guilty of no unpatriotic indifference to the fate of French colonies. Such phrases merely reflect the general body of mercantilist opinion.[49] Overseas possessions were not regarded by leading statesmen as new territory for the expansion of French society or for the spread of French culture. Concern for national prestige remained out of consideration.

Canada Voltaire judged as an unproductive colony in the temperate zone and defensible only by ruinous warfare. The surrender of this distant financial liability was in his estimation not too high a price to pay for the peace so vital to war-weary France. As he weighed his country's interests in his *Summary of the Century of Louis XV*:

Those fifteen-hundred miles, three quarters of which are glacial deserts, were not perhaps a real loss. Canada cost a lot of money and brought back scant returns. If a tenth-part of the funds swallowed up in this colony had been used to reclaim our wastelands in France, we would have gained considerably. But we wished to maintain Canada and we lost the labor of a hundred years along with money lavished without return.[50]

Nevertheless his keen disappointment at the capture of Pondichéry by the British in 1761 appears at variance with his habitual view of colonies as transmarine investments. French trade posts in India had long proved a losing venture. The reorganized East India Company had made manifest an utter inability to support itself on the profits of commerce alone. The commanding position it enjoyed was due to state protection and what dividends it paid were derived solely from a tobacco monopoly. This last was unconnected with the hazards of Oriental trade. Such facts Voltaire as a historian admitted:

At last nothing was left to the French in this part of the world except the regret at having spent for over forty years immense sums to keep up a company which had never made the least profit, which never paid its stockholders or creditors anything at all from the gains of its business; which in its Indian administration subsisted only on a secret brigandage and which was only maintained by a part of the tobacco monopoly the King had granted it; a memorable and perhaps useless example of the lack of understanding the French nation has had up to now of the huge and ruinous Indian commerce.[51]

Even so, by their inability to defend and maintain Pondichéry, Voltaire felt that his countrymen had failed to meet the demands of world progress. His national sentiment, it appears, was offended. So he took revenge on Britain by uttering some unaccustomedly harsh words about Shakespeare.[52]

The successful operation of the French East India Company he beheld as one step toward the uniting of the world through luxury, the solving of economic problems through an enterprise capable of enriching both the citizens and the State. The potential value of the French colony at Pondichéry he never underestimated. Efficiently managed, such an enterprise, he believed, could have proved at least as successful as the Dutch and English Far Eastern trading-posts.

In his *Accounts of a Few Revolutions in India* of 1773 he contrasted the greed for personal gain manifested by French colonial administrators with the loyalty to the common interests seemingly characteristic of the British.[53] After exposing French corruption and administrative jealousy, he came to the following conclusion about his countrymen as colonizers:

In actuality, the French have in their character and too often in their government something which prevents them from successfully forming large associations: for the English companies, the Dutch and even the Danish ones prospered with their commercial monopoly.[54]

With France, in colonial competition, the loser, the continuous expenditure for the tea and spices of the Indies was making Frenchmen poor and acting as a ruinous form of self-imposed taxation.

Thus the same Voltaire who had written verses in praise of the "superfluous so necessary"[55] now decried the uselessness of luxury articles which either lured Europeans to their death at the opposite ends of the earth or contributed to their financial ruin in Paris.[56] Far from fostering peace and mutual assistance between nations, the trade in the Far East had merely opened up new theaters of warfare.

Commercial expansion may well point the way toward progress. The nations of the world, including France, are not always able to follow in this difficult direction. In the face of these circumstances, Voltaire discouraged his European contemporaries from colonial endeavors in the Indies. On colonization in the Western Hemisphere he ventured, however, one interesting prediction.

In the British colonial possessions in North America situated amid fertile territories, interwoven with wide navigable rivers so favorable for commerce, he sensed a great power in embryo. These British dependencies, he seems to have realized, represented the expansion not merely of trade, but of European society. The inhabitants were not isolated trappers and garrisoned military men, but families, settled communities of Englishmen and other nationalities, all seeking a political freedom denied them in their native lands. In the expansive vitality of such a colony the historian glimpsed a possible threat to the mother country. He even hinted that under her yoke so thriving a dominion might in time grow restless.[57]

Like all mercantilists, Voltaire thought that colonies should have no economic life apart from the mother country and that these dependencies should strive accordingly to serve her interests. Scarcely could he perceive that in his own country this old-fashioned mercantilistic conception of colonies was being revolutionized. So he failed to grasp the theoretical significance of the new colonial tactics used by Dupleix. The plan of this administrator was to win for France territorial supremacy in India. This he tried to do by gaining political control of the local Indian rulers and inducing them to appoint agents to their courts. Through such agents he fomented quarrels with native potentates and, in return, for his intervention, received from the princes he helped, both armies and money. These resources he would use for the conquest of additional colonial territory.[58]

That Dupleix was an imperialist, that in his *Memoir* of justification he set down the rules for a new system of colonization based on internal control and military exploitation of Indian affairs,[59] no eighteenth-century historian could foretell. Thus Voltaire merely commented on a phenomenon which seemed to him picturesquely unfitting: "Here is an agent of a commercial company turned sovereign, and having sovereigns under his command."[60]

Voltaire, like the heads of the French East India Company, viewed Pondichéry as the local branch of a business firm which held headquarters in Paris. Thus the agent of a commercial company had no right to embark on a campaign of conquest. Nor should he seek to transform this economic organization into a political and territorial dominion maintained by protectorates over Indian princes. A similar conviction was expressed in the article "Colonies" of Diderot's *Encyclopedia*: "Commercial colonies would betray their essential principle should they embark on a campaign of conquest."[61]

Voltaire, however, had words of appreciation for the genius of Dupleix.[62] The political experiments of this administrator he explained by his inability to compete with the rival British trading station at Madras and, at the same time, meet all company expenses on only such money as his Paris superiors managed to send him on ships that arrived late or not at all. The policy of Dupleix was imperialistic, but his motives and inspiration were entirely mercantilistic. To the colonial problem of lack of funds he had arrived in desperation at a new answer. Yet in the opinion of Voltaire this answer was unacceptable.

The author of *Candide* looked with marked disfavor on actions which a later century would call imperialistic. In the following words he described such European attempts to exploit for selfish national purposes the native governments of India:

We have laid waste their country; we have irrigated it with our blood. We have shown them how far we surpass them in courage and wickedness and how, in wisdom, we are inferior to them. We, the European nations, have mutually destroyed each other in this same land where we go to seek gain and where the first Greeks traveled only for purposes of instruction.[63]

The principle of empire, of the political dominion of the mother country over lands inhabited by other races, was contrary to Voltaire's whole philosophy.[64] As a believer in "natural law" he held as his first axiom that men, regardless of race, color or different living conditions, all share the dignity of the human status and as thinking beings all possess certain inalienable rights. Yet colonization, on the basis of overseas empire, must owe its successful existence to the violation of these same prerogatives. For such colonies were maintained, first by Negro slave labor, and, secondly, by the no less forcible enslavement of the native population.

The practice of Negro slavery Voltaire ridiculed in his *History of the Travels of Scarmentado*. With his customary wit, he proved how a racial enmity based on personal appearance could boomerang back against white Europeans if, by any ill chance, they ceased to be the "strongest." Then whites might be captured by blacks, and treated, in their turn, as so many heads of runaway livestock.[65]

Again in *Candide* and in the *Essay on the Manners and Minds of Nations,* Voltaire made a stand against the violations by Europeans of the "natural rights of dark-skinned races,"[66] their brothers in the world-wide fraternity of reason. The enslavement of one branch of the human family to another was contrary both to the factual brotherhood of man implicit in "natural law" and the mystic Brotherhood of men's souls expounded by Christianity. So he flayed white Christians who converted to a religion of immortality those peoples they treated as less than mortal: "We tell them that they are men like us, that they were redeemed by a God who died for them and then we make them toil like beasts of burden."[67]

It is safe to say that Kipling's imperialistic concept of the "white man's burden" would have seemed to Voltaire like sheer hypocrisy. For far from raising Orientals to a higher level of civilization, Europeans, so the eighteenth-century thinker charged, merely infected these peaceful peoples with their sinisterly superior vices, with their superior white skill and cleverness in harming their fellow-men.[68] If from the contact between East and West there did arise any so-called moral and intellectual benefits, these certainly fell not to the share of the Orientals. Here again, as in the case of the material advantages, the East was the loser.[69]

The attachment of Voltaire to his native land is reflected in his personal belief that colonization, on any terms, is barely feasible.[70] For such overseas settlements exacted as their price the individual happiness of the colonizer. A future away from French society, French culture, and all the amenities of French living, the epicurean philosopher could desire neither for himself nor for any other Frenchman. To him the "white man's burden" consisted not in the moral uplift of supposedly "inferior" races, but in the burdensome necessity which forced the white man to live so far from Paris.

The national garden, he therefore believed, should be cultivated on home soil and within hereditary boundaries. On the earthly salvation, whether of the State or the citizen, there exists no more perfect expression of his thoughts than the saying: "Let us cultivate our garden."

Voltaire felt persuaded that the wealth of a nation consists first of all in the earth of *la patrie* made productive through agriculture. Yet, unlike the Physiocrats, he valued land not as a sole source of income, but as a primitive capital from which the profits could be reinvested in industry, commerce, and manufactures, all branches of national activity as important as agriculture. The economic development of the state would reach its maximum when every available field in France was made to contribute to the sustenance of the nation. Such a condition, though, could be achieved only in a well populated country and when farm-laborers devoted to the soil they tilled a care inspired by ownership. Thus the author of the *Philosophic Dictionary* would abolish serfdom and welcome in its place a newly created class of peasant proprietors. As he stated in his article "Property":

It is certain that the possessor of a piece of land will cultivate his own heritage better than that belonging to someone else. The spirit of property doubles the force of man. One works for oneself and one's family with more vigor and pleasure than for a master.[71]

The same reasoning had led him to choose a republic as the strongest, the most "natural" and "ideal" form of government.[72] In the article "Property" he declared: " 'Liberty and Property': this is the English cry. It is worth more than Saint George and my right, Saint Denys and Montjoie. This is the cry of human nature."[73]

Each man should be allowed to work, on no matter how small a scale, for his own just interests. Then the soil of France would show a hitherto undreamed of productiveness. For the more carefully the individual plots were tended the more the national garden would prosper.

As a result, industry and commerce, in their turn, would benefit.[74] The first aimed to increase the value of all "natural" products, while the second strove to secure for these enhanced raw materials a favorable rate of exchange in the market.[75] An improvement in the quality and distribution of primary products would enable industry and commerce to attain at high profit their given objectives. So agricultural productivity was the first step in achieving that perfect coordination of all the major economic forces so necessary to the prosperity of the State.

Furthermore, a fulfillment of the ideal of "Liberty and Property," Voltaire argued, would enrich the nation in so dynamic a form as increased population. For the security of the individual and his joy in ownership would act as an important inducement to marriage.[76]

The rapid growth of man power among the peasantry could indeed be counted upon to strengthen all classes of French society. The crown would be supplied with soldiers, and the nobleman with large numbers of agricultural workers who could make their own fortune and that of their nation in armies for defense, in the workshops of trade, and in the mills of manufacture. To the author of the *Philosophic Dictionary* economic power was man power.

As he concluded: "Population will have produced this great good; and the possession of lands granted to cultivators under a system of rent which enriches the lords will have produced this population."[77]

In the opinion of Voltaire the reservation of the finest lands in the realm as Church property was a prodigious squandering of his country's resources. Within Church domains crop failure was frequent. For the clergy, sworn to poverty and chastity, had no stake in the earthly advancement of *la patrie*. This class he despised, for the most part, as parasites on the State who, as owners of one-third of the lands in France, served loyally the interests of neither God nor man. Secure in their rôle as celestially favored beings, such idle unproductive members of the social order grew rich on the labor of their fellow men.[78] The function of government was to prevent this abuse of power and to utilize these valuable ecclesiastical territories for the common good.[79]

Voltaire viewed property as the most important single factor in the economic development of the nation. Prosperity, he felt persuaded, would reach its maximum when the monarch cherished all of France as his sovereign property, when small segments of peasant-owned land tripled in value the estates of the nobility, when the farm-worker, free to choose the most profitable conditions of labor, was sustained in his toil by the hope of ownership.

As he observed in his article "Property": "Thus from the scepter to the sickle and the shepherd's crook, everything comes alive, prospers and gathers new force through this pulse-spring alone."[80]

For the materialism implicit in the bourgeois motto of "Liberty and Property" Voltaire felt scant aversion. As a humanist he fought for man's earthly happiness. As a realist he recognized that this happiness was largely composed of peace, security, and bourgeois comfort. His insistence on the greatest good of the greatest number may indeed have been materialistic. Yet his goal, the philosopher was well aware, could be attained only through such ethical or spiritual qualities on the part of society as foresight, incorruptibility, self-sacrifice.

Nevertheless the public welfare, he feared, would not be served should there arise a growing class of parvenu nobility. To prevent the misuse of power by those unused to exercising it, he advocated such reactionary measures as legal restrictions on the purchase of land by plebeians. As in the *Philosophic Dictionary* he observed:

In more than one kingdom it has happened that the enfranchised serf, becoming rich through his industry, usurps the place of his former masters whom their luxury has made poor. He buys their land and takes their names. The former nobility has been degraded and the new is only envied and scorned. All classes have been jumbled together. The people who have endured these usurpations have been the playthings of the nations who have preserved themselves from this scourge.[81]

The aristocracy Voltaire looked upon as patrons of the arts and custodians of the nation's culture. From them Enlightenment should proceed, and their civilizing example should instruct and uplift the middle and lower ranks of society.

The economic emancipation, upon which working-class enlightenment must depend, should likewise be progressive and gradual. For such freedom brings power, and with each increase in power the individual should be mentally and morally prepared for an equal increase in responsibility.

"Liberty and Property," Voltaire would conserve as the basic premise of the social order. Yet for the social contract to be fulfilled, material progress, he believed, should be regulated so as to aid, not impede, national advancement in the realm of ethics, art, and intellect.

# Conclusion

V OLTAIRE based his concept of *la patrie* less on territorial attachment to a native land than on world-wide principles of social justice. These, he believed, should be enforced by all government. A France where inalienable human rights were daily unrespected he refused to accept as his homeland. Yet love for this land bequeathed to him by history, and pride in all the distinguishing features of his own nationality, inspired him to strive unceasingly to establish within French boundaries a trustworthy State.

His political philosophy was in harmony with democracy, for he believed that the State exists for the citizen, as opposed to the authoritarian dictum that the citizen exists for the State. The aim of the political organization should be to uphold individual welfare and rights. These "natural" and inalienable prerogatives, which he referred to throughout his writings, may be loosely summarized as liberty of person and property, trial by due processes of the law, freedom of speech and assembly, liberty to worship God as dictated by the individual conscience, and the equal right of all human beings to pursue their happiness or self-interest. Such claims of human nature, he argued, were as old as history and formed the basis of society. In order to erect a citadel within which their universal rights could be maintained against all outside perils, men had first banded together to form communities or nations.

Membership in the nation is therefore inherently contractual.

The duty of the State is to provide the individual with liberty and security, while in exchange for these benefits, the individual owes the State his loyal protection and support. Voltaire recognized that in the France of his day this bond between the nation and the citizen was not infrequently broken. The persecuted, the enslaved, the destitute could have no true homeland, nor could they love the country in which they dragged out their dreary existences. Toward these men, deprived of their "natural rights," the State had failed to keep its part of that basic social agreement which had originally summoned it into being.

On the contrary, hired soldiers, adventurers, and intriguers had no country. For they defaulted in the duties and responsibilities which their union with the nation required of them. Nor had the rich idle clergy and parasitic nobles, in any vital sense, a homeland. Such persons merely resided in the nation without making any active contribution to the life of the organization or helping to advance its initial purpose. The implicit social pact demanded from both the State and the citizen an equal interchange of advantages and services. This equitable balance, the French philosopher insisted, should be preserved by the sovereign.

The tragedy of France under the Bourbons lay in the fact that the royal authority, which constituted the State, failed to support the interests of the vast majority of Frenchmen. Thus, instead of adhering to the accepted though outworn conception of patriotism as devotion to a ruling house, Voltaire pledged his lifelong allegiance to the rights of the people, to the principles which advanced their welfare. Once these principles ruled the nation, he felt persuaded that the tie of unity would be not compulsion but willing allegiance. Then public spirit and love of country would overcome local and private concerns.

His mature conception of a homeland included both the State and the land assigned to an individual by fate or history. In nearly all his major writings from the *Henriade* to the *Philosophic Dictionary,* he spoke of *la patrie* not as the provinces and classes subject to a single crown, but as a vast community of men, living in the land of their forefathers in spiritual contentment and in full enjoyment of their "natural rights." Only under such conditions could France become for Frenchmen the hearth of their human liberties or could an individual be said to have, in the classical liberal sense, a homeland or *patrie*.

Voltaire, like the authors of the Declaration of the Rights of Man and the makers of the American Constitution, looked unfailingly upon the individual as the unit of social organization. Yet for this same reason the fact of civilization seemed to him a paradox. The need to preserve their fundamental liberties as members of the human species had originally caused individuals to assemble in communities. Yet to the problem of man's dependence and personal inequality, society had been able to find no other answer than servitude.

Thus the aim of statecraft should be to regain for all citizens as much of their elementary birthright of liberty and equality as can be attained without severing or unduly straining those ties of interdependence which bind men together in the nation. Though in eighteenth-century France the ideal of equality of opportunity was hardly formulated, Voltaire worked unceasingly to further every condition which pointed the way toward this ultimate democratic goal. The social order he would construct so that individual talents could develop freely and productively, unhindered by the insuperable obstacles to self-realization imposed by superstition, arbitrary convention, or the unjust "right of the strongest." Then, if the individual would enormously profit, so, he believed, would the State; for the more abundantly the citizen contributes to the civilization of his country, the more the nation thrives and flourishes. The greater the benefits and services exchanged between the State and the citizen, the more successful is their political partnership.

The French philosopher therefore esteemed the republic as the most "natural" and "ideal" form of government. For such a self-governing people's state would give fullest expression to the fundamental equality of all men as members of the human species. A republic, as a perfect fusion of particular self-interest with the general public interest, would, he maintained, grow strong with the vigor of a liberated people, and, if successfully administered, gain through its citizens considerable wealth and power.

Nevertheless, while Voltaire admitted the logical and theoretical perfection of republican government, a true republic, he was well aware, could function only in Utopia. Nonexistent in eighteenth-century France were the education, equipment, or experience required for any form of self-government; and much less the integrity or will to keep self-interest enlightened. The mass of the French population consisted of miserable artisans and peasants as illiterate, inarticulate, and driven as the beasts they tended. The mere thought of foisting governmental responsibilities on men like these would have been regarded by all classes alike as not only dangerous but ludicrous.

In the face of these circumstances, the French thinker proceeded toward his ultimate democratic objectives not as a radical egalitarian, but by the safer more indirect path of liberalism. He felt persuaded that conditions pointing toward freedom and equality of opportunity could be best brought about through a wise application of the major liberal principles. These liberal principles he looked upon as the political expression of "natural rights," and he believed that they could be most successfully enforced by constitutional monarchy.

British constitutional monarchy Voltaire considered the form of government most trustworthy. For, in this land across the channel, the monarch ruled not by his "good pleasure," but according to a body of law as the First Magistrate of his people. The laws of the British constitution were designed to render inviolate the "natural rights" of each individual, in whatever his social sphere. Through relatively effective organs of representation the average citizen had a voice in those matters which vitally concerned him, such as, for example, taxation, and under the impartial, competent guidance of the king, both the nobles and the people would strive to reconcile their opposing interests for the sake of the common good.

The British system, nevertheless, could provide no conditions even approaching the democratic ideal of equality of opportunity. Yet this government which Voltaire called "royalist-republican," still managed to uphold a strict legal equality. To the author of the *Philosophic Letters,* legal equality signified the political recognition of all men as members of the human family and their equal claim to the rights and privileges of man's estate. Laws in relation to which master and servant stood as equals he regarded as the cornerstone of mutual protection in society and the first essential step toward the attainment of that larger measure of equality implied in true democracy. Imperfect as was British constitutional monarchy, the individual received from this system more liberty and justice than could be had from any other government known to Europe in the Age of Enlightenment.

In France, constitutional monarchy was not even a possibility. For French monarchs ruled by an authority which, with no irreverence intended, was generally known as "divine right." The Church and State were one. As a result, the abuses of the State would often receive sanction by the ecclesiastical order, while the ecclesiastical conscience remained likewise subject to all the pressures of lay politics. The union of the spiritual and temporal powers made the criticism of either governing body an official impossibility, and such "natural rights" as free speech and religious tolerance a matter for social abhorrence. Thus in his fight for liberal and democratic principles, Voltaire went fearlessly to the heart of the whole problem and struck his major blows for the separation of Church and State.

He argued that the nation, as an organization originally designed to meet the earthly need for happiness and security was an inherently lay institution. Therefore the temporal human dealings of the citizens with each other, such as the disposal of the revenue from land, marriage, the days set aside for devotional purposes and the conditions under which an individual should be allowed to enter monastic orders, ought all to come under the aegis of the State.

Education, likewise, should be lay and national. The young ought not to be handed over to priests who might unduly bind them to a supernatural authority, indifferent or hostile to all terrestrial progress. Youth should be trained by learned laymen to become citizens valuable to the national organization and as such capable of raising the standard of civilization within their native country.

Voltaire insisted that by virtue of the implicit pact which underlies all organized society, the first duty of an ecclesiast was to the nation. Accordingly reason and "natural law" decreed that the Church should be subservient to the State. The complete subjection of French Catholicism to Roman ecclesiastical domination was, in his eyes, incompatible with the rightful position of the Church as an adjunct of the civil power. So his writings consistently plead for Gallicanism and all the traditional liberties of the Gallican Church. He also argued that as members of the State and subjects of the king, the clergy should share the expenses of the nation, and in a measure befitting their wealth and eminence.

In his opinion, the true function of the Church should be to help the State accomplish its original purpose, which was the common good. The clergy should act as a sort of moral police force to the populace and urge the citizens to upright actions. While the State exists to defend men's rights, the Church, in its separate sphere, should inspire all classes to the willing fulfillment of their obligations, for every right, of necessity, entails an obligation. If rights are fulfilled, so also must be obligations.

Thus, from a rival and usurper of the civil power, Voltaire would change the status of the Church to an important and indispensable adjunct to the temporal authority. Yet such a transformation, he believed, could be brought about only by breaking the hold of superstition and fanaticism on the minds of the ruling class.

Charged with this conviction, the object to which he devoted the major energies of his long lifetime was religious tolerance. The liberty to profess in peace the religion of one's choice was regarded by the French thinker as the key to civilized living. This fundamental freedom was sanctioned by "natural right" and by a respect for the moral dignity of man.

Nevertheless, when a given sect provokes or abets socially undesirable actions or sedition, religious tolerance should, he maintained, under these special circumstances, be restricted. In his eyes, the highest law in the land was the public welfare, and the principle of tolerance was important only as it contributed to this end. This same point of view was upheld by the French *Declaration of the Rights of Man* of 1789 and by the American Constitution.

As a realist striving for the betterment of his superstition-ridden country, Voltaire made no outright appeal for the democratic concept of religious tolerance. Rather than equal recognition by law of all religions, he pleaded first and most urgently for the merely liberal principle of the toleration of all sects within the boundaries of the State. Such a degree of toleration he had seen successfully practiced in England. Though freedom of worship was actually established and enforced, honors and important positions were barred to all those who refused to profess the Anglican faith, an argument in favor of the official religion which, the French philosopher observed, made more converts than coercion or persecution.

His life and correspondence prove that his desire and ultimate hope was for the fullest possible measure of tolerance. Yet to express this wish in his *Treatise on Tolerance* he knew would weaken his case. Had he done so the combined powers of Church and State would have denounced such a proposal as anarchic, criminal, and destructive.

Instead, Voltaire saw more chances of success in demanding

for France at least as much religious tolerance as he had seen in highly workable effect in England, the mightiest state in Europe. As a liberal and a progressive, he believed that the winning of this mere toleration would prove an indispensable first step toward that greater democratic tolerance he desired.

Freedom of speech and press, like religious tolerance, was another invaluable safeguard of individual liberty. The right of the citizen to criticize, by word of mouth or on the printed page, his government, an organization originally founded to advance his interests, the French philosopher upheld as one of the inalienable rights of man. Still, he maintained that just as laws exist to protect the individual against wilfully malicious libel or slander, the State was likewise entitled to defend itself against overt appeals in print for the violent overthrow of the government.

The constructive criticism of public affairs and existing conditions within the nation could not fail to prove of benefit to the entire organization. Yet, as Voltaire remained lastingly convinced, no problems and conflicts could ever be solved by violence. Therefore he believed that in the public interest some legal restrictions should be placed on the liberty of the press to prevent the misuse of this right by heedless revolutionaries. Some such restrictions have been found essential in nearly every nation.

As regards economics, his policy was also one of liberalism. He stood firmly for free trade within the nation, and looked forward eagerly to a day when this principle could be applied to the international sphere. He likewise pleaded for the right of the worker to choose his conditions of labor. For this reason he applauded the destruction of those *maîtrises* and *jurandes* which fettered industry and kept the artisans in financial bondage to cruel tax-masters.

Voltaire felt persuaded that equality, in any democratic sense, could be most safely attained through the progressive liberation of social classes from ignorance and economic bondage. Since by historical determinism, the bourgeois had arrived first on the threshold of enlightenment, he considered this class the first in line to be educated. The wide-scale education of that third estate which acted as a lever in French society he viewed as a great national enterprise. To the eighteenth-century French thinker, the enlightenment of the middle class was the first advance toward the enlightenment of the people. By their educated example they could place the footsteps of the superstition-bound workers on the path of reason, tolerance, and humanity.

For the peasants and artisans, the French philosopher advocated just as much education as they could reasonably profit by and still maintain that labor on which the social structure depended. Such a degree of education he knew would be very slight. When, as in Geneva, he found that the learning of the watchmakers in no way injured their efficiency at their trade or ill-adapted them to life in their inescapable environment, he rejoiced. Experience then proved that more enlightenment for the people was compatible with the common good than he had at first suspected. In the light of this firsthand observation, he himself established a school for laborers' children at Ferney.

In general, though, he did not urge the direct or immediate emancipation of the proletariat masses from illiteracy and superstition. He feared that any wide-spread or extensive schooling would leave the people without moral anchorage. For their code of ethics, such as it was, rested solely on superstition. Furthermore, he inclined to the opinion that without offering the working class any new opportunities, their learned pursuits might render them failures at their bread-winning occupations.

He concluded that the intellectual state of the people could not be much improved until their material lot was alleviated. For this reason he battled so long and fiercely against feudal privilege. In his opinion, the ethical and patriotic duty of the first two estates of French society was to rescue the majority of their compatriots from a weight of taxation which was grinding them down to near-starvation and condemning them to perpetual ignorance. Not until this vital victory was won could the initial pact between the State and the citizen come anywhere near fulfillment.

Within the nation, all human dealings Voltaire would see governed by enlightened self-interest. This same delicate balance between egotism and altruism, he hoped, might eventually control relations between foreign powers. Since, to his way of thinking, all sovereign states are founded on human convenience, nations the world over are logically and inescapably committed to one and the same purpose. This fundamental purpose is the advancement of humanity.

Therefore, all attempts at national domination by military conquest Voltaire denounced as a sanguinary abomination and a crime far worse than highway robbery on the individual scale. Such efforts to rule by brute force were alike contrary to the Christian brotherhood of man and to the "natural law" which governs the universe. For this Divine Reason commands that the problems arising from human interdependence be solved in accordance with the Golden Rule.

The flouting of this principle was judged by the French philosopher as a wilfull denial of the ethical insight with which man has been endowed by the Supreme Being. Unfailingly he insisted that any such denial of the progressive instincts inherent in human nature must inevitably condemn mankind to primeval chaos and unending struggle on the brute level. In the increasing perfection of military weapons and the spread of war to distant colonial outposts in other hemispheres, the eighteenth-century thinker saw, if not an actual threat to civilization, at least a phenomenon of the most ominous possibilities.

Furthermore he looked upon the long dynastic conflicts which tore Europe in the seventeenth and eighteenth centuries as not only unethical and unreasonable but exceedingly unprofitable. The annexation of territory captured by military violence could offer the citizens of the aggressor state no material advantages whatsoever. While in the classical world, conquest meant the appropriation by the victors of the spoils and resources of the vanquished, in the modern world, conquest, in most cases, meant nothing more than a formal rounding out of national boundaries to include some insignificant province or seaport. This materialistic argument Voltaire used to impress ambitious sovereigns.

Nevertheless, despite his contempt for violence as a way to solve problems, the French philosopher readily admitted that liberty can not survive without force to defend it. In the article "Venice" of the *Philosophic Dictionary* he declared that all charters which defined and guaranteed "natural rights" had been signed at the point of the sword; that no nation could remain free without the means and the courage to withhold the usurper. In his *Century of Louis XIV* he paid full tribute to the soldier for his heroism and self-sacrifice. Nor did he minimize the glory won by Louis XIV and Charles XII in their grandiose and senseless campaigns. This indeed was *la gloire,* though of an undesirable type.

Since the "right of the strongest" was so much easier to apply than the stern law of reason, Voltaire looked upon war as an inescapable condition of existence. Yet he saw no sense in that "preventive" war so rashly counselled by Montesquieu. The idea of attacking to prevent being attacked seemed to the author of *Candide* like the lowest form of international hypocrisy. For, while attempting to protect his homeland, Montesquieu would make of his nation the aggressor.

Instead of risking national ruin by what may be best described as a "war to begin wars," Voltaire appealed to statesmen to meet any implicit threat by peaceful means. If the neighboring nation owed its might to the skillful exploitation of national resources, to extensive arming, or to a sagacious choice of alliances, it remained only for the homeland to follow this example.

The leader of eighteenth-century Enlightenment would stop the wars which in his eyes were a senseless fratricide between the sons of Europe. This he believed could best be done by maintaining that precarious equilibrium between jealous hostile nations generally referred to as the "balance of power." Such a known agreement among sovereign states often served as a powerful deterrent to a would-be conqueror. For whenever the international balance was threatened, an armed coalition could be counted upon to resist his aggression.

Only thus Voltaire believed could there be won a few years of peace on the continent. For such a system of mutual protection between nations was based on reason and enlightened self-interest. In compliance with this rule, all states were obliged, to some extent, to reconcile their differences and bring their national interests into harmony with those of the European community as a whole. A patriot who was also a philosopher would want his own particular nation to be of a size and a strength to aid and not upset the general balance and stability. Imperfect as were the results of such moves toward international cooperation, the effort in itself was a signpost toward progress.

If Voltaire condemned any advancement of his country by armed force, in economic power and cultural supremacy he beheld the sole legitimate means of national domination. Unlike the external, artificial aggrandizement brought about by military conquest, economic strength was a product of that superabundance of national vitality resulting from a fulfillment of the social contract. The wealth of the nation, he argued, depends on population, on the skilled utilization of human ability, on the development of natural resources, on the intelligent coordination of agriculture, manufacture, industry, and commerce. These key factors in the life of the State are inseparably related to individual happiness.

While economic power results from the robustness of the political organization, cultural supremacy, the French thinker believed, was the infallible mark of the greatness of a people and a reliable indication of their spiritual strength. Nevertheless, as a poet who had come of age during the reign of the Sun King, he remained lastingly persuaded that genius does not bloom unaided or untended. The encouragement of a discerning monarch is needed, as is also a minister of finance whose economy and efficiency place at the disposal of the monarch a full national treasury.

True to this belief, Voltaire honored Louis XIV and his minister, Colbert, as at once the authors and architects of his country's greatness. His delight in that superb flowering of French art and science—which he credited his king and his minister with having summoned into existence, often blinded him to their antihumanitarian policy toward foreign states. Above all, a cultural patriot, the author of the *Century of Louis XIV* desired for his country artistic eminence. A national glory won by art and culture would not bring ruin to foreign lands, but contribute to their ultimate enrichment. For outstanding cultural achievements are expressive of *l'esprit humain* and, as such, the enjoyment of them belongs to the world.

In his theories on the relations of his country with foreign powers, Voltaire was always guided by two all-important considerations. The first of these was the peace and welfare of Europe; the second was the advancement of *la patrie*.

Free trade he regarded as an expression of that great "natural law" which commands that, in their pursuit of happiness, men offer each other mutual assistance. With Turgot and the Physiocrats he stood for the free exchange of commodities within the nation and, like these thinkers, he hoped for a day when the natural forces of supply and demand would be allowed to operate freely and unrestrictedly between foreign powers.

In the world market, though, trade barriers remained an ever prevalent reality. So Voltaire accepted the moderate protection of national industries as a matter of course. Exports, he maintained, should exceed imports, and imports should be severely taxed. For the immediate welfare of the nation such measures were indispensable.

A similar effort to balance patriotic and international interests is evident in his attitude toward the extension of national influence overseas. The potential value of certain colonies he estimated as high. Yet bold words from his pen called attention to the fact that these distant dependencies were costly, ruinously administered, and defensible only by continual warfare. Such outposts, he warned, were frequently maintained at the price of the public welfare at home, and by the violation of men's rights abroad. For the cultivation of these lands depended on slave labor.

Nevertheless the race for colonies was on, and the Far Eastern trade had become a powerful factor in the economic life of Europe. In this international competition he hated to see his native France the loser.

The philosopher who answered life's complexities with the words "We must cultivate our garden," held to the belief that the national garden could be best tended on home soil and within hereditary confines. The economic power of the State, he maintained, would reach its culmination when every available field in France was reclaimed for productivity and made to contribute to the support of French citizens. Such an aim would be furthered by an ever increasing population, and when free peasant proprietors cultivated their land with a patience and ardor born of ownership. In the English middle-class motto of "Liberty and Property," the author of *Candide* recognized a "cry of nature," indeed the irresistible demand of mankind for earthly happiness.

By his lifelong effort to improve the French state, advance French culture, and make France a safer and freer abode for Frenchmen, Voltaire stands revealed as a great humanitarian patriot. As Professor Carlton Hayes has stated in the *Historical Evolution of Modern Nationalism,* humanitarian patriotism was the earliest expression of the nationalist idea in the era before the French Revolution, and claimed such advocates throughout Europe as the English Bolingbroke, the Genevan Rousseau, and the German Herder. These thinkers believed that the prime duty of mankind is service to humanity. Yet this obligation can be best fulfilled by an effort to perfect human conditions within the framework of a given nation. Humanity, though, should always come first in the hierarchy of man's loyalties, and the interests of nations should be made to conform to the interests and welfare of that larger country, the world. His life, his writings and his intimate correspondence all prove that Voltaire should be classed with such patriots as these.

The cosmopolitan, humanitarian, patriotism of Voltaire offers an example of how reason and sentiment can function together in their separate spheres, yet in constructive harmony. Reason persuaded him that all nations can have but one legitimate aim— world progress, humanity. Therefore the organizing of an impartial State, based on universally applicable principles of justice in human relations, is less a national issue than an ethical obligation toward mankind. "Natural rights" represent the invariable claims of reason and humanity. Yet, as the eighteenth-century thinker believed, these universal liberties can be best enforced by men who feel a pride and pleasure in their homeland—leaders like Henri IV, whose will was sustained by a disinterested love of country.

This love of country, though, could not be artificially generated. So public glorification of a "divine right" monarch, patriotic spectacles, or uncritical worship of national heroes were powerless and puerile means to serve this end.

Instead, the author of the *Henriade* remained persuaded that the more the State succeeds in bettering the lot of the citizen, the stronger becomes the citizen's attachment to his homeland, and as national sentiment increases, the more the individual, in his turn, will strive to raise the material and intellectual standard within his native land.

Accordingly Voltaire would have had scant sympathy with that philosophy of modern nationalism which Professor Carlton Hayes defined as "the paramount devotion of human beings to fairly large nationalities and the conscious founding of a political nation on linguistic and cultural nationality." To the eighteenth-century skeptic, nationality or the bond between individuals who speak the same language and possess in common the same culture, mores, history, and traditions would have seemed an insufficient basis for social union. For the State, as he conceived it, was an association which men entered and participated in by free consent and by spontaneous preference. They were not assigned to it by such historical factors outside their control as race or geography. National character and its distinguishing features he viewed as matters of habit, inheritance, or private predilection. As such, they should have no bearing on the impartial fulfillment of the implicit social agreement between the citizen and the State.

The France known to Voltaire was by no means strictly national. For about five hundred years French kings had extended their sway over Bretons, Burgundians, Gascons, Bearnais, and other minor nationalities, each with their own particular *patois* and folkways. Yet into this conglomerate mass the French philosopher would bring uniformity by laws based on "natural law." To these diverse peoples cowering under the Bourbon scepter he would bring unity and solidarity by a monarchical government identified with their interests, which they could trust and to which they could give their active allegiance. He contributed to nationalist philosophy by advancing the belief that a man should depend for his well-being, the possession of his rights, his hope of self-improvement, not on God, the king, or his class, but on his nation, *la patrie*. Such a lifework, though, was animated by a deeply personal source of inspiration. This inspiration was his devotion to all that made up the dominant French nationality.

The love of Voltaire for his native France was not primarily territorial. The advancement of his principles for the State and his genius for quarreling often and inevitably drove him to seek refuge outside his national boundaries. Yet on foreign soil he found his permanent consolation in serving the French language, in advancing French culture, and in enjoying Parisian society far from his home capital. In England, his effort to endow France with a corrected and embellished edition of his national epic poem consoled him for his banishment from Paris, just as years later, work on his magnificent *Century of Louis XIV* cheered and sustained him throughout the trials of his semi-compulsory stay with Frederick the Great. Shakespeare he enjoyed as no detached "amateur" of "belles-lettres." Just as Louis XIV and Colbert had exploited foreign artists for the greater glory of the French kingdom, Voltaire meant to use the Bard as a means of instructing his compatriots on how to inject fire and action into their dramas. With artistic secrets stolen from the curious English poet, he would add to the already excellent French literary tradition a few new ornaments.

Though he felt no deep, instinctive bond with the soil of his native country, there are incredibly few instances when Voltaire left France voluntarily. Even then, as in 1722, when he chose of his own free will to take a trip to Holland, he started forth not to observe a foreign nation. He went—alas—to visit Jean-Baptiste Rousseau, a great French poet he had once claimed as his "master," and also to consider a Dutch printing of the *Henriade*. Parisian society he took with him in the person of Mme de Rumpelmonde.

Similarly, years later, when not fear of the censors but the Du Châtelet lawsuit dragged him to Brussels, he grumbled but made the best of it. He called this city "the land of insipidity," and for intellectuals at once an inferno and a limbo. Yet he enjoyed French wit and urbanity at its best in the company of Mme du Châtelet.

Again at Lunéville, with Stanislaus, the dethroned king of Poland (where he went to show off to Versailles how well he stood with King Louis's father-in-law), at Potsdam where he labored to win for his nation's Hall of Poetic Fame a king of the Vandals, he found French society, French culture, French amusements, and French intrigue. Dearer to him than the soil of France was the spiritual atmosphere of his native country.

In any people the feeling of nationality arises through the memories which they share of a common past and, at the same time, through their expectations of sharing together, as a group, one and the same future. This sentiment, which indeed existed in eighteenth-century France, Voltaire felt to a marked degree. In the *Henriade* he reminded his compatriots of the triumphs for peace and liberalism which a national hero had once won for French citizens. In the *Century of Louis XIV* he strove to inspire Frenchmen to new levels of attainment by tabulating for them the great national achievements of the preceding century, when under the competent direction of the Sun King French genius had flowered. In spite of all her errors, frivolities, and corruptions, he believed in the essential greatness of his nation, in her unconquerable vitality, and in her great civilizing role in Europe and the world. He looked upon *la patrie* as morally and even materially indestructible. Despite their many reverses he had faith in the inherent soundness of the French people, in their ability to emerge triumphantly even after the most formidable blows.

France he described as a "patient" with an excellent constitution. When, during the Seven Years' War, prophets of evil announced to him that the House of Austria was becoming all powerful, and that France accordingly was doomed, his profound trust in the national character assured him of the contrary. "Well, Sirs," he replied, "an archduke captured Amiens, Charles V reached Compiègne, Henry V, King of England, was even crowned in Paris. Do not worry! You need not fear the eclipse of France, whatever blunder she might make."

# Notes

ALL REFERENCES to Voltaire's writings are to the Moland edition of his complete works (see Bibliography) unless expressly stated otherwise.

## INTRODUCTION

1. Bellesssort, *Essai sur Voltaire,* p. 2.
2. Brunetière, *Voltaire,* p. 1.
3. Faguet, *La Politique comparée,* pp. 6-7.
4. Brunetière, *Discours,* I, 156.
5. Cornou, *Trente années de luttes,* p. 128. "Monarchiste par principe, il [Fréron] a la raison-d'être du monarchiste, le patriotisme, sentiment qu'ignorera toujours Voltaire et que méconnaîtront fréquemment à sa suite ses lieutenants et ses amis."
6. Champion, *Voltaire,* pp. 125-138.
7. Aulard, *Patriotisme français,* p. 63.
8. Seligman and Johnson, *Encyclopedia of the Social Sciences,* XII, 26.
9. Voltaire, I, 236.
10. Voltaire, I, XLIV (Jugements sur Voltaire).
11. Voltaire, I, XLIX (Jugements sur Voltaire).
12. Chateaubriand, *Le Génie,* I, 191: "Il est très décidé en faveur de l'ordre social sans s'apercevoir qu'il le sape par les fondements en attaquant l'ordre religieux. Ce qu'on peut dire sur lui de plus raisonnable, c'est que son incrédulité l'a empêché d'atteindre à la hauteur où l'appelait la nature, et que ses ouvrages, excepté ses poésies fugitives, sont demeurés au dessous de son véritable talent."
13. Chateaubriand, *Le Génie,* I, 137-44.

14. Lamartine, *Histoire des Girondins,* I, 15: "Ce que le Christianisme appelait révélation, la philosophie l'appelait raison. Les mots étaient différents, le sens était le même. L'émancipation des individus, des castes, des peuples, en dérivait également. . . . La philosophie politique de la Révolution n'avait pas même pu inventer un mot plus vrai, plus complet et plus divin que le Christianisme pour se révéler à l'Europe, et elle avait adopté le dogme et le mot de fraternité."

15. Lamartine, *Histoire des Girondins,* I, 21.

16. Voltaire, I, LIII (Jugements sur Voltaire).

17. Thibaudet, *Histoire de la littérature française,* p. 273.

18. Michelet, *Histoire de la Révolution française,* I, 80-81: "J'entends ce mot sortir des entrailles de l'ancienne France, mot tendre, d'accent profond: 'Mon roi!'—C'est ici un trait singulier de la France. Ce peuple n'a compris longtemps la politique que comme dévouement et amour."

19. Voltaire, I, LIV-LV (Jugements sur Voltaire).

20. Taine, *Origines de la France contemporaine,* I, 221, 222, 240.

21. Taine, *Origines,* I, 221-328.

22. Taine, *Origines,* I, 347.

23. Taine, *Origines,* I, 347-48.

24. Taine, *Histoire de la littérature anglaise,* I, XXIII.

25. Cf. Hayes, *Historical Evolution,* pp. 182-83.

26. Thibaudet, *Histoire de la littérature française,* pp. 417-21.

27. Renan, *Oeuvres,* I, 903-04: "Une nation est une âme, un principe spirituel. Deux choses qui, à vrai dire, n'en font qu'une constituent cette âme, ce principe spirituel. L'Une est dans le passé, l'autre dans le présent. L'Une est la possession en commun d'un riche legs de souvenirs; l'autre est le consentement actuel, le désir de vivre ensemble, la volonté de continuer à faire valoir l'héritage qu'on a reçu indivis."

28. Renan, *Oeuvres,* I, 905: "Les nations ne sont pas quelque chose d'éternel. Elles ont commencé, elles finiront. La confédération européenne probablement les remplacera." Brunetière's lecture, "L'Idée de patrie" of 1896 later reprinted in the volumes of his *Discours de combat,* is almost entirely a refutation of Renan's lecture of 1882. He declares: "Renan qui pendant trente ans, avait enseigné que l'observation de la loi morale ne va pas sans une singulière

étroitesse d'esprit, et que le plus grand saint n'est, après tout, qu'un assez pauvre homme; Renan dont toute la religiosité tant vantée n'a consisté qu'à faire des oraisons jaculatoires au néant; Renan a bien vu qu'il entrainait l'idée de patrie dans la ruine commune de la religion et de la morale." I, 155.

29. Brunetière, *Discours*, I, 127.

30. Brunetière, *Discours*, I, 128.

31. Brunetière, *Discours*, I, 127: "Ni la nature ni l'histoire, à mon avis du moins, n'ont en effet voulu que les hommes fussent tous frères.

32. Brunetière, *Discours*, I, 150.

33. Brunetière, *Discours*, I, 156.

34. Brunetière, *Discours*, I, 157.

THE BOND WITH *La Patrie*

1. Voltaire, XVI, 493; XX, 182-83.

2. Voltaire, XX, 182: "Tout ce qui n'est pas cette habitation d'hommes n'est-il pas quelquefois une écurie de chevaux sous un palefrenier qui leur donne à son gré des coups de fouet? On a une patrie sous un bon roi; on n'en a point sous un méchant."

3. Foulet, *Correspondance de Voltaire, 1726-1729*, p. 61.

4. As early as 1740 Voltaire stood for the right of the individual to choose *la patrie*. To Maupertuis then called to the court of Frederick the Great he wrote, XXXV, 486: "Si vous aviez à vous plaindre de votre patrie, vous feriez très bien d'en accepter une autre."

5. Voltaire, IV, 110.

6. Voltaire's love for Paris and also his habitual exasperation with this city for proving too exciting for his nervous temperament is well illustrated in the following poem of his youth, XXXIII, 37.

> Revoyez la ville chérie
> Où Venus a fixé sa cour
> Est-il pour vous d'autre patrie?
> Et serait-il dans l'autre vie
> Un plus beau ciel, un plus beau jour
> S'i l'on pouvait de ce séjour
> Exiler la Tracasserie?

7. Sée, *Idées politiques*, p. 83.

8. Voltaire, XXIII, 502.

9. Voltaire, XX, 181-82.

10. Lanson, *Voltaire,* p. 10: "Ainsi sans sortir du logis paternel l'enfant qui devait être Voltaire mettait le pied dans trois mondes: celui des grands seigneurs, celui de la noblesse parlementaire et celui des gens de lettres."

11. Lanson, *Voltaire,* p. 11, states of the Jesuits' religious education: ". . . là où ils ne plantaient pas la foi obéissante qui ne raisonne pas, le fondement de la morale manquait; il ne restait que des habitudes de complaisance au monde, de compromis avec les moeurs du siècle et les tentations intérieures, toute cette pratique relâchée dont leur adroite religion savait faire un pieux usage, à la gloire de Dieu et au profit de l'église."

12. Martin, *French Liberal Thought,* p. 27: ". . . it is reported that Louis in the midst of the defeats of the War of the Spanish Succession cried, 'The Lord might have remembered what I have done for him.' "

13. Lanson, *Voltaire,* pp. 11-12.

14. Voltaire, XI, 112.

15. Voltaire, XVII, 32; XX, 107.

16. Voltaire himself acknowledged his lasting cultural debt to the Jesuits and remained friendly with them for over thirty years. He broke with them only in 1759 when Jesuit agitation in the *Journal de Trévoux* brought about the suppression of vols. I-VII of Diderot's *Encyclopédie,* chief organ of eighteenth-century enlightenment. Cf. Desnoiresterres, *Voltaire et la société,* V, 412-13.

17. Voltaire, VII, 334.

18. Desnoiresterres, *Voltaire et la société,* I, 48, states that Voltaire's father intended to buy him a parliamentary office. Yet the thinker who was to devote so much of his life to a campaign against the venality of these judgeships refused. True to his later convictions, the young man replied: "Dites à mon père que je ne veux point d'une considération qui s'achète, je saurai m'en faire une qui ne coûte rien."

19. Lanson, *Voltaire,* p. 9: "L'amour des lettres est une partie de la politesse, M. Jourdain et Turcaret se dégrossissent."

20. Torrey, *Spirit of Voltaire,* pp. 17-20.

21. Desnoiresterres, *Voltaire et la société,* I, 91. Tallentyre, *Life of*

*Voltaire*, p. 8, states that Abbé Chaulieu drew a revenue of thirty thousand francs from his benefices to pay for his excesses.

22. Hazard, *La Crise de la conscience européenne*, I, 169-70.
23. Voltaire, X, 221.
24. Cf. Torrey, *The Spirit of Voltaire*, "Voltaire and Humanism," pp. 261-84.
25. Tallentyre, *Life of Voltaire*, p. 21.
26. Chase, *The Young Voltaire*, p. 37.
27. Chase, *The Young Voltaire*, pp. 42-43.
28. Desnoiresterres, *Voltaire et la société*, I, 157.
29. In a letter to Mme de Mimeure he petulantly confided, XXXIII, 35: "Il serait délicieux pour moi de rester à Sully s'il m'était permis d'en sortir."
30. Voltaire, XXXIII, 54.
31. Voltaire, XXXIII, 149.
32. Desnoiresterres, *Voltaire et la société*, I, 356, reproduces the account of the Rohan affair as written up by the Maréchal de Villars, who severely blamed Rohan for having committed a crime punishable by death, ". . . en faisant battre un citoyen" and likewise blamed the government for not having punished this ill deed. Desnoiresterres states, "Cela mérite bien d'être signalé à cette date [the sympathy of a "grand seigneur" for a commoner], ainsi que le mot de citoyen, ce mot terrible, qui soixante-quinze ans plus tard retentira dans toute la France et sera la seule appellation du Français affranchi."
33. Voltaire, I, 308, Letter of Maurepas to de Launay. Desnoiresterres, *Voltaire et la société*, I, 360-61.
34. Voltaire, *Lettres Philosophiques* (Lanson), I, 106.
35. Voltaire, *Lettres philosophiques* (Lanson), I, 103.
36. Voltaire, *Lettres philosophiques* (Lanson), I, 91.
37. Voltaire, *Lettres philosophiques* (Lanson), I, 107.
38. Voltaire, XIX, 296.
39. Voltaire, *Lettres philosophiques* (Lanson), I, 122.
40. Chase, *The Young Voltaire*, pp. 159-60.
41. Foulet, *Correspondance de Voltaire*, p. 61.
42. Cf. Chase, *The Young Voltaire*, p. 119.
43. Chase, *The Young Voltaire*, pp. 159-60.
44. Voltaire, XLI, 91, 92.
45. Voltaire, IV, 502; II, 316-18.

46. Voltaire, VIII, 353.

47. Voltaire, VIII, 357.

48. White, *Voltaire's Essay on Epic Poetry,* pp. 82-83.

49. Naves, *Le Goût de Voltaire,* p. 495, states that Voltaire had slight interest in his own posthumous reputation. He wanted to succeed with his age and nation. Says Naves: ". . . cette société ne laisse pas d'être éphémère et bornée; au dessus d'elle, il y a son propre idéal, et aussi un idéal plus large, qui admet certains apports de l'humanisme et du cosmopolitisme; le vrai goût sera donc, non seulement un choix capable de plaire, mais un choix qui puisse concilier les grandes aspirations de l'humanité civilisée."

50. White, *Voltaire's Essay on Epic Poetry,* p. 135.

51. Voltaire, II, 314.

52. Voltaire, IV, 502.

53. Foulet, *Correspondance de Voltaire,* p. 176: ". . . écrivez-moi, je vous prie, plus souvent que je ne vous écris. Je vis dans une retraite dont je n'ai rien à vous mander, au lieu que vous êtes dans Paris où vous voyez tous les jours des folies nouvelles qui peuvent réjouir votre pauvre ami assez malheureux pour n'en plus faire."

54. Voltaire, X, 85.

55. This account of Voltaire's relations with Frederick the Great is based for the most part on Desnoiresterres, *Voltaire et la société,* II, III, IV; and on Tallentyre, *Life of Voltaire;* also Henriot, *Voltaire et Frédéric II.*

56. Voltaire, XXXIV, 107.

57. Cf. Voltaire, XLIII, 175.

58. Voltaire, XXXV, 354.

59. Voltaire, XXXVI, 27.

60. Voltaire, XXXVI, 35.

61. Voltaire, XXXVI, 28-29.

62. Dorn, *Competition for Empire,* pp. 142-47.

63. Dorn, *Competition for Empire,* p. 142.

64. Cf. Caussy, "Mission diplomatique de Voltaire," LXV, 551-52. Also "Lettres secrètes," LXV, 673-96.

65. Caussy, "Mission diplomatique de Voltaire," LXV, 551-52, states that the only items Voltaire gathered from secret sources were reports on the financial resources of Holland and news of a loan of

400,000 florins made on the bank of Amsterdam by Frederick the Great. These matters were confided to him by Podewils.

66. To Podewils Voltaire wrote details of the courage, resolution, and efficiency with which the French and Louis XV were carrying on that war with England which Frederick had demanded of them as allies. Cf. Caussy, "Lettres secrètes," LXV, 686, 688.

67. Caussy, "Lettres secrètes," LXV, 688-89.

68. Cf. Desnoiresterres, *Voltaire et la société,* III, 424-25. Cf. Tallentyre, *Life of Voltaire,* pp. 159-63.

69. Voltaire, XXXVI, 344.

70. Voltaire, XXXVI, 357

71. Voltaire, XXXVI, 346.

72. The feeling of excitement and exasperation which court life habitually inspired in Voltaire is well summed up in a letter to Cideville of March, 1742, XXXVI, 120; also, letter to Thiriot of February 27, 1745, XXXVI, 346.

73. Voltaire, XXXVI, 364.

74. Voltaire, XXXVI, 343.

75. Aulard, *Patriotisme français,* p. 16, 111.

76. Voltaire, XXXVI, 143-44; cf. XXXV, 564-65.

77. On September 4, 1749 Frederick the Great had written to Voltaire, XXXVII, 60: "Vous êtes enfin comme l'éléphant blanc pour lequel le roi de Perse et l'empereur du Mogol se font la guerre, et dont ils augmentent leurs titres quand ils sont assez heureux pour le posséder. Adieu, si vous venez ici, vous verrez à la tête des miens; Fédéric, par la grâce de Dieu, roi de Prusse, électeur de Brandebourg, possesseur de Voltaire."

78. Voltaire, XXXVII, 78.

79. Voltaire, XXIII, 468.

80. Voltaire, XXIII, 467.

81. For Voltaire's sentiments on his departure, cf. XXXVII, 135; XXXVII, 120.

82. Voltaire, XXXVII, 154.

83. Voltaire, XXXVII, 161.

84. Voltaire, XXXVII, 161.

85. Sainte-Beuve, *Causeries du lundi,* III, 151: "De la littérature allemande, il en est à peine question avec Frédéric; il en sent très bien

les défauts qui étaient encore sans compensation à cette date, la pesanteur, la diffusion, le morcellement de dialectes, et il indique quelques uns des remèdes. Il présage pourtant à cette littérature nationale de beaux jours, et il prédit: 'Je vous les annonce, ils vont paraître.' "

86. Voltaire, XXXVII, 160-61.

87. Voltaire, XXXVII, 217.

88. Voltaire, XXXVII, 218.

89. In this letter Voltaire begged Richelieu, his former comrade at the Lycée Louis-le-Grand, to use his influence with the king and Mme de Pompadour to make possible his return. Yet at the idea of retirement and the disapproval of his friends and enemies in Paris, he exclaimed, XXXVII, 167: "Mais alors quel triste rôle! Quelle condition équivoque! Quelle dépendence de ceux qui pourront me faire sentir que j'ai eu tort de m'en aller et tort de revenir."

90. Henriot, *Voltaire et Frédéric II*, p. 114, offers the following conclusive evidence of royal guilt in the Frankfurt affair: "Le 14 juillet de cette meme année 1753, Freddersdorf, secrétaire intime et factotum de Fréderic addressait à M. le baron de Freytag, ce satisfecit, où la fourbe royale se découvre: 'Vous avez agi en fidèle serviteur du roi, conformément à ses augustes ordres.' "

91. Voltaire, XXXVII, 192.

92. Without official permission either to return to Paris or remain in Colmar, Voltaire asked D'Argenson to sound the King's indulgence in order to find out if he might travel. Cf. Tallentyre, *Life of Voltaire*, pp. 294-96; also, 60,000 francs of his income came from annuities or bonds on the city of Paris of which the king might deprive him whenever he saw fit.

93. Voltaire, XXXVIII, 195. Also, in an earlier letter Voltaire had declared in a letter to the same Swiss acquaintance (Polier de Bottens) his desire to end his life in a free country, XXXVIII, 165: ". . . sous un gouvernement doux, loin des caprices des rois et des intrigues des cours. J'ai toujours pensé que l'air de Lausanne conviendrait mieux à ma santé que celui d'Angleterre."

94. Voltaire, XXXIX, 47; cf. Chaponnière, *Voltaire chez les Calvinistes*, p. 13.

95. Chaponnière, *Voltaire chez les Calvinistes*, pp. 84-85.

96. Tallentyre, *Life of Voltaire*, p. 337.

97. Voltaire, XXXIX, 549.

98. A letter of December 29, 1760 to his former secretary, Colini (and therefore unmotivated by any desire to impress or dissemble) well attests Voltaire's quiet happiness at Ferney, XLI, 127: "Il faut que je cultive mon petit territoire; j'ai environ deux lieues de pays à gouverner. Les choses sont bien changées de ce que vous les avez vues; je n'ai jamais été si heureux que je la suis, quoique malade et vieux."

99. Lettre à Thiriot, Aux Délices, 24 decembre, 1758, XXXIX, 558: "Vous vous trompez, mon ancien ami, j'ai quatre pattes au lieu de deux. Un pied à Lausanne, dans une très belle maison pour l'hiver; un pied aux Délices, près de Genève, où la bonne compagnie vient me voir: voilà pour les pieds de devant. Ceux de derrière sont à Ferney et dans le comté de Tournay, que j'ai acheté par boil emphy-téotique, du président des Brosses."

100. For the response of Frederick, cf. XLIV, 341-42.

101. Voltaire, XLIV, 358.

102. Voltaire, XLIV, 397.

103. Cf. Desnoiresterres, *Voltaire et la société*, VI, 505-6.

104. Tallentyre, *Life of Voltaire*, 495.

105. Tallentyre, *Life of Voltaire*, p. 493.

106. Caussy, *Voltaire seigneur de village*, pp. 251-53.

107. Cf. Torrey, *Spirit of Voltaire*, p. 201.

108. Torrey, *Spirit of Voltaire*, pp. 201-2.

109. Though as usual Voltaire hoped for the favor of the Court he also showed his usual independence of action. He made a public display of his admiration for Louis XVI's disgraced minister, Turgot. Condorcet claimed that on this last meeting he saw the French philosopher and Turgot fall on each other's neck and that the former cried out emotionally: "Laissez-moi baiser cette main qui a signé le salut du peuple." Desnoiresterres, *Voltaire et la société*, VIII, 277-78.

110. Desnoiresterres, *Voltaire et la société*, VIII, 205. On this last visit to Paris Voltaire received the visit of Benjamin Franklin who brought with him his grandson: "Les deux vieillards s'embrassèrent en pleurant. Franklin présenta alors son petit-fils à l'auteur de *la Henriade*, et lui demanda sa bénédiction pour l'enfant qui se mit à genoux. Le patriarche étendant ses mains sur ce front de quinze ans, lui dit: 'Dieu et la liberté, *God and liberty*, et le serra sur son coeur."

111. L, 383-84.

THE CONCEPT OF *La Patrie*

1. Palmer in his article, "The National Idea in France before the Revolution," I, 101, states that a few conservative patriots did challenge the ideas of the French "philosophes." An adversary of Rousseau defended revealed Christianity in a work which he entitled *Offrande aux autels de la patrie* (1764). In the same year a scholar named Réal completed a work called *La Science du gouvernement* in which he maintained that the French monarchy was the best government in existence. In 1774, the year Louis XVI ascended the throne, there was published at Amsterdam *Discours philosophique et patriotique sur la soumission dans l'ordre politique* by Paumerelle. These conservative writings, to mention only a few, were animated with sincere patriotic feeling.

2. The aim and ideal of the "philosophe" party was to improve the earthly lot of man and to accomplish this end through the medium of the State. Aulard in *Patriotisme français,* pp. 42-64, ranges Montesquieu, Voltaire, Diderot, and Rousseau among the liberal, humanitarian patriots. Hayes in *Historical Evolution,* pp. 22-27, devotes a section to Rousseau as a humanitarian patriot and the intellectual leader who prepared the way for Jacobin nationalism.

3. As early as 1775 Abbé Coyer, a liberal though militant patriot, already showed his awareness of the duties which the nation owes to the individual. In *Dissertation sur la nature du peuple,* he deplored the misery and abasement of the common people, comparing their lot to that of domesticated animals. To remedy this evil he advocated a tax reform by which the *rentiers* who merely consumed without producing and who rendered no service to the State would be more heavily taxed. Cf. Green, *Eighteenth-century France,* pp. 70-110. Convinced that the government of France should uphold the material well-being and interests of the French people, Turgot, spokesman and representative of the "philosophe" party, pleaded with Louis XVI to rid the nation of some of the most flagrant economic abuses resulting from "privilege." Cf. Lavisse, *Histoire de France,* Vol. IX, Part I, pp. 41-51.

4. Bossuet in *Politique tirée,* I, 373, formulated with superb finality the theory of service to the nation under the rule of a "Divine Right" monarch. To the great churchman the king was the

living embodiment of *la patrie*—"tout l'Etat est en la personne du prince." Hence: "Il faut faire concourir ensemble le service qu'on doit au prince et celui qu'on doit à l'Etat comme choses inséparables."

5. Aulard, *Patriotisme français,* p. 16, reminds the reader that Joachim du Bellay in his *Deffence et illustration de la langue française* of 1549 introduced into the French language the warm emotional word "patrie," a word which coincided with a new effort toward French unity. As Aulard declares: "Il exprime aussi une nouvelle manière d'aimer la France, une manière de l'aimer comme les Athéniens aimaient Athénes ou comme les Romains aimaient Rome. L'humanisme restaure en s'appliquant à notre pays, le patriotisme antique, d'où la francisation du mot latin *'patria.'* Ce patri otisme antique à la manière grecque, à la manière romaine, se greffant sur le patriotisme moderne tel qu'il s'était dévelopé en France au XV⁰ siècle, produira le patriotisme de la Révolution française, à la fois national par l'histoire et greco-romain par la tradition de collège."

6. Aulard, *Patriotisme français,* p. 37, declares of the word nation: "C'est au XVIII⁰ siècle que le mot nation est usuellement employé, surtout dans le sens de peuple souverain, voir les remontrances du Parlement; les écrits politiques des philosophes; enfin comme résultat du mouvement pour l'émancipation de la nation, le serment décrété par la Constituante, le 22 decembre 1789: 'La Nation, La Loi, le Roi.' "

7. Voltaire, XIX, 296: "Voice à quoi la législation anglaise est enfin parvenue: à remettre chaque homme dans les droits de la nature dont ils sont dépouillés dans presque toutes les monarchies." For another summing up of the fundamental human liberties, see XXVII, 382.

8. This "natural right" upon which Voltaire expressly insisted, XX, 182-83, was also an inevitable corollary of the doctrine of popular sovereignty so warmly preached by Rousseau in the *Contrat social.* As Hayes asserts in *Historical Evolution,* p. 24: "Just as Rousseau's doctrine provided directly for a determination of the form of government by 'the people,' so it involved indirectly the national self-determination of peoples." Thus leaders of the French Revolution ardently upheld the right of the individual to choose *la patrie.*

9. Voltaire, II, 80. Cf. Voltaire's denial of the possibility that man

could have supernatural perceptions in *Le Traité de métaphysique* of 1734, XXII, 204 ff.

10. Voltaire, II, 93.

11. Voltaire, II, 77. Compare with the following lines from Pierre Corneille, "le Cid," *Oeuvres complètes,* I, 233:

> Mourir pour le pays n'est pas un triste sort:
> C'est s'immortaliser par une belle mort.

or with these lines from Racine, "La Thébaide," *Oeuvres complètes,* I, 439:

> Etéocle: Ce prince le dernier de la race royale
> S'est appliqué des dieux la réponse fatale,
> Et lui-même à la mort il s'est précipité
> De l'amour du pays noblement transporté.

In the above mentioned lines Corneille, Racine and Voltaire all make use of patriotism as a theatrically effective "beau sentiment." All three poets likewise use the word "pays" in the sense of "patrie."

12. Voltaire, II, 77.

13. In such works as *Le Temple du bonheur, Pensées philosophiques,* and *Entretien d'un philosophe avec la Maréchale D.* and other works too numerous to mention, Diderot regarded virtue as meaningful only in the form of service to one's fellow men. In *Dieu et l'Homme of 1771,* IV, 93, he made the following appeal in favor of lay morality: "Ne savez-vous pas que vous voulez être heureux, que les autres ont le même désir que vous; qu'il n'y a de félicité vraie pour vous que par le besoin que vous avez les uns des autres, et que par les secours que vous espérez de vos semblables et qu'ils attendent de vous, que si vous n'êtes pas aimés, estimés, considérés vous serez méprisés et hais; et que l'amour, la considération, l'estime, sont attachés à la bienfaisance. Soyez donc bienfaisant."

14. Voltaire, *Lettres philosophiques* (Lanson), I, 89.

15. Voltaire, VIII, 3. Same observation, though in different words is expressed in first letter to Frederick the Great, XXXIV, 107. The idea that epic poetry should be used to enlighten and elevate royalty had also been widespread in the seventeenth century. Cf. Duchesne, *Histoire des poèmes épiques,* pp. 59-61.

16. Voltaire, X, 243. In 1774 this very same expression was used by Vergennes, Louis XVI's Minister of Foreign Affairs, who, like Turgot, did his utmost to uphold a policy of humanitarian idealism

in dealings with other European nations. Says Aulard, *Patriotisme français,* p. 70: "Il [Vergennes] déclare que Louis XVI n'est pas un roi conquérant mais 'un roi citoyen.' Il ne veut pas accroître la patrie par des annexions violentes."

17. Voltaire, X, 244.

18. Duchesne, *Histoire des poèmes épiques,* p. 34, states that despite popular applause and encouragement, Ronsard, dissatisfied with his own effort, *La Franciade* (1567), left his epic poem unfinished.

Tilley, *From Montaigne to Molière,* pp. 110-11, states that in 1656 there appeared *La Pucelle* by Chapelain. In eighteen months this work went through four French editions and two Dutch ones. Then popular enthusiasm waned. The general public opinion was well expressed by Mme de Longueville: "Cela est parfaitement beau, mais cela est bien ennuyeux."

19. Voltaire, VIII, 254-57.

20. Voltaire, VIII, 43.

21. Hayes, *Historical Evolution,* recognizes in Bolingbroke a founder of modern nationalism, though an exponent of that humanitarian nationalism which he states, p. 17, "was the earliest and for some time the only kind of formal nationalism."

22. Cf. Palmer, "National Idea in France," I, 99: "In *Dissertation on the Ancient Word, 'Patrie,'* 1755, Abbé Coyer expressed a simpler more militant form of patriotism than that of the cosmopolitan, humanitarian philosophers of Enlightenment, who in general sympathized with his ideas. Coyer stressed the duties which the individual owes to '*la patrie*' in the sense of the public good. Also, with plentiful examples from antiquity he insisted that society should reward public service with crowns, triumphs, statues, tombs, funeral orations and large assemblies. His treatise was so admired by the '*philosophes*' that they reprinted large sections of it verbatim in the *Encyclopédie,* thus making up with added comments the article 'Patrie.' In 1788 the *Encyclopédie Méthodique* reproduced the article from the older encyclopedia, dropping the acknowledgment to Coyer and adding six new paragraphs of its own."

23. Voltaire, VIII, 180.

24. Aulard, *Patriotisme français,* p. 37.

25. Voltaire, VIII, 253-54. Hazard, *La crise,* II, 137. Professor

Hazard states in this work that the philosophy of reason which was already well formulated at the end of the seventeenth century and at the beginning of the eighteenth led to a new feeling of tenderness toward man and accordingly a new sensitivity toward man's common hardships. Deists and skeptics believed that earthly happiness was the goal to strive for. Therefore, they condemned war as an eternal obstacle to this end.

26. Voltaire, *Lettres philosophiques* (Lanson), I, 88-107.

27. Voltaire, II, 311.

28. Voltaire, II, 346.

29. Voltaire, II, 305-6.

30. Voltaire, II, 343.

31. Voltaire, XXIII, 527.

32. Voltaire, VIII, 352.

33. Voltaire, *Lettres philosophiques* (Lanson), I, 89.

34. Fénelon, *Télémaque,* I, 191. Mentor describing royal authority as practised by the King of Crete says: "Il a une puissance absolue pour faire le bien, et les mains liées dès qu'il veut faire le mal."

35. The similarity in style and wording between *Télémaque* and *Zadig* is striking, particularly in the passages in which the littleness of the earth is contrasted with the cosmic immensity of the universe and its countless spheres spinning on their axes through space. Cf. Fénelon, *Télémaque,* I, 346 and Voltaire, *Zadig,* XXI, 54-55; also *Micromégas,* XXI, 118.

36. Voltaire, XVI, 268.

37. Taine, *Histoire de la littérature anglaise,* I, xxiii.

38. Voltaire, XVI, 132.

39. Voltaire, XVI, 132.

40. Voltaire, XVI, 264-65.

41. Voltaire, XVI, 130, 351.

42. Voltaire, XVI, 393-94.

43. Voltaire, XVI, 264-65; 559-60.

44. Voltaire, XVI, 508-9.

45. Voltaire, XVI, 130.

46. Voltaire, XXXV, 508.

47. Voltaire, XVI, 220, 221, 351.

48. Voltaire, XVI, 493.

49. Voltaire, XVI, 493.

50. Voltaire, V, 526-27. Not only was Voltaire the author of some eloquent lines on patriotism, but he was one of the first to dignify national history by making it a subject of tragedy. Brenner in an article entitled *L'histoire nationale dans la tragédie française*, XIV, 309-310 states: "Les commencements de la tragédie historique française telle qu'elle existait au dix-huitième siècle se trouvent dans le *Zaire* (1732) de Voltaire. Le même auteur fournit encore de contributions à ce genre dramatique par son Adélaïde du Guesclin (1734) et son *Tancrède* (1760).

51. Cf. Voltaire, III, 93; IV, 110.

52. Voltaire, IV, 375

53. Voltaire, V, 253.

54. Voltaire, VIII, 377.

55. Voltaire, VIII, 377.

56. Voltaire, XX, 184.

57. Voltaire, XX, 184.

58. This same idea is expressed by Rousseau in the *Contrat social* (Collection Selecta des Classiques Garnier), p. 247: "Ce que l'homme perd par le contrat social, c'est sa liberté naturelle et un droit illimité à tout ce qui le tente et qu'il peut atteindre; ce qu'il gagne, c'est la liberté civile et la propriété de tout ce qu'il possède." Voltaire in the *Dictionnaire philosophique* and Rousseau in the *Contrat social* both made a plea for the nation as an organization designed to guarantee "natural rights." Yet Voltaire was more concerned with the successful result than with the mode of attainment. Rousseau, on the other hand, concentrated primarily on the technique of democracy and the reasonableness of democratic principles.

59. Voltaire, XX, 184.

60. Rousseau declares, in the *Contrat social,* p. 246: "Afin donc que ce pacte social ne soit pas un vain formulaire, il renferme tacitement cet engagement qui seul peut donner de la force aux autres, que quiconque refusera d'obéir à la volonté générale y sera contraint par tout le corps: ce qui ne signifie autre chose sinon qu'on le forcera à être libre." Both Voltaire and Rousseau were in agreement on the contractual nature of society, only the former more or less takes the social contract for granted. The latter stresses and features it.

61. Voltaire, XIX, 296.

62. Voltaire, XX, 182.

63. Voltaire, XX, 182. The quotation and discussion of these ideas take place in the following chapter.

In Diderot's *Encyclopédie*, XXIV, 472, in that article "Patrie" which was officially written by the Chevalier de Jaucourt but actually founded on Abbé Coyer's treatise one reads: "Le rhéteur peu logicien, le géographe qui ne s'occupe que de la position des lieux, et le lexicographe vulgaire prennent *la patrie* pour le lieu de la naissance, quel qu'il soit; mais le philosophe sait que ce mot vient du latin *pater,* qui représente un père et des enfants, et conséquemment qu'il exprime le sens que nous attachons à celui de *famille,* de *société,* d'*Etat libre,* dont nous sommes membres et dont les lois assurent nos libertés et notre bonheur. Il n'est point de patrie sous le joug du despotisme."

64. Voltaire, XX, 183.

65. Voltaire, XX, 181-82.

66. Voltaire, XX, 183.

67. Voltaire, XX, 182.

68. Voltaire, XX, 182.

69. In the *Contrat social,* p. 254, Rousseau likewise insisted that the pact between the individual and the nation was binding only when mutually respected: "Les engagements qui nous lient au corps social ne sont obligatoires que parce qu'ils sont mutuels; et leur nature est telle qu'en les remplissant on ne peut travailler pour autrui sans travailler aussi pour soi."

70. Voltaire, XXXIII, 466.

71. Voltaire, XX, 183.

72. Voltaire, *Dictionnaire philosophique* (Benda et Naves), II, 283.

73. Voltaire, XIV, 518; XXIII, 252.

74. Voltaire, *Dictionnaire philosophique* (Benda et Naves), II, 176.

75. Voltaire, *Dictionnaire philosophique* (Benda et Naves), II, 176.

*La Patrie* AND THE PRINCIPLES OF DEMOCRACY

1. Voltaire, XX, 182.

2. Voltaire, *Dictionnaire philosophique* (Benda et Naves), II, 127.

3. Voltaire, *Dictionnaire philosophique* (Benda et Naves), I, 81-82.

4. Voltaire, *Dictionnaire philosophique* (Benda et Naves), II, 174.

5. Voltaire, XXIV, 424-25.

6. Voltaire, XX, 182.

7. As previously mentioned, Voltaire based his whole conception of virtue on service to one's fellow men. *Dictionnaire philosophique* (Benda et Naves), II, 283. The *fraternité* preached by leaders of the French Revolution is indeed implicit in the following statement, p. 284: "La vertu entre hommes est un commerce de bienfaits; celui qui n'a nulle part à ce commerce ne doit point être compté."

8. Voltaire, *Dictionnaire philosophique* (Benda et Naves), I, 246.

9. Rousseau believed that all laws based on force violate the natural law of fundamental human liberty and equality. In the *Contrat social,* p. 239, he states: "Puis aucun homme n'a une autorité naturelle sur son semblable et puisque la force ne produit aucun droit, restent donc les conventions pour base de toute autorité légitime parmi les hommes."

10. Voltaire, XXVI, 78-85; XIX, 378-81.

11. Voltaire, XIX, 296 ff. *Dictionnaire philosophique* (Benda et Naves), II, 174.

12. Voltaire, XXIII, 527. On this point Rousseau has exactly the same opinion as Voltaire. He states in the *Contrat social,* pp. 239-40, "Renoncer à sa liberté, c'est renoncer à sa qualité d'homme, aux droits de l'humanité, même à ses devoirs. Il n'y a nul dédommagement possible pour quiconque renonce à tout. Une telle renonciation est incompatible avec la nature de l'homme; et c'est ôter toute moralité à ses actions que d'ôter toute liberté à sa volonté."

13. Voltaire, XXIII, 527.

14. Voltaire, XVIII, 475. Rousseau, *Contrat social,* p. 65, likewise attributes social inequality to man's dependence: "Sans prolonger inutilement ces détails, chacun doit voir que les liens de la servitude n'étant formés que de la dépendance mutuelle des hommes et des besoins réciproques qui les unissent, il est impossible d'asservir un homme sans l'avoir mis auparavant dans le cas de ne pouvoir passer d'un autre." Yet, unlike Voltaire, Rousseau seems to look upon primitive nature as limitlessly bountiful, for he concludes ". . . situation qui n'existant pas dans l'état de nature y laisse chacun libre du joug et rend vaine la loi du plus fort."

15. Voltaire, XVIII, 477.

16. Voltaire, XVIII, 475.

17. Voltaire believed that human actions in accord with Natural Law were those based on enlightened self-interest, XXVII, 331: "C——Il n'y a donc point de loi naturelle? Il y en a une sans doute, c'est l'intérêt et la raison." "Sin," he explained in the following way, p. 338: "C——Mais pourquoi dit-on que l'homme est toujours porté au mal? A——Il est porté à son bien-être lequel n'est un mal que quand il opprime ses frères."

18. Voltaire, XXIII, 527.

19. His despair at changing the irrational social inequalities of the ruling order is reflected in the parable of the cardinal's cook, Voltaire, *Dictionnaire philosophique* (Benda et Naves), I, 246. Though the servant of this exalted personage may indeed state his fundamental human equality with his master, he is still obliged to play the part of the menial. The author concludes: "Tout ce discours est raisonnable et juste: mais, en attendant que le Grand Turc s'empare de Rome, le cuisinier doit faire son devoir, ou toute société humaine est pervertie."

20. Voltaire, XI, 528.

21. Voltaire, XXIII, 527. Montesquieu, *De l'esprit des lois*, I, 110-11, thus explains the difference between a sane equality and confusion of rank and function: "Telle est la différence entre la démocratie réglée et celle qui ne l'est pas, que dans la première on n'est égal que comme citoyen, et que dans l'autre, on est encore égal comme magistrat, comme sénateur, comme juge, comme père, comme mari, comme maître."

22. Seligman and Johnson, *Encyclopedia of Social Sciences*, V, 76.

23. Voltaire, XXVII, 348.

24. Voltaire, XXIV, 424.

25. Voltaire, XXIII, 527.

26. Voltaire, XXIV, 425.

27. Voltaire, XVIII, 476-77.

28. Voltaire, XIV, 532.

29. Laski, *The Rise of European Liberalism*, p. 214.

30. Encyclopedia Britannica.

31. Seligman and Johnson, The Encyclopedia of Social Sciences, IX, 437.

32. Voltaire, XX, 291.

33. Voltaire, XLIX, 543.

34. Voltaire, XVII, 26.

35. Laski, *Rise of European Liberalism*, pp. 162-75.

36. Voltaire, XX, 293.

37. Cf. Lavisse, *Histoire de France*, Vol. IX, Part 1, p. 41.

38. Voltaire, XX, 291; 291-94.

39. Sée, *Esquisse d'une histoire*, p. 254. Nevertheless this author calls attention to the fact that some of the more radical thinkers and the people themselves demanded more education. "Combien un enseignement national faisait défaut, c'est ce que montre le projet attribué à Turgot par le *Mémoire sur les* municipalités, rédigé par Dupont de Nemours. Beaucoup de cahiers de paroisses en 1789, réclament 'un maître d'école dont les enfants ont été privés jusqu'ici.'"

40. Sée, *Esquisse d'une histoire*, p. 254.

41. Sée, *Esquisse d'une histoire*, pp. 349-60. The author asserts, p. 355, that the average working day of the artisans lasted from dawn to sunset.

42. Voltaire, XXIV, 425.

43. Laski, *Rise of European Liberalism*, pp. 214-15.

44. Voltaire, XLIV, 256; 248.

45. Voltaire, XLII, 404.

46. Voltaire, XLIV, 256.

47. Voltaire, XLIV, 256.

48. Voltaire, XLV, 164.

49. Chaponnière, *Voltaire chez les Calvinistes*, pp. 195-96.

50. Chaponnière, *Voltaire chez les Calvinistes*, pp. 216-25.

51. On the words Voltaire addressed to the "Natifs" on this occasion, see Chaponnière, *Voltaire chez les Calvinistes*, p. 232.

52. Chaponnière, *Voltaire chez les Calvinistes*, pp. 229-30.

53. Chaponnière, *Voltaire chez les Calvinistes*, p. 231.

54. Voltaire, XLVI, 112.

55. Voltaire, XVIII, 476. Voltaire, *Lettres philosophiques* (Lanson), I, 91.

56. Tallentyre, *Life of Voltaire*, p. 410.

57. No evidence of Voltaire's humanitarianism to the underprivileged is more conclusive than the monument which stands in the town of Ferney. Norman L. Torrey, *The Spirit of Voltaire*, p. 188, reproduces the inscription which bears no flowery tribute to a de-

parted philosopher, indeed nothing more than a concise yet eloquent summary of facts: " *'To the Benefactor of Ferney.* Voltaire built more than a hundred houses. He gave the town a church, a school, a hospital, a reservoir and a fountain. He loaned money without interest to neighboring communities. He dried up the swamps of the countryside. He established fairs and markets. He nourished the inhabitants during the famine of 1771.' "

58. In the struggle of the bourgeoisie for political expression Rousseau stirred the "Représentatifs" to a flaming consciousness of their rights. Yet after the storm provoked by his *Lettres de la montagne,* he retired from the scene with unctious words as to his high and noble intentions, *Correspondance générale,* Paris, Colin, 1930, XIII, 43. Nevertheless uneasy at the discord he had created and unwilling to take any further stand in the quarrel between the *"Représentatifs"* and the *"Négatifs"* he advised the bourgeois to rely solely on his rival and enemy Voltaire; Rousseau, *Correspondance générale,* XIV, 358-59.

59. Voltaire, XXIII, 502.

60. Voltaire, XLIV, 256.

61. Voltaire, XX, 456.

62. Laski, *Rise of European Liberalism,* p. 215.

63. Voltaire, XLIII, 175.

64. Voltaire, XXVII, 347: "J'aime à voir des hommes libres faire eux-mêmes les lois sous lesquelles ils vivent . . . C'est un plaisir pour moi que mon maçon, mon charpentier, mon forgeron, qui m'ont aidé à bâtir mon logement, mon voisin l'agriculteur, et mon ami le manufacturier s'élèvent au dessus de leur métier et connaissent mieux l'intérêt public que le plus insolent chiaoux de Turquie."

65. Voltaire, XI, 528-29; XVIII, 333-34.

66. Voltaire, XI, 528. Montesquieu, *De l'esprit des lois,* I, 45 states: "Comme l'égalité des fortunes entretient la frugalité, la frugalité maintient l'égalité des fortunes. Ces choses quoique différentes, sont telles qu'elles ne peuvent subsister l'une sans l'autre; chacune d'elle est la cause et l'effet, si l'une se retire de la démocratie, l'autre la suit toujours."

67. Sée, *Idees politiques,* p. 83, declares: "Voltaire considère que l'essentiel pour garantir vraiment la liberté individuelle, c'est de connaître les droits de l'homme. On peut penser que c'est de Voltaire

que s'inspirera le plus directement la Déclaration des droits de l'homme de 1789."

68. Palmer, "The Nationalist Idea in France," I, 110.

69. Voltaire, XXIV, 415.

70. Voltaire, XVI, 538.

71. Voltaire, XVI, 538.

72. Voltaire, XVI, 538.

73. *Textes sacrés de la liberté,* p. 48.

74. *Textes sacrés de la liberté,* p. 49.

75. Voltaire rebuked Rousseau for saying in the *Contrat social* that executive officers are not the masters of the people but merely their officials, that the people could therefore appoint and dismiss them at their good pleasure. This Voltaire maintained, XXIV, 421, would be "le code de l'anarchie." Instead, he asserted, "Il est vrai que les magistrats ne sont pas les maîtres du peuple; ce sont les lois qui sont maîtresses." The people should have a voice in the choosing of magistrates, yet the latter ought not to be dismissed without due processes of law.

76. Voltaire, XXVII, 353.

77. Voltaire, XX, 104; XI, 155.

78. Voltaire, XXV, 40: "Le droit humain ne peut être fondé en aucun cas que sur ce droit de nature; et le grand principe, le principe universel de l'un et de l'autre, est, dans toute la terre: 'Ne fais pas ce que tu ne voudrais pas qu'on te fît.' "

79. Despite their obvious differences in methods and approach, Voltaire and Rousseau were essentially in agreement on the aims of government. As the former asserted in the *Idées républicaines,* XXIV, 416: "Le gouvernement civil est la volonté de tous executée par un seul ou par plusieurs, en vertus des lois que tous ont portées."

80. Voltaire, XXIV, 416; XXVII, 338-39.

81. Voltaire, XXVII, 351. Montesquieu, *De l'esprit des lois,* I, 6: "La loi en général est la raison humaine en tant qu'elle gouverne tous les peuples de la terre; et les lois politiques et civiles de chaque nation ne doivent être que les cas particuliers où s'applique cette raison humaine."

82. Voltaire, XXIV, 415.

83. Voltaire, XIX, 625.

84. Voltaire, XLII, 404, 506-7.

85. Voltaire, XLIII, 138; XVIII, 471. D'Alembert, *Encyclopédie,* VIII, 496, article "Collège," also makes a plea that young men be trained by those studies "par lesquelles ils doivent un jour se rendre utiles à leur patrie." He deplored the time and effort spent by the colleges in teaching youth to compose prose and poetry in a dead language, thus turning loose on society, VIII, 498, "une nuée de versificateurs latins," no one of which was worth reading. Instead, he asserted, p. 497, "Ce temps serait bien mieux employé à apprendre par principes sa propre langue, qu'on ignore toujours au sortir du collège et qu'on ignore au point de la parler très mal."

86. Voltaire, XX, 272; XXIII, 467; XXIV, 415.

87. Voltaire, XVIII, 438.

88. Voltaire, IX, 459; XIX, 625-626.

89. Voltaire, XIX, 626.

90. Montesquieu, *De l'esprit des lois,* II, 102-3.

91. Voltaire, XXVIII, 133.

92. Voltaire, XV, 480.

93. Voltaire, XX, 518.

94. Voltaire, XXV, 37.

95. Voltaire, XXIV, 432.

96. Voltaire, XLII, 281, 409, 505.

97. Voltaire, XXV, 96.

98. *Textes sacrés de la liberté,* p. 51.

99. Voltaire, XXV, 33. The editors Kehl in a footnote, XXV, 48, call to the attention of the reader the care taken by Voltaire not to ruin his case for tolerance by statements which might have been called radical: "Il faut regarder cet ouvrage comme une espèce de plaidoyer où M. de Voltaire se croyait obligé de se conformer quelquefois à l'opinion vulgaire."

100. Voltaire, *Lettres philosophiques* (Lanson), I, 61.

101. Voltaire, XXV, 37.

102. Faguet, *Politique comparée,* p. 23.

103. Faguet, *Politique comparée,* p. 23.

104. Faguet, *Politique comparée,* p. 23.

105. Voltaire, XXVII, 360.

106. Voltaire, XIX, 583-84.

107. Voltaire, X, 423.

108. Voltaire, XLI, 76; XXV, 418-19.

109. Faguet, *Politique comparée,* pp. 24-25.

110. Voltaire, XXIV, 418.

111. Voltaire, XXV, 418-19.

112. That war-cry of the American Revolution: "No taxation without representation," is foreshadowed in the article "Impôt" of the fourth edition of the *Questions sur l'Encyclopédie,* dated 1774, XIX, 440: "Dans les républiques, et dans les Etats qui, avec le nom de *royaume,* sont des *républiques,* en effet, chaque particulier est taxé suivant ses forces et suivant les besoins de la société. Dans les royaumes despotiques ou pour parler plus poliment dans les Etats monarchiques, il n'en est pas tout à fait de même. On taxe la nation sans la consulter."

113. *Textes sacrés* p. 51.

114. Voltaire, XIV, 523.

115. Martin, *French Liberal Thought,* pp. 228-35.

116. Voltaire, XLIX, 89.

117. Voltaire, XV, 329.

118. Voltaire, XIX, 296.

119. Voltaire, *Lettres philosophiques* (Lanson), I, 105-6.

120. Cf. Pollard, *The Evolution of Parliament,* pp. 338-40.

121. Cf. Porritt, *Unreformed House of Commons,* pp. 340-48.

122. In his scathing pamphlet, *Remontrances du grenier à sel* of 1771, Voltaire has Parlement thus define to the king the exact nature of their role in the government of France, XXVIII, 404: "Nous sommes entre vos sujets et vous, un corps intermédiaire, semblables à ces humeurs corrompues que forment un dépôt dans le corps humain, et se nourissent de sa substance. Aussi anciens que la monarchie, nous avons, seuls le privilège exclusif de connaître ses lois, de les interpréter...."

123. Voltaire, XX, 173: "Toute compagnie, tout citoyen a droit de porter ses plaintes au souverain par la loi naturelle qui permet de crier quand on souffre."

124. Voltaire, XV, 487-90.

125. Lavisse, *Histoire de France,* Vol. IX, Part 1, p. 41. In January 1776 Turgot declared in the edict introducing the reform of the *corvée* that it was high time that non-property holders were relieved of this hated tax, which robbed them of their time and work. "...

leur temps et leur travail, leurs seules ressources contre la misère et la faim, pour les faire travailler au profit de citoyens plus riches qu'eux."

In regard to an adversary of Turgot who combatted his steps toward fiscal equality and invoked the ancient constitution of France, Voltaire declared, XLIX, 540, in a letter to de Vaines of March 1, 1776: "Ce factotum de maître La Croix paraît très insidieux; il écarte toujours avec adresse le fond de la question, et le principal objet de M. Turgot, qui est le soulagement du peuple."

THE STATE AS A DOMINANT POWER: *Part 1*

1. Voltaire, VIII, 352.
2. Voltaire, XX, 182.
3. Voltaire, XXIII, 530.
4. Voltaire, *Dictionnaire philosophique* (Benda et Naves), II, 28.
5. Voltaire, XIV, 218.
6. Voltaire, *Dictionnaire philosophique* (Benda et Naves), II, 25.
7. Voltaire, XIV, 525.
8. Voltaire, *Dictionnaire philosophique* (Benda et Naves), II, 24.
9. Montesquieu, *Lettres persanes,* (Barckhausen), I, 235: "C'est le destin des héros de se ruiner à conquérir des pays qu'ils perdent soudain ou à soumettre des nations qu'ils sont obligés eux mêmes de détruire: comme cet insensé qui se consumait à acheter des statues qu'il jetait dans la mer et des glaces qu'il brisait aussitot."
10. Voltaire, XIV, 525.
11. Voltaire, XIV, 234. However, in 1777 the aged Patriarch had bold words to say about any so-called *"raison d'état."* In the *Prix de la justice et de l'humanité* (Beuchot), L, 314: ". . . un crime est toujours crime soit qu'il ait été commandé par un prince dans l'aveuglement de sa colère, soit qu'il ait été revêtu de patentes scellées de sang-froid avec toutes les formalités possibles. La raison d'état n'est qu'un mot inventé pour servir d'excuse aux tyrans. La vraie raison d'état consiste à vous précautionner contre les crimes de vos ennemis, non pas à en commettre."
12. Voltaire, *Dictionnaire philosophique* (Benda et Naves), II, 25.
13. Voltaire, XX, 184.
14. Voltaire, XIV, 241.

15. Voltaire, XIV, 320.
16. Voltaire, Cf., XIV, 287, note K.
17. Voltaire, XIV, 309.
18. Voltaire, XIV, 260-66.
19. Voltaire, XIV, 323.
20. Voltaire, XIV, 307.
21. Voltaire, XIV, 383; 419: "Il faut avouer que Louis XIV eut toujours dans l'âme une élévation qui le portait aux grandes choses en tout genre."
22. Voltaire, XIV, 383; 419.
23. Voltaire, XIV, 256.
24. Voltaire, XIV, 268.
25. Voltaire, XIV, 269.
26. Voltaire, XVI, 351.
27. Voltaire, XI, 146.
28. Voltaire, *Dictionnaire philosophique* (Benda et Naves), II, p. 28.
29. Voltaire, *Dictionnaire philosophique* (Benda et Naves), II, p. 28.
30. Voltaire, *Dictionnaire philosophique* (Benda et Naves), II, p. 28.
31. Voltaire, *Dictionnaire philosophique* (Benda et Naves), II, 26-27. Voltaire believed that a religion based on "natural law" discouraged war-time atrocities. Yet he failed to recognize the debt of the modern world to Christianity in stopping, to a certain extent, such savagery. Montesquieu, however, acknowledged this debt; Cf. *De l'esprit des lois,* II, 103.
32. Voltaire, XXVII, 352.
33. Voltaire, XXVII, 353.
34. Voltaire, XXVII, 353.
35. Voltaire, *Dictionnaire philosophique* (Benda et Naves), II, 29.
36. Voltaire, *Dictionnaire philosophique* (Benda et Naves), II, 295. However in regard to that treaty of "perpetual peace" between nations imagined so fondly by the Abbé de Saint-Pierre, he declared (Beuchot), XLVI, 57, that between rulers of various political states such an agreement would be no more respected than it would have been between elephants and rhinoceroses.
37. Voltaire, XV, 426.

38. Voltaire, *Dictionnaire philosophique* (Benda et Naves), **II**, 25, 28. Voltaire defined war even more savagely in *Candide,* XXI, 184: "Un million d'assassins enregimentés courant d'un bout de l'Europe à l'autre, exerce le meurtre et le brigandage avec discipline pour gagner son pain, parce qu'il n'a pas de métier plus honnête."

39. Voltaire, XI, 257-61.

40. Voltaire, *Lettres philosophiques* (Lanson), I, 90; XIX, 295.

41. Voltaire, XIII, 56-57.

42. Voltaire, XIV, 384. Also Voltaire concludes his short poem on the art of military strategy, *Poème de la tactique* of 1773, with the following lines, X, 193:

> Mais je vous l'avouerai, je formai des souhaits
> Pour que ce beau métier ne s'exerçât jamais
> Et qu'enfin l'équité fit régner sur la terre,
> L'impraticable paix de l'Abbé Saint-Pierre.

43. Cf. Fuller, "Voltaire's Tank," CLXV, 336-37. About the great Frenchman's projected *char de guerre* this modern military expert concludes: "We know that it was moved by two horses and that its crew was two men. It was therefore a smaller vehicle than its Scottish ancestor [Scottish War Cart of 1456] and probably the first two-man tank ever devised. That it was only suitable for level ground is acknowledged; consequently its limitations were considerable. It was a great idea born before its age." Voltaire also urged his invention on Catherine the Great in her struggle against the Turks.

44. Montesquieu, *De l'esprit des lois,* I, 133-34: "Mais entre les sociétés, le droit de la défense naturelle entraîne quelquefois la nécessité d'attaquer, lorsqu'un peuple voit qu'une plus longue paix en mettrait un autre en état de le détruire, et que l'attaque est dans ce moment le seul moyen d'empêcher cette destruction."

45. Voltaire, XIX, 322.

46. Voltaire, XIX, 322.

47. Voltaire, XIX, 322.

48. For Voltaire's ideas on the question of "just wars," cf. *A B C* dialogue of 1768, XXVII, 372.

49. Seligman and Johnson, *The Encyclopedia of Social Sciences,* II, 396-97.

50. Voltaire, XXIII, 576.

51. Tallentyre, *Life of Voltaire,* pp. 334-35.

52. Dorn, *Competition for Empire*, pp. 297, 302, declares that both those master statesmen, Count Kaunitz and Frederick the Great, viewed France and Prussia as natural allies. This author quotes, p. 302, the latter as saying: " 'Alsace-Lorraine and Silesia are two sisters of whom France has married one and Prussia the other. This connection forces them to pursue a common policy. Prussia can not suffer France to be deprived of Alsace or Lorraine, and Prussia is in a position to defend France by penetrating at once into the heart of the Austrian dominions. For the same reason France cannot suffer Prussia to be deprived of Silesia. That would weaken excessively a French ally who is useful in the north and in the Empire and who can protect Alsace or Lorraine by means of a diversion.' "

53. Voltaire, XXXIX, 321. Pellissier, *Voltaire philosophe*, p. 227, quotes one of the critics most hostile to eighteenth-century philosophers, none other than the conservative Brunetière as saying in his *Etudes critiques:* ". . . les défaites de la royauté de Versailles allaient bientôt cesser d'être celles de la patrie . . . la guerre de Sept ans nous donnera le spectacle—peut-être unique dans l'histoire—d'un peuple . . . faisant en quelque manière cause commune avec les ennemies de sa puissance et de sa gloire."

54. Voltaire, XXXIX, 299.

55. Desnoiresterres, *Voltaire et la société*, V, 355.

56. Voltaire, XL, 242.

57. Desnoiresterres, *Voltaire et la société*, V, 272, states that Abbé Bernis, one of the authors of the Austro-French alliance, was essentially in agreement with Voltaire on the need for peace with Prussia. Though, as the tool of Louis XV, he could not go contrary to his master's wishes, as author of the unpopular alliance, Bernis felt responsible for the *impasse* into which he had led his country. Discreetly he worked for peace in his correspondence with the French ambassador at Vienna."

58. Dorn, *Competition for Empire*, pp. 353-57.

59. Montesquieu, *De l'esprit des lois*, I, 130, likewise asserts: "La vraie puissance d'un prince ne consiste pas tant dans la facilité qu'il y a à conquérir que dans la difficulté qu'il y a à attaquer; et si j'ose parler ainsi dans l'immutabilité de sa condition. Mais l'aggrandissement des Etats leur fait montrer de nouveaux côtés par où on peut les prendre."

1. Voltaire, XIV, 525-26.

2. Voltaire, XXIII, 502-3.

3. In his *Histoire de Pierre Ier, Empereur de Russie,* Voltaire commended his hero for attaching so much importance to the economic upbuilding of his kingdom rather than to alliances and embroilments with other powers, XVI, 570: "Il [Pierre] savait que les négotiations, les intérêts des princes, leurs ligues, leurs amitiés, leurs défiances, leurs inimités éprouvent presque tous les ans des vicissitudes et que souvent il ne reste aucune trace de tant d'efforts de politique. Une seule manufacture bien établie fait quelquefois plus de bien à un état que vingt traités."

4. Voltaire, *Lettres philosophiques* (Lanson), I, 120, 121.

5. Voltaire, *Lettres philosophiques* (Lanson), I, 120 cf. note.

6. Weulersse, *Physiocrates,* p. 20, states that the Physiocrats did not really become influential until 1767 when Mercier de la Rivière published his *Ordre naturel et essentiel des sociétés politiques.* The Physiocratic doctrine was very compatible with enlightened despotism. For all the sovereign needed to do was to place his domains in harmony with the iron rule of natural forces. The Physiocrats enjoyed the patronage of Louis XV and Louis XVI. Weulersse, pp. 23-24, quotes Mercier as declaring of his "nouvelle discipline": "Elle ne veut régner que par le concours de ceux-là mêmes qui résistent à ses lois; elle respecte toutes les puissances et n'attaque que ces trames civiles appelées privilèges et contrepoids."

7. Voltaire, XIII, 180-83.

8. Martin, *French Liberal Thought,* p. 230, thus describes the position of the leading Physiocrats: "Quesnay's conviction that a natural order of society lay within our reach, if the Creator's ordinances were followed, was built, just as Locke's had been, upon his training and experience as a doctor. He believed, as one of his disciples put it, that 'natural laws extended far beyond the bounds hitherto assigned to them' and applied to the circulation of money just as they did to the circulation of the blood."

9. Cf. Hearnshaw, *Social and Political Ideas,* pp. 205-15.

10. Weulersse, *Physiocrates,* p. 36.

11. Carré, *Consistance de Voltaire,* pp. 98-99, thus explains Vol-

taire's idea of progress: "La part du devenir historique, en effet est énorme et recouvre la nature mais ne la détruit pas, et dès qu'on la voit en fait toujours fondamentalement constituée d'égoisme et bienveillance—il y aura progrès dans la mesure où plus d'hommes pourront jouir plus pleinement de leur nature sans opprimer celle d'autrui, et sans déchirer le lien social qui permettront, si les choses allaient au mieux, que tous développent paisiblement leur nature."

12. Voltaire, X, 84.

13. Voltaire, X, 91.

14. Weulersse, *Physiocrates,* p. 158, asserts that the Physiocrats believed free trade within the nation scarcely sufficient to insure national prosperity without a removal of the restrictions on foreign exportation: ". . . suivant nos auteurs, sans la liberté d'exporter, la circulation intérieure elle-même ne s'établirait jamais bien, ne fût-ce qu'en raison des entraves dont presque inévitablement le cabotage resterait chargé. 'Le commerce extérieur effectif peut et doit être souvent inutile; mais la liberté du commerce est indispensable pour soutenir la communication.' "

15. Voltaire, XXIII, 506.

16. Voltaire, XLIX, 286: L, 545-46.

17. Gaffiot, "La Théorie du luxe et Voltaire," XIV, 341. Voltaire, XIV, 498-99, 524.

18. Voltaire, XXI, 307.

19. Voltaire, XIV, 531. Cf. Seligman and Johnson, *Encyclopedia of Social Sciences,* X, 337-39.

20. Voltaire, XXIII, 502.

21. Voltaire, XII, 406-7; XXIV, 575.

22. Voltaire, XIV, 531-32.

23. Voltaire, XXIII, 502.

24. Voltaire, XXIII, 503.

25. Voltaire, XXIII, 505-6; XIV, 526-27; XV, 165-66.

26. Voltaire, XXIII, 501.

27. Cf. Lavisse, *Histoire de France,* IX, Part 1, 41-51.

28. Voltaire, XIV, 518. Nisard, *Histoire de la littérature française,* IV, 357-58, points to the national pride implicit in the *Siècle de Louis XIV* and calls it the fruit of Voltaire's intimate inspiration: "L'idée de placer la France du XVII<sup>e</sup> siècle à la tête de l'Europe intellectuelle, de faire accepter de tout le monde l'appellation du *'Siècle de Louis*

*XIV,'* de présenter à l'esprit humain, comme sa plus parfaite image, l'esprit français personnifié dans nos écrivains, nos savants et nos artistes, cette idée là ne vint à Voltaire, ni d'un besoin public, ni d'une invitation de la mode. Ce fut son ouvrage personnel. . . ."

29. Voltaire, II, 544-45.

30. Voltaire, II, 542.

31. Voltaire, XIV, 563-64. Of Voltaire's admiration for Louis XIV and his court, Condorcet declares, I, 291: "On l'accuse d'avoir trop loué le faste de la cour de Louis XIV: cette accusation est fondée. C'est le seul préjugé de sa jeunesse qu'il ait conservé. Il y a bien peu d'hommes qui puissent se flatter de les avoir secoués tous. On l'accuse d'avoir cru qu'il suffisait au bonheur d'un peuple d'avoir des artistes célèbres, des orateurs et des poètes: jamais il n'a pu le penser." Condorcet states that Voltaire merely saw in art a softening, refining influence on the rulers and the ruled alike.

32. Lavisse, *Histoire de France,* Vol. VII, Part 2, pp. 83, 83-84 footnote. Cole, *Colbert and a Century of French Mercantilism,* I, 318.

33. Cf. Morize, *l'Apologie,* p. 69.

34. Voltaire, X, 92. Cf. Montesquieu, *De l'esprit des lois,* I, 96: "Si les riches n'y dépensent pas beaucoup, les pauvres mourront de faim. Il faut même que les riches y dépensent à proportion de l'inégalité des fortunes, et que, comme nous avons dit, le luxe y augmente dans cette proportion."

35. Voltaire, XXII, 363.

36. Voltaire, XXIII, 503.

37. Voltaire, XXIII, 503.

38. Voltaire, XIV, 426. Voltaire not only wrote verses about the delicate pleasures of luxury, but he was an early campaigner for public hygiene. In such articles of the *Dictionnaire philosophique* as "Charité" and "Enterrement," he pleaded for new and clean hospitals, for sanitary burials. XVIII, 137, 550.

39. Lavisse, *Histoire de France,* Vol. VII, Part 1, p. 170.

40. Cf. Sée, *Esquisse d'une histoire,* pp. 274-84.

41. Sée, *Esquisse d'une histoire,* pp. 274-84.

42. Voltaire, XIV, 323-24.

43. Dorn, *Competition for Empire,* pp. 260-64.

44. Dorn, *Competition for Empire,* p. 264.

45. Voltaire, XIV, 498-99.

46. Voltaire, XIV, 498-99.
47. Voltaire, XXXIX, 440.
48. Voltaire, XXI, 196; XXXIX, 440.
49. Dorn, *Competition for Empire,* pp. 259-60.
50. Voltaire, XV, 369.
51. Voltaire, XV, 368.
52. Voltaire, XLI, 91-92.
53. Voltaire, XXIX, 149.
54. Voltaire, XXIX, 162.
55. Voltaire, X, 84.
56. Voltaire, XXIX, 88-89.
57. Voltaire, XV, 374: "Les côtes anglaises dans l'espace de six cents lieues sont traversées par des fleuves navigables qui leur portent leurs marchandises jusqu'à 40 et 50 lieues dans leurs terres. Les peuples d'Allemagne se sont empressés d'aller peupler ces pays, où ils trouvent une liberté dont ils ne jouissaient point dans leur patrie. Ils sont devenus Anglais, et si toutes ces colonies demeuraient unies à leur metropole, il n'est pas douteux que cet établissement ne fasse un jour la plus formidable puissance."
58. Dorn, *Competition for Empire,* pp. 275-79.
59. Dorn, *Competition for Empire,* p. 276.
60. Voltaire, XXIX, 95-96.
61. Diderot et D'Alembert, *Encyclopédie,* VIII, 521.
62. Voltaire, XXIX, 93-94.
63. XXIX, 89.
64. Aulard, *Patriotisme français,* states the ideas of Turgot, whom Voltaire much admired, on imperialism. Aulard, p. 69, quotes Dupont de Nemours as saying: "Il [Turgot] ne pensait point que l'Europe dût gouverner l'Asie; il désirait au contraire qu'elle se bornât à lui procurer le bonheur de se gouverner elle-même. Il trouvait digne de la France et de son roi de protéger la liberté sur toute la surface du globe et de ne l'opprimer nulle part."
65. Voltaire, XXI, 131.
66. Voltaire, XXI, 180; XII, 417.
67. Voltaire, XII, 417.
68. Voltaire, XXIX, 89-90.
69. Voltaire, XXIX, 103.
70. Voltaire, XXIX, 90.

71. Voltaire, XX, 291.
72. Voltaire, XXIV, 424.
73. Voltaire, XX, 291.
74. Voltaire, XX, 292.
75. Voltaire, XX, 291-92.
76. Voltaire, XX, 292-93.
77. Voltaire, XX, 292.
78. In his *Histoire de Pierre Ier, Empereur de Russie,* XVI, 419, Voltaire praised Catherine the Great for taking some of the wealth and lands of Russia away from the monasteries. Also by depriving them of serfs, she forced the monks to till their own soil.
79. Voltaire, XX, 293.
80. Voltaire, XX, 293.
81. Voltaire, XX, 293-94.

# Bibliography

T O EXTRACT a theory of statesmanship from the works of Voltaire
it has been necessary to reexamine all his major ideas on politics,
economics, and social classes. Not only these ideas themselves but the
motives behind them must be explored. This work is based as far as
possible on primary sources. The researcher is indebted to such indispensable aids to Voltaire scholarship as the Moland and Beuchot
editions of his complete works and the bibliography of his writings
compiled by Georges Bengescu.

For the thorough knowledge of Voltaire's life that such a work
entails, the present researcher has consulted all the principal Voltaire
biographies from the early summing up of his lifework by his friend
and disciple Condorcet to such excellent contributions of nineteenth-
century scholarship as the biography by Desnoiresterres, and the comparatively recent twentieth-century work by Noyes. Certain studies of
a particular period of Voltaire's life have proved informative, such as
the work on the young Voltaire by Chase and the book on his
Genevan experiences by Chaponnière. As one of the most brilliant
and authoritative discussions of Voltairean aims and outlook, the
essay by John Morley must be given special mention.

Many secondary sources have also proved helpful. Chief among
these are the writings of Black (in a volume edited by J. F. C.
Hearnshaw), Carré, Brailsford, Pellissier, and Torrey—to name only
a few.

For the political background of the eighteenth century, no book
has proved more valuable than the work of Walter Dorn's entitled
*Competition for Empire.*

EDITIONS OF WORKS OF VOLTAIRE

Benda, Julien et Raymond Naves, eds. Le dictionnaire philosophique. Edition critique avec préface et notes. 2 vols. Paris: Garnier, 1936.

Beuchot, M., ed. Voltaire, oeuvres complètes. 72 vols. Paris: Lefèvre, 1834-40.

Havens, George. Candide on l'optismisme. New York: Henry Holt, 1934.

Lanson, Gustave, ed. Voltaire, Lettres philosophiques. 2 vols. Paris: Hachette, 1930.

Moland, Louis, ed. Voltaire, oeuvres complètes. 52 vols. Paris: Garnier, 1883-85.

GENERAL REFERENCES

Abbott, Lawrence. Twelve Great Modernists. New York: Doubleday, 1927.

Ascoli, Georges. "Voltaire et l'Angleterre," Revue des cours et conférences, 1924-25, XXV, 128-44, 275-315.

Aubry, Jean. Voltaire: Lettres d'Alsace à sa nièce, Mme Denis. Paris: Gallimard, 1938.

Aulard, Alphonse. Le patriotisme français de la Renaissance à la Révolution. Paris: Chiron, 1921.

Baldensperger, Fernand. "Voltaire à l'étranger," Revue de littérature comparée, XI, 581-606.

Barr, Mary Margaret. A Bibliography of Writings on Voltaire, 1825-1925. New York: Institute of French Studies, 1929. Supplement, MLN, May, 1923; MLN, December, 1941.

Barzun, Jacques. Of Human Freedom. Boston: Little Brown, 1939.

——Race, a Modern Superstition. New York: Harcourt, Brace, 1937.

Beaune, Henri. Voltaire au collège. Paris: Amyot, 1867.

Bellessort, André. Essai sur Voltaire. Paris: Perrin, 1925.

Bengescu, Georges. Voltaire: Bibliographie de ses oeuvres. 4 vols. Paris: Perrin, 1882-90.

Bossuet, Jacques Bénigne. La politique tirée des propres paroles de l'écriture sainte, Oeuvres. 4 vols. Paris: Firmin Didot, 1852.

Brailsford, Henry N. Voltaire. London: T. Butterworth, 1935.

Brandes, Georg. Voltaire. New York: A. and C. Boni, 1930.

Brenner, Clarence D. "L'histoire nationale dans la tragédie française," *Publications in Modern Philology,* XIV, 195-329. Berkely: University of California Press, 1929.

Brunetière, Ferdinand. Discours de combat. 3 vols. Paris: Perrin, 1914.

——Voltaire, Etudes sur le XVIIIe siècle. Paris: Hachette, 1911.

Carré, J. R. La consistance de Voltaire le philosophe. Paris: Boivin, 1938.

Caussy, Fernand. "Lettres secrètes et inédites de Voltaire," *La Grande Revue,* LXV (February, 1911), 673-96.

——"La mission diplomatique de Voltaire (1743-45)," *La Grande Revue,* LXV (February, 1911), 547-63.

——Voltaire, seigneur de village. Paris: Hachette, 1912.

Cayroll, M. de. Lettres inédites de Voltaire. Paris: Didier, 1856.

Célarié, Henriette. Monsieur de Voltaire, sa famille et ses amis. Paris: Colin, 1928.

Champion, Edmé, Voltaire (Etudes Critiques), 3d ed. Paris: Colin, 1921.

Chaponnière, Paul. Voltaire chez les Calvinistes. Paris: Perrin, 1936.

Chase, Cleveland B. The Young Voltaire. London and New York: Longmans, Green, 1926.

Chateaubriand, François de. Le Génie du Christianisme. Nouvelle édition, 2 vols. Paris: Garnier, 1926.

Cole, Charles W. Colbert and a Century of French Mercantilism. 2 vols. New York: Columbia University Press, 1939.

Condorcet, Antoine Nicolas. Vie de Voltaire, Voltaire, Oeuvres complètes. Moland ed. Paris: Garnier, 1880.

Corneille, Pierre. Le Cid, Vol. I of Oeuvres complètes. 2 vols. Paris: Lefèvre, 1834.

Cornou, François. Trente années de luttes contre Voltaire et les philosophes du XVIIIe siècle. Paris: Champion, 1922.

Cru, R. L. Diderot, a Disciple of English Thought. New York: Columbia University Press, 1913.

D'Alembert, Jean Le Rond: see Diderot, Denis et Jean Le Rond d'Alembert.

Desnoiresterres, Gustave. Voltaire et la société du XVIIIe siècle. 2d ed., 8 vols. Paris: Didier, 1871-76.

Diderot, Denis. Vol. IV of Oeuvres complètes. 20 vols. Paris: Garnier, 1875-77.

——et Jean Le Rond d'Alembert. L'Encyclopédie ou dictionnaire raisonné des sciences, des arts et des métiers. 36 vols. Lausanne et Berne: Chez les Sociétés Typographiques, 1781.

Dorn, Walter. Competition for Empire. New York and London: Harper, 1940.

Duchesne, Julien. Histoire des poèmes épiques français du XVIIe siècle. Paris: Thorin, 1870.

Encyclopedia Brittanica. 14th ed.; London: Encyclopedia Brittanica Co., 1929.

Faguet, Emile. La politique comparée de Montesquieu, Rousseau et Voltaire. Paris: Société française d'imprimerie et de librairie, 1902.

——Voltaire. Paris: Société française d'imprimerie et de librairie, 1900.

Fénelon, François de Salignac de La Mothe. Télémaque. 2 vols., nouvelle édition par Albert Cahen. Paris: Hachette, 1920.

Foulet, Lucien. Correspondance de Voltaire, 1726-1729. Paris: Hachette, 1913.

Fuller, J. F. C. "Voltaire's Tank," Spectator, CLXV (Oct. 4, 1940), 335.

Gaffiot, Maurice, "La Théorie du luxe et Voltaire," Revue d'histoire économique, XIV (1926), 320-43.

Green, Frederick C. Eighteenth-century France. New York: D. Appleton, 1931.

Havens, George. Candide ou l'optimisme. Critical, annotated edition; New York: Henry Holt, 1934.

Hayes, Carlton J. H. Essays on Nationalism. New York: Macmillan, 1928.

——The Historical Evolution of Modern Nationalism. New York: Macmillan, 1948.

Hazard, Paul. La crise de la conscience européenne. 3 vols. Paris: Boivin, 1935.

——"Voltaire et Leibnitz," Académie royale de Belgique. Classe des lettres et des sciences morales et politiques, 5th series, XXIII, 435-49, 1937.

Hearnshaw, J. F. C., ed. The Social and Political Ideas of Some Great French Thinkers of the Age of Reason. New York: Crofts, 1930.

——Social and Political Ideas of the Revolutionary Era. London: Harrap, 1931.

Henriot, Emile. Voltaire et Frédéric II. Paris: Hachette, 1927.

Higgs, Henry. The Physiocrats. New York: Macmillan, 1897.

Kohn, Hans. The Idea of Nationalism. New York: Macmillan, 1944.

Kozminski, Leon. Voltaire financier. Paris: Les presses universitaires de France, 1929.

Lamartine, Alphonse de. Histoire des Girondins. 6 vols. Paris: Hachette, 1913.

Lanson, Gustave. "Les premières manifestations de l'esprit philosophique," Revue des cours et conferences 1907-1908, XVI, 389-98.

——Manuel bibliographique de la littérature française moderne: XVIe, XVIIe, XVIIIe et XIXe siècles. Paris: Hachette, 1921.

——Voltaire. Paris: Hachette, 1906.

Laski, Harold J. The Rise of European Liberalism. London: Allen and Unwin, 1936.

Lavisse, Ernest. Histoire de France. 9 vols. Paris: Hachette, 1900-11.

Lichtenberger, Andre. Le Socialisme au XVIIIe siècle. Paris: Alcan, 1895.

Longchamp, G. et Wagnière. Mémoires. Paris: André, 1826.

Martin, Kingsley. French Liberal Thought in the Eighteenth Century. Boston: Little Brown, 1929.

Michelet, Jules. Histoire de la révolution française. 7 vols. Paris: Flammarion, n.d.

Montesquieu, Charles de Secondat. De l'esprit des lois. Classiques Garnier. Paris: Garnier, n.d.

——Lettres persanes. Edited by H. Barckhausen. Paris: Hachette, 1913.

Morize, Andre. L'Apologie du luxe au XVIIIe siècle et "le mondain" de Voltaire. Paris: Didier, 1909.

Morley, John. Voltaire. New York: Macmillan, 1923 (first printed 1872).

Mornet, Daniel. La pensée française au XVIIIe siècle. Paris: Colin, 1926.

——Origines intellectuelles de la révolution française. Paris: Colin, 1933.

Naves, Raymond. Le Goût de Voltaire. Paris: Garnier, 1938.

——Voltaire et l'Encyclopédie. Paris: Les Editions des presses modernes, 1938.

Neserius, Philip G. "Voltaire's Political Ideas," *The American Political Science Review*, 1926, XX, 31-51.

Nicolardot, Louis. Ménages et finances de Voltaire. Paris: Dentu, 1887.

Nisard, D. Histoire de la litterature française. 4 vols. Paris: Firmin-Didot, 1883.

Noyes, Alfred E. Voltaire. New York: Sheed and Ward, 1936.

Oulmont, Charles. Voltaire en robe de chambre. Paris: Calmann-Levy, 1936.

Pagès, G. La Monarchie d'ancien régime en France. Paris: Collection Armand Colin, 1928.

Palmer, Robert R. "The National Idea in France before the Revolution," *Journal of History of Ideas,* I (1940), 95-111.

Parton, James. Life of Voltaire. Boston: Houghton Mifflin, 1881.

Péguy, Charles. Notre patrie. Paris: Editions de la nouvelle revue français, 1915.

Pellissier, Georges. Voltaire philosphe. Paris: Colin, 1908.

Pollard, A. F. The Evolution of Parliament. London: Longmans, Green, 1920.

Porritt, Edward. The Unreformed House of Commons. Cambridge, England: Cambridge University Press, 1909.

Price, William R. The Symbolism of Voltaire's Novels. New York: Columbia University Press, 1911.

Prod'homme, J. G. Voltaire raconté par ceux qui l'ont vu. Paris: Stock, 1939.

Racine, Jean Baptiste. La Thébaide in Vol. I of Oeuvres. Paris: Hachette, 1865.

Réau, Louis. L'Europe français au siècle des lumières. Paris: Michel, 1938.

Renan, Ernest. Oeuvres complètes. 5 vols. Paris: Calmann Levy, n.d.

Rousseau, Jean-Jacques, Le Contrat social: le discours sur l'inegalité. Collection Selecta. Paris: Garnier, 1914.

——Correspondance générale. 20 vols. Annoté par Théophile Dufour. Paris: Colin, 1924-34.

Sainte-Beuve, Charles Augustin. "Frédéric le Grand, littérateur," *Causeries du lundi*. 15 vols. Paris: Garnier, 1851.

Sakmann, Paul von. Voltaires Geistesart und Gedankenwelt. Stuttgart: Frommanns Verlag, 1910.

Sales, Raoul de Roussy. The Making of Tomorrow. New York: Reynal and Hitchcock, 1942.

Sée, Henri. Esquisse d'une histoire économique et sociale de la France. Paris: Alcan, 1929.

——L'Evolution commercial et industrielle de la France sous L'ancien régime. Paris: Giard, 1925.

——La France économique et sociale au XVIIIe siècle. Paris: Colin, 1925.

——Les Idées politiques en France au XVIIIe siècle. Paris: Hachette, 1920.

——"Que faut-il penser de l'oeuvre de Colbert?" Revue historique, CLII, 181-94. Paris: Alcan, 1926.

Seligman, E. R. and Alvin Johnson (eds.). The Encyclopedia of Social Sciences. 15 vols. New York: Macmillan, 1931.

Soltau, R. H. French Political Thought in the Nineteenth Century. London: E. Benn Ltd., 1931.

Sorel, A. L'Europe et la révolution française. Paris: E. Plon, 1927.

Taine, Hippolyte. Histoire de la littérature anglaise. 8th ed., 4 vols. Paris: Hachette, 1892.

——Origines de la France contemporaine. 20th ed., 6 vols. Paris: Hachette, 1896-1904.

Tallentyre, S. G. The Life of Voltaire. New York: Putnam, 1938.

Tawney, R. H. Religion and the Rise of Capitalism. New York: Harcourt, Brace, 1926.

——Equality. New York: Harcourt, Brace, 1931.

Textes sacrés de la liberté. Editions de la maison française. New York: 1942.

Thibaudet, Albert. Histoire de la littérature française. Paris: Stock, 1936.

Tilley, Arthur. From Montaigne to Molière. London: John Murray, 1908.

Torrey, Norman L. The Spirit of Voltaire. New York: Columbia University Press, 1938.

——Voltaire and the English Deists. New Haven: Yale University Press, 1930.

Wade, Ira. Voltaire and Mme du Châtelet. Princeton: Princeton University Press, 1941.

Weulersse, S. G. Les Physiocrates. Paris: G. Doin, 1931.

Wharton, Edith. French Ways and Their Meaning. New York and London: D. Appleton, 1919.

White, Florence D. Dissertation on Voltaire's Essay on Epic Poetry. Albany: Brandow, 1915.

# Index

# Index